W9-BLK-547

LOVE IN BLACK AND WHITE

LOVE IN BLACK AND WHITE

THE TRIUMPH OF LOVE OVER PREJUDICE AND TABOO

MARK AND GAIL MATHABANE

 HarperCollins*Publishers*

Thanks to all the interracial couples
whose candor and courage made this book richer.

Special thanks to our editors Craig Nelson and Jenna Hull, and to our agents, Kevin McShane and Fifi Oscard, for their encouragement, suggestions, and support.

LOVE IN BLACK AND WHITE. Copyright © 1992 by Mark Mathabane and Gail Mathabane. All rights reserved. Printed in the United States of America. No part of this book may be used or reproduced in any manner whatsoever without written permission except in the case of brief quotations embodied in critical articles and reviews. For information address HarperCollins Publishers, Inc., 10 East 53rd Street, New York, NY 10022.

Designed by Cassandra J. Pappas

Library of Congress Cataloging-in-Publication Data

Mathabane, Mark.
    Love in Black and white : the triumph of love over prejudice and taboo / Mark Mathabane, Gail Mathabane. — 1st ed.
        p.   cm.
    Includes index.
    ISBN 0-06-016495-6
    1. Mathabane, Mark. 2. Mathabane, Gail, 1962– . 3. Interracial marriage—United States. 4. Blacks—United States— Biography. 5. United States—Biography. I. Mathabane, Gail, 1962– . II. Title.
E185.97.M38A3 1992
306.84'6'0922—dc20   91-50454

To our children, Bianca and Nathan,
who are an affirmation of our love
and of our belief in the oneness of humanity.

It is not by wearing down into uniformity all that is individual in themselves, but by cultivating it, and calling it forth, within the limits imposed by the rights and interests of others, that human beings become a noble and beautiful object of contemplation; and as the works partake the character of those who do them, by the same process human life also becomes rich, diversified, and animating, furnishing more abundant aliment to high thoughts and elevating feelings, and strengthening the tie which binds every individual to the race, by making the race infinitely better worth belonging to.

—JOHN STUART MILL,
On Liberty

CONTENTS

Contents / x

PHOTO INSERT FOLLOWS PAGE 50.

PREFACE

What does it mean to be an interracial couple in America? For many years, decades, it has meant being analyzed, studied, categorized, labeled, and collected into statistics and theories—some bizarre and others downright ridiculous—aimed at answering a question at once simple and complex: Why do human beings fall in love?

There's little doubt that of all the kinds of mixed couples in America, the black and white relationships are among the most studied, psychoanalyzed, and discussed. They provoke the strongest reactions in people. They are constantly targeted by black and white opponents of "race mixing."

Sociological treatises and psychological studies abound about the problems of and the motives behind interracial relationships. They have fascinated and titillated society since the days of slavery. But despite extensive research into such relationships, there have been few human stories about why individuals from different and frequently antagonistic worlds defy formidable cultural prejudices and taboos to unite their lives in friendship and marriage.

There are about 200,000 married black-white couples in America, living in virtually every state of the Union. Amazingly, many of these couples are in the South, where until 1967 such marriages were forbidden by law.

In Virginia in 1959 a white man and his black wife were convicted by an all-white grand jury for violating the state's ban on interracial marriages. The penal code stated:

> If any white person intermarry with a colored person, or any colored person intermarry with a white person, he shall be guilty of a felony and shall be punished by confinement in the penitentiary for not less than one nor more than five years.

In his sentencing opinion the Virginia judge stated:

> Almighty God created the races white, black, yellow, malay and red, and he placed them on separate continents. And but for the interference with his arrangement there would be no cause for such marriages. The fact that he separated the races shows that he did not intend for the races to mix.

The couple appealed the decision, and in June 1967 the Supreme Court struck down the Virginia law, along with the anti-miscegenation laws of fifteen other states, on the grounds that the freedom to marry whom one chooses is one of the "vital personal rights" protected under the Fourteenth Amendment.

But attitudes change slower than laws: Twenty-five years after the Supreme Court ruling, stereotypes and misconceptions against mixed marriages are still rife. We have attempted, with this book, to explore and expose these attitudes.

Our book is not another "scientific" or "sociological" study of mixed couples. It is simply the story of two individuals who fell in love. From outward appearances Gail and I could not be more dissimilar—a blond American who grew up in relative comfort in the middle-class suburbs of Ohio, Texas, and Minnesota, and an African raised in segregated South Africa amid dire poverty, suffering, and racism.

With the publication of *Kaffir Boy* and *Kaffir Boy in America*, our relationship came under the spotlight. It was misunderstood, criticized, praised, and subjected to all the stereotyping that America's lingering and pervasive racism could conjure up.

This book is about our odyssey as a mixed couple in America. It is about what brought and keeps us together, how we have dealt with opposition from family members, hostility from opponents of "race mixing," hate mail, the birth of our children, the threats to our careers, our own grappling with the complex requirements and emotions of interracial love.

It is also about the moving personal stories of friends and

acquaintances who decided to break long silences about the true nature of their interracial relationships, often revealing painful secrets about careers, friendships, and families sacrificed for their undying conviction that humanity is one, that human love can and should be shared with everyone, regardless of color or creed. For years many of these courageous individuals had been prevented from telling their stories for fear of opening deep wounds, of provoking racist attacks, or worse.

Gail and I are far from assuming to speak for all mixed couples. Nor do we have all the answers for the complex process of falling in love that is as individual as our fingerprints. Nor do we expect our book to dispel all the stereotypes about mixed couples. In some cases these stereotypes may be validated. But of one thing we are certain: Interracial couples should cease being simply statistics, guinea pigs for social scientists and psychoanalysts to dissect and analyze. They should become human.

KERNERSVILLE, NORTH CAROLINA, 1991

PART 1

OUR STORY

HOW WE MET

MARK'S VIEW

Gail and I met in 1984 when I was twenty-four and she twenty-two. We were both graduate students at the Columbia Graduate School of Journalism in New York City. I had just committed what many considered the worst blunder of my life: I had abandoned my scholarship at the journalism school and a possible secure job afterward as a journalist.

I had few prospects except a half-completed, unpublished manuscript about my childhood and youth in Alexandra, a South African ghetto, and how I escaped from apartheid bondage to freedom in America. My leaving journalism school had partly to do with a fervid desire to finish the book, whose story had haunted me for years. A few publishers had expressed interest in the manuscript. But I held out little hope that the book, if published, would change my life—in other words, that it would be any different from the thousands published each year only to fade into oblivion, leaving the author as poor and insignificant as before.

Gail and I were living at International House—popularly known as I-House—on 122nd and Riverside Drive. Situated on the edge of Harlem and overlooking the Hudson River, the five hundred rooms of I-House offered affordable housing to students of various nationalities, from all over the world, who were in the United States pursuing advanced degrees or working as interns for multinational companies in New York City. Among them were Germans, Africans, Swedes, Mid-Easterners, Japanese, South Americans, French. Scores of American students were permitted to live in I-House to partake in the unique cultural exchanges.

I first became aware of Gail at a crowded dance party, hosted by the African cultural club, in the main hall of International House, an elaborate room with huge original oil paintings on the walls and French doors opening onto a terrace overlooking a small park.

Attending the party was a fluke. My upbringing and experiences in South Africa (which in no sense was a normal childhood) had led me to believe that life was mainly for working and learning. I had tried since arriving in the United States in 1978 to learn to relax and enjoy myself the way most Americans do, but to no avail. As a result, many women considered me a bore. At this party I merely stood awkwardly and abstractedly beside a pillar, occasionally attempting to engage this and that person in serious conversation, with little success.

Gail was joyously leaping about to the Reggae music, laughing and clapping her hands as if she had no cares in the world. She was the epitome of a free spirit. Because I frequently brooded over the fate of my impoverished family back home in South Africa, her carefree attitude was like a breath of fresh air in a stuffy hut. It gave me momentary relief from heavy and depressing thoughts.

Gail was dancing with a tall, gangly white fellow. A strange feeling akin to envy arose in me as I saw them sit down on a couch together to talk. I watched them out of the corner of my eye, wondering if they were more than friends. But what reason did I have to wonder at such things? I didn't even know her. Besides, she was white and we seemed to have little in common.

Some of the women I had dated through college had been white, and I had enjoyed and benefited from the experience, but I still hoped eventually to marry a black woman. Repeated attempts to establish serious relationships with compatible black women, however, ended in painful failure. Some considered me ascetic, too serious about life and too much of a bookworm. Others thought me too "feminine" because I openly expressed my feelings and disdained a macho image. Still others were bewildered and even ashamed at finding out about my background of poverty, squalor, and degradation.

This befuddled me as I thought we had much in common, emotionally at least, given our similar experiences under white oppression and common African culture. But many black women saw themselves as more American than African. They judged me and my worth in American terms, and because I had no prospects, no money, and no status and was a foreign student, I was presumably considered a risky investment for a long-term relationship.

Realizing this, and being somewhat wounded by it, I vowed to stick with the woman, whatever her race or color, who would see that beneath the poverty, seriousness, and lack of material success, there was a feeling, caring, and loving human being worthy of being befriended, loved, and depended on.

Gail and I continued to run into each other. At meals I saw her enter the cafeteria carrying her lunch tray, look around for an open table, and sit down at a distance from me. She seemed taller and stronger than other women; she wore her blond hair short and usually dressed in shabby men's clothing. Her favorite outfit consisted of a dark blue men's suit jacket she bought the previous summer at a yard sale in San Francisco's Haight-Ashbury district, denim jeans, army-style boots, dangling earrings, and multicolored scarves around her neck in the bohemian style reminiscent of the 1960s. Her devil-may-care manner of dressing was part of her charm. She would have been out of character in high heels and dresses.

One evening while doing my regular exercise routine of skipping rope and doing push-ups on the sixth floor, Gail happened to walk by. Without warning she dropped to the floor, did ten quick push-ups, smiled at me, and then vanished behind a closing elevator door.

I was perplexed. Who is this strange woman? Why is she so independent of societal pressures, especially the pressure many women felt to act weak and feminine? At the time I was rereading John Stuart Mill's classic essay "The Subjection of Women" and was strongly interested in feminism, particularly in comparing the role and struggles of women in South African and American societies.

My early introduction to feminism was through my mother and

grandmother. Though the two indomitable matriarchs daily groaned under the yoke of a triple oppression—they were women in a patriarchal culture, blacks in a white-dominated society, and unschooled in a world where education was increasingly vital—they remained strong, caring, loving, and compassionate individuals, full of earthy wisdom and resolute in striving to better their lives and those of their children. Granny had raised my mother and my mother's four siblings alone after her husband abandoned her for another woman. And my mother, following my father's emasculation by the apartheid system, effectively kept the family together.

My mother and grandmother were the first feminists I knew. Their characters, example, and deeds heavily influenced my values and outlook on life. They liberated the other important half of me, the feminine part, and made it grow and fully complement my masculine half. Whereas my father had sought to teach me that however deep the pain men never cry, ever, and that they should suppress, deny, and keep their emotions bottled up, my mother and grandmother taught me that a man can cry, love, care, change diapers, clean house, iron, and still be a man.

Once I came to know Gail well, I saw a lot of my mother in her. Her being white did not obscure the fact that she was intensely human. She felt deeply and cared about others. She possessed in full measure what in my mother's Tsonga culture is called *rirhandu* ("human love, kindness").

My first conversation with Gail was about women's issues. One day in the hot and humid laundry room in the basement of I-House, I overheard Gail telling Katie King, another journalism student, about her visit to a battered women's shelter in Harlem. I joined the conversation. My sympathy for women's issues and my hatred of male violence against women surprised Gail and Katie. But I was merely speaking from personal experience: My father used to beat my mother for such trifles as answering back when he lectured her, which he called "insubordination unbecoming the woman he bought." At the age of thirty-seven, he had paid about twenty cattle in *lobola* for my mother when she was seventeen and without a say in the matter. The patriarchal tribal culture at the time invested men with almost dictatorial powers over women. Wife beating was so widespread and accepted that many women considered it a sign of a man's affection.

Not my mother. She was a quiet, but determined, rebel.

As I mentioned at the beginning, about the time I met Gail I was leading a life, largely self-imposed, of an intellectual hermit. Having dropped out of Columbia J-school to concentrate on completing the manuscript for *Kaffir Boy*, I followed a rigid schedule of reading, writing, and exercising, and spent most of my time in my cell-like dorm room. I only went out to purchase fruit at a Korean fresh market on Broadway or to browse through my favorite used-book stores on Amsterdam Avenue and downtown at the Strand.

Because I had dropped out of school, my immigration status was precarious. Technically I could have been deported because I had ceased being a full-time student. I was in the process of applying for a green card. If that were denied, I was ready to request political asylum rather than return home, where the Pretoria regime had escalated its repression and killing and detention of blacks. Letters from home brought only bad news and entreaties for money. I had none. I was still unable to support myself and relied on my benefactor Stan Smith, one of the closest friends I have, black or white.

Shortly after quitting journalism school I published a few articles in the *St. Petersburg Times* sharply critical of apartheid and its brutal suppression of black dissent. Soon I began receiving anonymous threatening phone calls in the middle of the night.

I knew it was dangerous to write the truth about black life under apartheid, but I felt it was my duty, having had the rare opportunity of escaping from the bondage of legalized racism and segregation, to inform Americans, in human terms, that blacks in South Africa were fighting and dying for the same rights and freedoms that Americans could not imagine life without: the rights to vote, to live where one wished, to speak freely, to work for just pay, to have equal justice under the law.

One night around three, the ringing of the phone jarred me from a deep slumber. I picked up the receiver.

"Hello?" Silence. "Hello?"

A low, deliberate voice with an Afrikaner accent said, "You'd better watch out, *kaffir*."

"Who is this?" I demanded.

"We can stop you, if we have to."

"Who is this?"

No answer. The phone went dead.

I dropped the receiver into its cradle, switched off the lamp, and crawled back under the covers. But I could not sleep a wink. Fear, doubt, and anxiety tormented me.

I found comfort only in daylight and in routine. I rose each morning at seven, wrote until noon, ate lunch, read all afternoon, ate dinner, read, then worked out. One evening, not long after sunset, I carried my ball hopper and tennis rackets downstairs to the gym, hoping to bang out my fears and anger by practicing ground strokes against the wall. In Manhattan, tennis courts were scarce and private clubs were prohibitively expensive. To keep playing my favorite sport, tennis, I had resorted to hitting against the gym wall.

The mysterious telephone calls in recent nights had put me on edge. I trusted few people, and those I did trust, black or white, had earned my confidence.

As I approached the gym, I noticed the lights were on. I paused, for I rarely encountered anyone else during my solitary tennis sessions. I opened the door a crack and saw Gail, who was stretching out. It turned out she had just returned from a jog through Riverside Park, in snow and ice. I hesitated. Should I come back later? I decided to enter. I strode in nonchalantly, placed my rackets and ball hopper in their usual spot against the back wall, and slipped the cover off one of the rackets, gifts from Stan.

"Hello," Gail said as she bobbed over an outstretched leg, reaching for the toe of her well-worn, gray running shoe.

"Hi, how are you?"

"All right," she replied, turning to stretch her other leg. "I survived my run. It's too icy out there for running shoes, but the snow isn't deep enough for skis."

Never having skied before, I found this statement intriguing. "Do you ski in New York?"

"Whenever I can," she said. "But the snow is much better where I come from, Minnesota."

Not knowing what else to say, I started whacking tennis balls against the wall. The whole time I was thinking of what a comely, radiant face she had, boyish in shape but feminine in feature. Her shoulders were broad for a woman, probably those of a swimmer, and in her turtleneck, sweats, and parka, she appeared rustic, outdoorsy, and unself-conscious. Flustered and embarrassed by my attraction to her, which I was convinced was one way, I concentrated on establishing the rhythm in my strokes and smooth weight transference from the back to the front foot as I struck the ball. I did not look in her direction.

What made me uncomfortable about my attraction to her was that she was white. My predicament was this: Since coming to the United States I had come under increasing pressure to choose sides in America's racial battles. Militant blacks wanted me to prove my solidarity with their cause by disassociating myself from whites and confining my friendships to the black community. My refusal to adopt the attitude that all whites are racist by abandoning white friends who had earned my trust and respect led me to be labeled an Uncle Tom.

To regard all whites as racist by failing to judge them as individuals is as harmful as the white attitude of stereotyping all blacks. But this argument of mine fell on deaf ears. Bitterness, rage, suspicion, fear, and hate had largely supplanted reason, tolerance, and common sense in America's race relations.

Some whites, on the other hand, also victims of the racism and intolerance that pervaded society, were unable or unwilling to deal with me on my own terms, as an individual, rather than as one of the many stereotypes about blacks they had imbibed growing up self-segregated from black America.

Suddenly Gail jumped up, picked up one of my other rackets, and tested the grip size.

"Do you play?" I inquired.

"I used to play a lot when I lived in Austin, Texas."

"Let's see," I said, and tossed her two balls.

She hit the balls hard, stiffly, but with determination. They bounced back to her at odd angles, making her look ludicrous as she lunged and twisted and spun with little success in hitting the balls back. Both of us laughed uproariously.

"Hold the racket firmly but don't choke it," I said. "And don't forget to watch the ball carefully. And follow through, transferring your weight forward. Like this." I demonstrated.

She tried again, but control of the ball kept eluding her. I noticed she was frustrated and a bit embarrassed. I took the pressure off her by patiently demonstrating the proper technique. We took turns hitting. Gradually some of her old skills came back. Gail ran nonstop all over the gym attempting to return my best shots. Finally she dropped from exhaustion.

"Don't stop, you're doing great," I said. "You're a natural athlete."

"I'll never be a tennis champion."

"Are you still holding your racket properly?" I walked over to Gail, placed my hands gently on hers, adjusted her forehand grip, and guided her arm through the correct swing. I did not let go of her hand right away. Our eyes met.

GAIL'S VIEW

I wondered if he were intentionally looking into my eyes or if he had simply forgotten himself. I was puzzled by the way his dark brilliant eyes seemed to penetrate right through me. I stepped away from him and hit a few more balls.

I had never before been attracted to anyone of a darker race, and I did not know how to react to my own emotions. Interracial love, white society had loudly and insistently said, was taboo. I did not forget for a second that I was alone in a gym with a black man. But I also knew he was a remarkable human being from what I had heard from colleagues at the J-school, and I felt excited at the opportunity of finally meeting and talking to him. I gathered my belongings nervously and headed for the door, overcome with the strangeness of the situation. I had learned to relate to blacks with respect and as equals from interviewing them in Harlem and the South Bronx for journalism classes, but I was aware of the racist attitudes of many whites and wondered at my own subtle prejudices. Simply put, I dreaded getting involved, however platonically, with a black man.

"Leaving already?" Mark asked.

"Yes, I have to go."

He seemed to want to say something more, so I waited.

"Would you like to accompany me to a tennis match Sunday afternoon?" he asked.

I felt paralyzed with a potent mixture of joy and fear. I spoke from my heart, not my head, when I said, "I'd love to." Then I fled from the object of my emotional turmoil. I ran upstairs to my tenth-floor room and sat on my bed looking out the window at Riverside Church and the Hudson River and the gray sky, deep in thought.

I first became aware of Mark during a Monday morning lecture in the World Room of the journalism school. I saw a well-dressed black man, whose shirt had apparently been carefully ironed and whose short Afro had been neatly combed, stand up and question the speaker about an issue related to apartheid. He spoke with a strange British accent, and the speaker cleared his throat several times before attempting to evade the question and mumble some obscure, unrelated answer.

Michelle Nayman, a fellow journalism student from Australia, leaned toward me and whispered, "That was Mark Mathabane. Have you met him?"

"No," I said. "Who is he?"

"Oh, you've *got* to meet him," she whispered. "He's led an incredible life and he's writing a book about it. He escaped apartheid with the help of Stan Smith, the tennis player. He grew up in a ghetto outside Johannesburg in a shack made of tin, plastic, and brick, and slept most of his childhood on pieces of cardboard under the kitchen table. He's the eldest of seven, and in the winter his mother wrapped them in old newspapers to keep them warm."

"How awful! Couldn't they afford blankets?" I asked naively, unaware, like most Americans were at the time, of the horrible living conditions in South African townships.

"No, they were very poor. His father made only ten dollars a week," Michelle continued. "But most of the time he couldn't find work. The family had to scavenge for food at garbage dumps."

I shook my head in disbelief, then looked at Mark, several rows up. "You'd never know from looking at him that he's lived through all that."

"He has amazing determination," Michelle said.

Michelle's admiration for Mark sparked my curiosity. I yearned to hear more about Mark's life under apartheid, a system I understood only superficially from newspaper accounts.

A few weeks later I was having lunch with a Belgian journalism student named Geert when Mark joined us at our table. He directed his conversation to Geert, and gesticulated with his hands a lot when he spoke. Having seldom sat so close to a black person before, I was fascinated by the simple fact that his palms were a lighter color than the backs of his hands. He had the smallest, cutest ears I had ever seen, and I admired his large brown eyes and the way his gold-rimmed glasses, watch, and white sweater contrasted with his dark skin.

Geert asked him questions. Mark infused his replies with incisive observations about race and such poignant details about his life in the ghetto that an overwhelming feeling of empathy arose within me. I had never before heard of such horrors or such a graphic description of the plight and resiliency of South African blacks. He left a deep impression on me.

One evening as I rode the elevator to the tenth floor, the car stopped on the sixth floor to let someone off. As the doors opened, I saw Mark jumping rope in the hallway, wearing nothing but yellow running shorts and tennis shoes. He was taking a breather, and his muscular chest glistened with sweat. He smiled bashfully as he stepped aside to let people by. He must have been popular, for everyone greeted him with a "Hi, Mark," to which he replied with a slow and drawn out, "Hello, how is everybody?"

Then the doors slid shut and the elevator jolted upward. It had just lasted a few seconds, but that image of him stuck in my mind. As a former swimmer and cross-country runner during high school, I had always admired well-conditioned athletes. A few days later, as I headed for the sixth floor elevator, Mark was doing push-ups. I pressed the elevator button and waited, trying to act casual and keep my eyes off him. I had a sudden urge to show him that he wasn't the only athlete at I-House so I dropped to the ground and did ten quick push-ups, then dashed onto the elevator with a quick "'Bye." As the doors closed I saw a funny smile spread across his face.

I never imagined Mark would ever become my boyfriend, let alone my husband. At the time I had a steady boyfriend named Glen. Though we were both PKs (preacher's kids) from Minnesota, Glen and I had met, of all places, in Budapest in 1983. He was a blue-eyed graduate of the University of Minnesota with a full-blooded Norwegian ancestry and a middle name of Thor, after the Norse god. As soon as I was accepted to Columbia, he started applying for jobs in New York City so he could be near me. He got a job with a nonprofit group started by Ralph Nader that fought to keep consumer prices down and advocated safe, reliable, and affordable public transportation. I admired his devotion to the public good and his dedicated efforts to help the poor. He rented a small room in Brooklyn and we would commute by subway to see each other.

I excitedly told Glen about Mark and his remarkable odyssey from a violent and desperate South African ghetto to the journalism school. One night I happened to run into Mark when I was with Glen, so I introduced them.

"I've heard a lot about you," Glen said, shaking Mark's hand with enthusiasm. He did not have the slightest hint of jealousy in his voice, probably because Mark was black and, therefore, presumed not a threat.

Glen wanted us to live together and eventually get married. Commitment scared me. My career ambition was to become a foreign correspondent. I was applying for jobs at Reuters News Service in London, at Radio Free Europe in Munich, and at the U.S. Information Agency for an internship in Germany. In case I could not get a job abroad, I had sent résumés to papers all over the country: on forested islands off the coast of Alaska, near Hawaiian beaches, in the wilds of Arkansas and Louisiana, high in the Rocky Mountains. I poured my random desires into the mailbox and patiently waited for my future to decide for itself what I would do and where.

Glen liked me to wear a white scarf because he felt it made me look "pure." He sometimes had jealous dreams in which I told him I had been seeing someone else. He wanted me to be his and his alone. He made me feel that I could have no male friends. He could never forgive me for having had boyfriends before him. Instead of being proud of my accomplishments, he felt threatened by them. He hated the Ivy League, and all it stood for, and resented the fact that I had graduated magna cum laude from Brown University, an institution he pegged as a tool for perpetuating the elite ruling class. Envy gnawed at him when he learned I was taking a literature class at Brown taught by Susan Sontag. It came to a peak when he learned I was taking a law course at Columbia taught by Benno Schmidt, now president of Yale University, and *New York Times* columnist Anthony Lewis.

I should have terminated the relationship much earlier, but I was afraid to hurt him. So I stuck it out, growing more miserable each day, and silently longing for a man who would let me be myself and trust me enough to let me have male friends.

At Christmastime 1984, back in Minnesota, I skied alone through snow-filled woods, sliding silently between evergreens laden with ice crystals. I brushed the snow off a fallen tree and lay down on it, facing the deep blue sky and watching the steam rise from my body. As I lay there, thoughts came to me that changed my life: I grew convinced that I should develop my talents and creativity fully, let my spirit thrive uninhibited, and avoid any man who sought to stifle and kill that spirit, the only thing that gave purpose and meaning to my life. I would break up with Glen.

The new year came and I returned to New York. I had been back a week when I went for a run along the Hudson River through snow, listening to Corelli and Telemann on my Walkman and watching the sun set in a glorious serenity of colors whose beauty made the heart ache.

I was stretching out in the gym when Mark walked in. My heart beat faster. I could not resist watching in silent awe as he began hitting tennis balls against the wall. He seemed to glide across the floor, like a ballet dancer, as he steadily and gracefully struck the yellow tennis ball, hard and fast against the wall in a lulling rhythm of bounces and swats. His jaw was firm in concentration and his eyes were riveted on the ball. His smooth black arms and legs moved in a synchronized manner with precision and grace. It was beautiful to watch. I was thrilled when he invited me to the tennis match.

But alone in my room, guilt set in. How would I tell Glen I was going to a tennis match with Mark? Did I have the courage to break up with him? When Mark called to confirm the date, I said, "Can I take a rain check?"

"Sure," Mark replied.

"Who was that?" Glen asked as I hung up.

"That was Mark. He wanted to take me to a tennis game."

As I expected, Glen flew into a jealous rage. "You were going to go on a date with another guy!" he screamed. "What were you thinking? How would you feel if I told you I was going on a date with another woman?"

"It would be okay with me, because I trust you."

The next morning on the front page of *The New York Times* I saw a photograph of John McEnroe holding a huge, ornate silver trophy above his head in triumph: He had just won the Grandmaster's title. I regretted not having gone to the match at Madison Square Garden with Mark, and I worried that he might have ascribed my refusal to his being black. I wrote a short and honest note to him, explaining why I had decided not to go and adding, in no uncertain terms, that I admired his character. Upon rereading the note, I realized I might be making a fool of myself if he were already in love with someone else. My cheeks flushed red and my heart pounded as I added a timid postscript: "P.S. Do you have a girlfriend?"

The next day I found in my mailbox a letter written on pink stationery. It read

Dear Gail,

Many thanks for your candid letter. I do not know if you expected a reply, but my heart willingly gives one. Bear in mind it is my heart speaking, and as we mortals well know, hearts have a curious language of their own, intelligible only to a select few. Such persons have about them that rare wonder called "Beauty of the Soul." The thoughts in your letter tell me you're one of them. They're spontaneous, down-to-earth and unpretentious. Put differently, they're the essence of you. They make you extremely attractive intellectually, emotionally, and otherwise. It is a joy to know you.

True friends are too hard to come by for us not to open our hearts when someone special comes along. Of course opening our hearts entails risks, leaves us vulnerable to the vicissitudes of human nature. But I have yet to meet true friends who knowingly hurt one another. That's what I believe we have the potential of becoming: true friends.

Finally, I don't presently have a steady girlfriend. The reason: I've yet to meet a woman who sees me the way you've described me; a woman who understands that true friendship is the basis of a relationship; a woman who accepts the maxim that "love is that relation between man and woman in which the independence is equal, the dependence mutual, and the obligation reciprocal." I hope I'm not looking for an angel on earth.

With love,
MARK

Like two nervous high-school kids on a blind date, Mark and I met downstairs in the lobby of I-House the next day, bundled up against the arctic wind screaming outside. But to us it might as well have been spring. We sauntered to Broadway where we boarded a bus for the Cloisters, an old medieval monastery on a cliff beetling over the Hudson that had been converted into an ancient art museum. Mark wore an amusing pink-and-green plaid tie. We strolled through the warm monastery, discussing unicorns and tapestries, brass statues and carved doors, and much more that was communicated without words by shy, sidelong glances and sheepish smiles.

That evening, alone in my overheated room, I wrote in my journal: "The sun has just set over the Hudson, and I have just fallen in love with another man. He is refined and highly educated though he grew up in a ghetto. He sees with his soul and writes with his heart. His thoughts sometimes roll by me as I struggle to pursue their meaning, his mind teems with philosophy and noble ideas, his shelves overflow with great literature, his face shines with the radiance of his convictions. He is a great artist, an independent spirit, a rebel in disguise, a believer in truth and right in a world full of deception and cynicism."

The phone rang, breaking my concentration. It was Glen. I told him I wanted to date "someone." We argued.

He rode the subway all the way uptown to talk to me in person. I told him I had spent the day at the Cloisters with Mark.

"You two have been seeing a lot of each other lately, haven't you?" he fumed.

"If you call one day 'a lot,' " I replied.

He paused, then asked, "Did he kiss you good-bye?"

"Yes."

"On the lips?"

"Yes."

Glen started trembling all over. Soon he was shaking so violently he put on his coat. "You have to choose between me and Mark," he said, "and I want the answer right here and *now*."

I didn't know what to say.

Glen hurled his shoulder bag at the wall, then grabbed it and left, his face flushed with anger. He called me later to say he was cold, wet, lonely, and terrified of losing me. He said he had been wandering around the city like a madman and had wet feet and was shivering in a phone booth. I felt awful.

"How could you just throw us away like that?" he demanded.

"Your biggest fault is that you can be so damn coldhearted some-times. I can't stand the thought of losing a woman to another man. If you leave me my life is over."

The next few months my joy at getting to know Mark was over-shadowed by my guilt at having hurt Glen. Glen seemed to think I was just going through a passing phase and would soon come to my senses. The fact that I had left him for a black seemed to make him even more desperate to win me back. He wrote long, tortured letters. He called me at odd hours to make sure I was in my room. He com-posed depressing poems I could not interpret. He waited for me out-side my classes with bouquets of flowers.

I wished Glen could just let go. Our relationship was over. All my devotion was now directed at Mark, whom I knew I could never stop loving. I carried my pain over the breakup inside me, and did not share much of it with Mark. But without my saying a word, Mark could always tell when I was upset or troubled. He would stop what-ever he was doing to listen to me, comfort me, try to understand.

"I don't understand why you stayed with him for nearly two years," Mark said.

"What do you mean?" I asked.

"You're so brilliant, such a free spirit, that it pains me to see you feeling confined and depressed. You deserve all the opportunities to grow. There's nothing wrong with stopping to ask yourself whether you're happy and trying to change your life if you're not."

I recall these memories not to revel in the pain I inflicted on someone I once cared deeply about, but to address a pervasive stereotype about mixed couples. Many whites believe that a white woman would only stoop to loving or marrying a black man if she were too ugly, too ignorant, or too poor to find herself a white mate. This could not be further from the truth. I've met dozens of bright, attractive white women from respectable families who have fallen deeply in love with good men who just happen to be black.

Another popular theory is that white women who date blacks have low self-esteem and want to degrade themselves as much as possible by prostituting their hearts, souls, and bodies to black men, who will supposedly take them for granted and treat them like trash. This, too, is a racist stereotype. Most white women I've met who date black men are more confident, self-assured, and independent than average. They are strong-willed and open-minded individuals who choose to go against the social grain rather than give in to pressure from parents, friends, coworkers, and society to break up with men they admire, respect, and love.

In my case, my friendship with Mark has been an uplifting experience, not a degrading one. Mark has been unstinting in his support of me as a writer. He constantly encourages me to do my best without fear of criticism or rejection. He has instilled in me one of his mother's favorite maxims: In life you never fail as long as you keep trying. He was even more of a feminist than I, and convinced me that women, like blacks, should strive to realize their potentials without letting prejudice and discrimination define, rule, and ruin their lives.

"Most obstacles to self-actualization can be overcome," he said. "If I did not believe that, I would still be in South Africa."

Mark was all the things I had ever hoped for in a man—an intellectual, a lover of books and philosophy and classical music, an athlete, a fellow writer, a sensitive and compassionate human being, and a loyal friend. To be honest I had not expected my ideal man to be black, but the fact that he was did not keep me from falling in love with him.

That spring Mark and I spent hours in one of the soundproof study rooms off the library, facing each other across a huge table covered with books and papers. We talked deeply and intensely about topics ranging from injustice, fate, and the Cold War to apartheid, history, and writing. He would read me *Dover Beach, The Prelude, The Rubaiyat of Omar Khayyám, Adonais,* and other favorite poems. He shared with me the history of Africa's contributions to literature, art, music, dance, science, religion, and warfare so that I gained a greater respect and sensitivity for truly one of the world's great civilizations.

I heard so many tales of his painful childhood that I knew his life story by heart long before *Kaffir Boy* was published. On my part I told him what it was like growing up in the Midwest as the daughter of a Presbyterian minister: how I always had a congregation of adoring faces smiling down on me, how my father would take us sailing every Sunday, how I spent my summers mountainclimbing in the White Mountains, and several of my off-beat adventures.

"What a vivid storyteller!" Mark exclaimed. "You're the writer, not I!"

I laughed at his childlike enthusiasm and wished I had half the confidence he had in my potential.

Mark heightened my desire to write and made me regularly think about life's deeper meaning. I thought of all the people who toil through life, suppressing their emotions and ideals, forsaking or shunning those eager to love them, single-mindedly pursuing their careers up some mythical ladder with blind persistence, only to grow old and die, leaving nothing behind but a hole in a corporate structure. I realized that the importance of life lies deep in one's relationship to others. People make our lives meaningful. Human interaction is the essence of our being. When we die, we are kept alive only by the memories of those who loved us, only by those whose lives we touched.

When Mark and I talked about writing we sometimes whipped ourselves into amazing states of optimism and euphoria. Writing, to us, was a religion. Great writers were our prophets. We modeled our relationship after that of the poet Percy Bysshe Shelley and his wife, Mary, the daughter of Mary Wollstonecraft and the author of *Frankenstein*, whom we saw as two perfectly matched nonconformists and free spirits.

I admired Mark's discipline so much that soon I acquired many of his habits: I drank no caffeine, ate no red meat or sugar, woke up around seven and typed journal notes or articles, ate piles of fruits and vegetables, and worked out every other day. We went for runs together through Riverside Park from 122nd to 72nd and back up again.

Mark, in turn, wanted me to share elements of my life with him. I was doing my master's thesis on foreign artists living in the East Village. I took him to a few art openings packed with artists with spiked hair that had been dyed fluorescent pink, in galleries reached only by passing prone derelicts, drug dealers, and rotting garbage. The paintings on the walls burst with color and expression, but neither of us could make any sense of their meaning or relevance to reality.

One winter evening, after hearing the New York Philharmonic play Stravinsky and Debussy at Carnegie Hall, Mark and I walked to a rustic restaurant crowded with heavy wooden tables on which burned thick white candles surrounded by piles of dripping wax. The place reminded me of the wine cellar under the Budapest Castle. Mark sat across from me in his meticulously clean and ironed white shirt with his gold necktie pin, telling me about his childhood and youth. Neither of his parents had gone to school, yet he consistently came out first throughout primary and high school, which he attended after winning a government scholarship. After a childhood deprived of books, he fell in love with English, his fifth language, and by his early teens books had become his only solace, his best friends, the liberators of his mind and soul.

My eyes filled with tears as he spoke, but I tried to hide them so he would not see my distress. His eyes too seemed glazed with tears at bringing overpowering memories back to life. He had once told me that he had trouble finding the right woman because many women thought him lachrymose, mistook his sensitivity for a sign of latent homosexuality.

I told him that his not being afraid to feel, to cry, to care, made him more human, and thus more of a man to me.

Here before me, I thought to myself, *is a wise and sensitive spirit, born in black skin and surrounded by the dirt and sorrow of utter poverty and powerlessness. But since the human spirit can have no race or color, he rose steadily and naturally, led not by what others told him he was or was not, but by what he believed himself to be. He is an admirable, yet most intimidating, companion.*

OVERCOMING STEREOTYPES

2

MARK'S VIEW

If someone had told me while I was growing up in a South African ghetto that I would someday end up marrying a white woman, I would have thought them insane. For much of my childhood I didn't know, let alone believe, that whites were even human, capable of emotions such as love, care, and compassion. The only image I had of them was as policemen and soldiers. Akin to predators, they were to be feared and hated. The oppression they daily and ruthlessly enforced robbed me of my innocence and trust by forcing me, in order to survive the raging hell of ghetto life their racist policies had created, to begin thinking, feeling, and acting like an adult while still a child.

I was about five years old when I had my first brutal encounter with the police. They had launched one of their midnight raids into the ghetto. I was awakened from my cardboard bed under the kitchen table by a tremendous din outside our tiny shack. Sirens blared, dogs barked, windows smashed, doors shattered, and children screamed. I instantly knew that the police had invaded the neighborhood. Terror seized me as I recollected that during previous raids my mother and father had to flee their own home to escape arrest because they did not have a permit allowing them to live together as husband and wife under the same roof. Their nocturnal flights always left me feeling helpless, confused, and afraid, especially as I had to care for my siblings, Florah, three years old, and George, one year old.

Repeated raids crystallized my hatred of whites. Once I was beaten by the police after they forced their way into the shack, for failing to open the door on time. I had delayed in order to give my parents time to hide or escape. Another time I felt rage and hatred well inside me as I saw them humiliate my father by marching him naked out of bed and interrogating him in the middle of the shack, in front of his bewildered and whimpering children.

For many years of my childhood my only contact with whites continued to be with the police and soldiers. Because of the Groups Areas Act, which mandated rigidly segregated neighborhoods, blacks were forbidden from entering white suburbs without permits. Without meeting whites who were different, I came to regard the inhumanity and bigotry of the police and soldiers as typical of their race.

This stereotypical image of whites was reinforced by, among other things, my father's virulent hatred of whites, and by a constant diet of violent movies shown at the ghetto's only cinema.

My father's emasculation and suffering at the hands of the police and his employers, who confined him to menial jobs and paid him a pittance of ten dollars a week, not only made him a bitter man but he came to hate white so much he would forbid the eating of white bread in the house. As for the movies, I took their violence and mayhem as a true representation of life in the white world I was forbidden to enter by apartheid laws.

The first undermining of this stereotype of whites as all bad came when I was about seven years old. Some black and white missionaries pitched a tent in our neighborhood and invited us to come hear "good news" so glorious, so warming to the heart, so uplifting and comforting to a suffering soul, that our lives, our hearts, the situations in our homes, would be changed forever for the better. The fact that blacks and whites cooperated to spread the gospel, to do good, rather than to inflict pain and suffering on blacks, as the black and white policemen did, made an impression on me. It was an early indication that skin color doesn't determine the goodness or badness of an individual; it is the color of one's heart that matters.

Another instance of this maxim came when a white nun at the local health center altered my destiny by helping my mother in her quest to enroll me at the local tribal school. To do so my mother needed a permit from the authorities certifying that my parents were legal residents of Alexandra. They weren't. The only way I could get around the law was if I had a birth certificate showing that I was born in Alexandra. I didn't. I had been born, like many black children in the ghetto, at home, my mother having been unable to afford maternity care.

Once my mother determined that the only way to save me from the dead-end life of the streets and gangs was by taking me to school, she went to the authorities and begged for a permit. They told her to bring my birth certificate. She went to the clinic and begged for one. They told her that they couldn't issue it without a permit from the authorities. This continued for almost six months, with my mother getting up around three in the morning and waiting in long lines, being humiliated and insulted by unfeeling bureaucrats till the white nun intervened after my distraught mother implored her: "Please Sister, help my child."

After hearing my mother's catalog of woes, the white nun, tears trickling down her face, stormed into the office, and briefly argued with the black officer. In a jiffy my mother was called to the window and the birth certificate was thrown into her face.

As we walked back home, my mother singing songs of praises for the white nun and calling her God's angel, she turned to me and said, "Child, you see, not all white people are bad. Remember that." The most indelible image that remained with me of the white nun were her tears. Some white people do cry, I remember thinking; they are human after all. Though I continued to meet and to suffer at the hands of racist whites, the stereotype that whites were all bad had been forever shattered.

At age eleven another milestone was reached in my battle against stereotypes. Granny took me on my first visit to the white world, to meet the Smiths, a white English family for whom she worked as a gardener. Though paternalistic, the Smiths turned out to be kind, respectful, and loving toward Granny. They had a son about my age. From this family I began receiving secondhand clothing, toys, and books, which became powerful weapons in my struggle to

liberate my mind from mental slavery, an oppression I believe to be
most formidable because it had caused me to make peace with my
servitude, to accept a racist society's definition of my humanity.
These revolutionary books had names like *Treasure Island* and
David Copperfield.

It was also from the Smiths that I got my first tennis racket.
Determined to master the sport that had brought world fame to
Arthur Ashe, the first free black man I had ever seen, I began teaching myself the game at the dilapidated ghetto sand courts. Soon I
became good enough to attract notice. An open mind led me to
befriend some liberal whites at a nearby tennis ranch. They invited
me to train and play at their facilities. They respected me as an athlete, and I respected them for treating me like a human being. My
white tennis partners and coaches gradually became steadfast
friends.

I knew from the start that my association with whites would
alienate me from black militants. Many of my black peers in the
ghetto had an us-against-them attitude that had been hardened by
repeated encounters with the police and soldiers. They didn't believe
me when I said some whites were different. They pressured me to
cease contact with whites. One night on my way home from playing
tennis at the ranch, a black gang waylaid me. I would have been
knifed to death had I not outrun them. A brick that smashed into my
face, knocking out my front tooth, reminded me of the risks I was
running for my refusal to consider all whites racist and to judge
them according to the concept of collective guilt.

Had I done so I never would have had the courage to lean across
a fence one hot afternoon in November of 1977, to watch U.S. tennis
champion Stan Smith, one of my idols, practice with Bob Lutz, a doubles partner and Davis Cup teammate, during the South African
Breweries Open in Johannesburg. If I had been consumed with a
blind hatred of all whites, I would not even have been at the tournament.

As it turned out Stan invited me onto the court to hit some balls.
Later I accompanied him and his wife, Margie, to a restaurant where
I was the only black. That encounter, that friendship, that human
contact, between individuals who had grown up in worlds as different as night and day, led to Stan arranging a tennis scholarship for

me to attend college in the United States, at a time when I was at the end of my tether and in danger of being detained by the police as a student activist.

In America I discovered that many blacks believed that all whites were racist. As my South African experiences had taught me otherwise, I was again called on to defend my conviction that there were among whites, as among all people, both good and bad, and that to realize fully my own humanity, it was my duty to acknowledge and respect the humanity of others. This meant judging people as individuals, by the contents of their character, rather than by the color of their skin.

My open-mindedness in relating to whites incurred me the resentment and enmity of militant blacks. My motives were often misunderstood and I was sometimes called an Uncle Tom. Though these accusations hurt, I had come a long way from the days when rage and hate had consumed and almost destroyed my life. I had acquired values and convictions that my conscience told me had to be defended at all cost, because they were a part of my soul and formed the essence of my humanity. One of these convictions is that neither blacks nor whites have a monopoly on racism or love. Anyone with a feeling heart is capable of love and anyone who is blind to the fact that his humanity is inextricably tied to his respect of the humanity of others is capable of racism.

International House was the perfect setting for putting my beliefs to practice. Every day I interacted on a level of equality and mutual respect with men and women of every race and religion. I had friends from the Far East, the Mid-East, Africa, South America, Europe, Australia, the United States, and Canada. In the lounge I saw Indian saris, Muslim turbans, and African tribal dress and heard the babble of a dozen different languages. We partook in each other's culture and found that we had a great deal in common and that our differences were more enriching than threatening. In such an environment it was easy to forget cultural and racial differences and interact on a purely human plane. It was on that important level that my friendship with Gail began.

GAIL'S VIEW

The white partner in an interracial relationship usually has ample, if subconscious, stereotypes to overcome. I did. Like Mark, I believe that these stereotypes began in my childhood, as did my battle against their influence on my life. To explain fully the turbulence of emotions I felt when I found myself falling in love with an African, I need to recount a few childhood experiences that shed some light on my past attitudes toward race.

On the outskirts of Austin, Texas, in the early 1970s, in a new housing development surrounded by cracked mud flats infested with rattlesnakes and composed of identical $30,000 stucco homes with burglar bars, sun-burned yellow lawns, and prickly cactus gardens, I grew from an innocently confident little minister's daughter adored by flocks of staid Presbyterian churchgoers into a shy and bewildered adolescent who found out she had a lot to learn about race and sex.

In the dry heat of Austin I grew tall quickly, Texas-style, like the wheat in the vast fields I saw stretching out in every direction toward the horizon. I grew wise quickly too. I had to in order to survive as a minority "honky" in an overcrowded junior high school. I watched in jealous silence as gangs of blacks and Mexicans patrolled the school halls and kept the panic-stricken, mostly white teachers in line.

Nineteen seventy-four found me a scrawny twelve-year-old with shoulder-length blond hair that hung in straight, uncombed wisps like straw. I was a fearless tomboy. It thrilled me to wear my brother's cowboy boots, play capture the flag and soccer and half-court basketball with the boys, and hunt for armadillos at night by crouching on the mud flats in my faded jeans and shining my flashlight between the tumbleweed and cactus plants.

Gnarled, stunted trees lined the banks of the creek where I watched water moccasins glide stealthily in the murky depths. I was stung by scorpions, fell from trees, slid down moss-covered dams, jumped at the sight of black widow spiders, stood frozen while a copperhead snake wrapped my ankle in a slithering embrace as I stood barefoot in the deep mud, watching in breathless fear as his black tongue darted in and out.

The Texas sun beat down on our neighborhood. Every other house had a pool or plastic tub in the backyard, some container large enough to hold a sweaty body underwater against the unbearable one-hundred-degree heat. Every third house was identical.

The neighborhood was divided along racial lines. White families lived on the hill, up on Greensboro Drive, and blacks were down in the valley, along the streets where smaller homes were still under construction. Black boys sometimes came up the hill to play basketball with the white boys in our neighborhood, slam-dunking balls through dozens of hoops mounted over garage doors. There were three black brothers who always came up the hill together: Dookey, Tiki, and Mojo. Their names sounded strange to me, and I could not understand much of what they were saying.

"I's gonna dot yo eye in a minute, boy. I ain't *even* messin' witchoo. I's fixin' to knock you flat."

I was afraid of blacks. For the first ten years of my life I had lived in lily-white communities in Cincinnati and Springfield, Ohio, and knew nothing about the people my Texas girlfriends casually called "niggers." In the halls between classes at Pearce Junior High School I clung to the walls and tried to be as inconspicuous as possible, tiptoeing away from gang fights with my eyes down and my books pressed against my flat chest. I would try to cling to the walls and glide unnoticed past the groups of tough-looking, weather-beaten students who filled the halls. Occasionally I would have difficulty getting to my classroom, blocked by a massive hall riot of leaping, tangled, thrashing bodies. Whenever I saw blood splattering on the lockers, I would seek an alternate route.

Pearce was, in the early 1970s when I attended and when busing first began, a racially torn and violent public school circled by fourteen portable classrooms and a parking lot that glittered with broken glass smashed during rumbles—massive fights between white and black students. The student body was 55 percent black, 25 percent Mexican, and 20 percent white.

During classes, blacks sat in the back, mostly braiding and combing each other's hair with big metal Afro rakes. I had been terrified of those rakes since the day I walked innocently into the girls' bathroom and found one being waved in my face. Three black girls, sitting on the bathroom sinks, watched with amused expressions on their faces.

"Give me some money," one of them said, tightening her grip on the rake as if it were a gun.

"M-Money?" I stammered.

"Yeah, you know, the stuff you use to buy things with."

The other girls burst out laughing at my nervous naïveté. They seemed so confident and sure of themselves while I, new to the school and unacquainted with robbery, felt so timid and uncertain. I quickly emptied my pockets and gave her all the lunch money I had, then made my escape with the sound of snide laughter, which resounded in the concrete chamber, still ringing in my ears. I did not eat lunch that day, and I never again entered a school bathroom. I became very good at holding it until I got home. One day I saw a white girl with six perfectly straight scars across her face, and I knew she had offended someone wielding an Afro rake.

My fear of blacks was mingled with admiration. They could braid their hair in neat rows from their faces to their napes; they could sprint so much faster than whites that the track team was virtually all black; they were tough and confident and had the temerity to tell a teacher to shut up; and they could dance so well I dared not even try a single step for fear of being laughed at.

My admiration developed into a mild envy. Perhaps it was simply a minority's desire to fit in, but I sometimes wished I were black. All the popular girls in school were black and had names like Felicia and Rhonda and Janelle and Paulette. All the cheerleaders were black, and danced along the sidelines doing the bump, knocking their hips together and singing

> Boogie down, our team don't mess aroun',
> We got the spirit now, we gonna show you how,
> To boogie down, boogie down, boogie down,
> Right now!

A shiny chrome jukebox stood in the corner of the school cafeteria, belting out songs by the Jackson Five and Barry White and Marvin Gaye as crowds of black students boogied and jived and did the bump and the robot. They would dance on the tabletops to such funky, irresistible tunes as: "She's a dance, dance, dance, dance, dancin' machine. Watch her get down, watch her get down."

Rednecks, goat-ropers, and kickers looked on in scornful amusement. They were the whites who refused to be intimidated by their minority position. They usually wore ten-gallon cowboy hats, snap-down work shirts, heavy belt buckles, pointed-toe snakeskin cowboy boots, and military buzz-style haircuts. Their lower lips bulged to one side and brown drool seeped from the corners of their mouths as they looked around for a suitable place to spit their wads of Skoal. Their favorite target was the back of a well-raked Afro.

The only way you could tell a kicker (derived from "shitkicker" and the old Texas expression "to kick a nigger's ass") from a regular redneck or goat-roper was to look at their pickup trucks. If the bumper sticker read "Goat-ropers need love too," then the answer was obvious. If they drove viciously around the parking lot hurling empty LoneStar beer cans at clusters of blacks, then you knew they were kickers. Rednecks were a little less violent unless they had been out honky-tonking too long and started a fight by accusing someone at the bar of being an NL (nigger lover).

One day a kicker managed to get near the jukebox, surreptitiously dropped in a quarter and pushed A-4, "I'm Proud to be an Oakie from Muskogee." He laughed as he was chased from the school by an angry mob of blacks threatening to kill him if he ever put on such "honky trash" music again.

Desperate to reduce racial tensions, the school launched a campaign called Partners. Every student was supposed to find someone of another race to be their partner, and the school would provide free transportation and food for a picnic at Barton Springs or Lake Travis. I was afraid to ask any of the black girls in my classes. They were too cool, too tough, and too popular and I was just a skinny white girl who came from the North and had no idea what was "goin' down." The picnic was canceled when a Partners meeting turned into a race riot. It always scared me to see kids climbing onto the tops of lockers so they could have better aim when they jumped, knife in hand, into the middle of a hallway fight.

At the sound of the three o'clock bell, I would rush out of the school ahead of the others. If I were lucky my bicycle tires would still be inflated and I could escape before the crowds of students made their mass exodus to see the after-school fighting sessions in the parking lot of the Baptist church across the street.

One boy at school was neither white nor black. He had a light brown Afro and skin that was covered with dark brown and very white splotches. Looking back on it, he was probably the product of a genetic fluke similar to albinism. His schoolmates teased him mercilessly. They nicknamed him "Patches."

"How did he get like that?" I asked my friend Kelly.

"I bet his mom is white and his daddy's a nigger," she replied.

"Is that what happens when whites and blacks . . . you know . . . do it?" I asked.

"Sure," she said sagely. "What'd you think?"

From that day on, for at least two years, I thought the children of mixed marriages were covered with black-and-white patches.

Ironically, Mexicans dated either whites or blacks and no one cared. Mexican boys, with their long, shiny black hair and heavy Spanish accents, were very popular among white girls. They had romantic names like Felicio and Fernandez and Emilio. My friend Kelly's older sister, a beautiful Baptist with green eyes, dated a Mexican. She drove a baby blue Mustang with her long blond hair flying in the wind and made all the white boys hot with desire. But she turned them all down and remained true to her Mexican companion.

Dating Mexicans was fine, even "cool," at least among white students, but if a white girl did so much as speak for more than five minutes with a black boy she was labeled an NL. Blacks and whites never touched each other, never danced together, never came in close contact with each other except through sports like football and wrestling. If a white did not laugh at a racist joke, he was shunned as an outsider. Racist jokes (which I recount here only to reveal the twisted attitudes of white adolescents during that period in Texas) usually ran like this:

"How can you find a nigger in the dark?"
"Tell him to smile."

"Why do blacks always have sex on their minds?"
"Because their pubic hair is on their heads."

The taboo against touching a white was so powerful that some blacks took it as a dare. At the public swimming pool my friends and I always had to be on guard against adventurous black boys. One scorching summer day Jill, Kelly, and I—three young blonds—were bobbing up and down, splashing, laughing, and chasing each other in the shallow end of an Olympic-style swimming pool complete with three diving boards and several lifeguards. Kelly and Jill were developing more quickly than I was, and their bikini tops were just starting to get round while mine hung flat and shapeless. Suddenly I felt a hand squeeze me between the legs. I screamed. So did Jill and Kelly. We whirled about and saw three black boys swimming away underwater.

"Goddamned niggers!" Jill shrieked, pounding the water furiously with her fists. "I'm gonna tell my brother!"

"You horny black bastards!" Kelly shouted.

The three boys, no older than fourteen, climbed out of the pool, shook the beads of water from their Afros, slapped each other's backs, and looked back at us, laughing triumphantly. "White pussy!" one of them shouted, jogging along the side of the pool with his fist in the air. "I got me a handful of white pussy!"

From that day on I stayed away from the swimming pool and ran through the sprinkler in our backyard instead.

One night when my mother was working late and I had cooked my father and brother Dan a meal of Hamburger Helper and frozen string beans—the one meal I could prepare—I rode my bike down to the twenty-four-hour Minit Mart to buy some candy. Like most twelve-year-olds, I was addicted to Life Savers, Sugar Babies, M&M's, Clark bars, and Zots—the hard candy that fizzes in your mouth. When I reached the store I realized I had forgotten my money. I looked at the candy longingly, then left the store and headed home.

It was about eight at night and already dark. I had to ride through the valley first, then ascend the hill to Greensboro Drive. Too tired to ride uphill, I got off and walked my bicycle. Suddenly I heard a male voice behind me.

"Want some money?"

I turned around and saw a black boy of about fourteen riding a ten-speed bicycle. He was so dark I could only see his clothes and the bicycle. I'd never been addressed by a black before; I'd never been alone with a black before. Frightened, I started walking faster.

"Girl, I seen you in the candy store," he said, getting off his bike, dropping it on the curb and hurrying after me. "I seen you lookin' at the candy. You din't buy nothin'. Why come? Don't you got no money? I'll give you some."

"I don't need any," I said over my shoulder, quickening my pace. "I'm going home."

"What's your name?"

"Jane Smith," I lied.

"I know that ain't right. What's yo *real* name?"

"Who wants to know?"

"Tiki."

One of those boys with the funny names. I wondered how long he had been following me.

"I been watchin' you." He grabbed me by the arm and started dragging me away from the street. My bike made a clanging sound as it hit the curb. I tried to run, but he clutched me firmly. I struggled. He tightened his grip.

"What do you want?" I asked, feeling helpless.

"I wanna give you some."

I knew he was not talking about money. He pulled me across the yard between two houses, then pushed me up against the brick wall and pressed himself against me. His thick lips seemed to cover my whole face. I could barely breathe. I had never been kissed before and was not sure what he was doing to my face with his mouth. I thought about screaming, but I was afraid people would come and see what this black boy was doing to me. Shame would follow me all the days of my life. I pleaded with him instead.

He shoved a clumsy, fumbling hand under my shirt and felt my flat, boyish chest. He immediately let go of me and stepped back. Apparently he did not realize I was so young and undeveloped. He seemed apologetic.

"Want some gum?" he said, handing me a stick of Wrigley's spearmint.

I stared at him in disbelief, then ran back to the street, grabbed my bike and bolted, trembling with shock and fear and, I must admit, a bit awed that a boy had kissed me.

"Don't be like that!" Tiki called after me. "I din't mean no harm."

No one was home: My father had gone to a meeting and my brother had gone out with friends. I ran over to Jill's house, breathless and shaken. I told her that the black boy down the street, Tiki, had forcibly kissed me.

Jill looked horrified. "You let that nigger *kiss* you?" she cried.

"No, I didn't *let* him. He pulled me—"

Her father called to her from the next room.

"Yes, sir, I'm coming, sir," Jill said. Like many of my friends in Texas, she had to address her parents as "sir" and "ma'am."

I tried explaining what actually had happened, but Jill said, "You'd best leave now." I wondered why she was so abrupt. I went home to an empty house and brooded.

The next day the news was all over the neighborhood. Everyone but the adults knew. Jill had told her sisters and brothers, who had told Kelly's sisters, who had told the boys next door and down the street. I was an outcast. Jill and Kelly did not want to be seen with me, yet Jill's brother Eric continued to play basketball with Tiki, Mojo, and Dookey.

My parents and two older brothers were rarely home, and some neighborhood boys knew it. My father was juggling several jobs at once: as the minister of a tiny white church near the Gulf of Mexico, as a professor at Austin Theological Seminary, and as a full-time graduate student in psychology at the University of Texas. My mother, who was working on a master's degree and had a full-time job as an elementary school teacher for kids with special learning disabilities, came home late and sometimes with bruises from hulking eighteen-year-old sixth graders with "emotional problems."

One evening when I was home alone the doorbell rang. I left the chain on the door and opened it cautiously. I saw Tiki's face and immediately tried closing the door. His foot was in the crack.

"I gotta use your phone," he said urgently. "It'll just take a minute."

"Leave me alone," I said.

"Please, it ain't gonna take but a minute. I gotta call someone. It's important. Our phone's busted and I don't know no one 'round here."

"I can't let you in."

"You still mad 'bout what I done, ain't you? Like I tole you, I din't mean no harm. All I wanna do is use your phone. I won't mess witchoo."

I was used to obeying my father and brothers, and I was also used to trusting people, so when he persisted, I finally undid the chain, let him in, and showed him to the kitchen phone. He picked up the receiver, dialed a few numbers, then hung up.

"I gotta check something first," he said, then ran down the hall, flicking on all the lights and looking into each room. It was not hard for him to tell my brothers' rooms from mine. He stared around my yellow room, then turned out the lights and just sat there.

"What are you doing?" I asked from the hallway, keeping a safe distance from him.

"Shhhh! Just a minute."

He sat there in the darkness, peeping through my curtains from time to time and telling me to "Hush up!" every time I asked what he was doing. A few minutes later he stood up, walked down the hall and left the house. I locked the door again, wondering why he had never finished making his phone call. He was up to something, but I was too young and naive to realize he was ingeniously trying to convince his friends he was having a white girl. A few minutes later the doorbell rang again. This time it was a black boy I had never seen before. I left the chain secured.

"Why don't you give *me* some?" he said.

"What do you mean?" I asked.

"How come you give *him* some but not nobody else?"

I looked beyond him and saw Tiki and a group of young blacks standing in a circular pool of light under a street lamp. It was then that I realized why Tiki had insisted on getting inside the house, turning on my bedroom light, turning it off and waiting. He had fooled his companions. I slammed the door in the boy's face.

The summer that followed was painful for me. My friends no longer called, and when they saw me coming they turned the other way. They made jokes about my family, particularly my mother, who subscribed to *Ebony* so she could better understand her black pupils and would reprimand anyone who used the word *nigger* in her presence. I spent my time alone, bewildered, wondering what I had done wrong. Nothing I said seemed to change my friends' poor opinion of me for having been kissed by a black boy. I did not tell my parents what had happened out of fear of being scolded: I was not supposed to ride my bike to the candy store after dark.

Fortunately we moved from Texas to Minnesota in August, and I was able to start a new life free from the stigma of being an NL.

We settled in a predominantly white suburb of Minneapolis with the idyllic name of Golden Valley, next to New Hope and Crystal.

Everywhere I looked I saw whiteness: white people, white snow, white sidewalks, Scandinavians with hair so blond it looked white. Everyone's last name seemed to end in "son" or "sen"—Anderson, Danielson, Swensen, Erikson. Suddenly there was no "color problem." I forgot about race. It was taken for granted that whites went to the Dinosaur roller-skating rink on Saturday night and blacks on Friday.

I knew there were sections of Minneapolis where blacks and Native Americans lived, but I was in the suburbs where it is easy to forget inner-city problems like poverty, violence, and racial strife. The only time I had to deal with black men was in encountering them on my way to Blake School, when I transferred from the suburban bus to the city bus in front of a windowless building on Hennepin and Twelfth called Rap-N-Romp. To avoid them I waited for the Number Six in a nearby post office, but even there I was not safe from the mildly retarded white man who daily tried to guess the color of my underwear.

I had heard of the "Minnesota Pipeline"—the network of pimps who lure young blonds of Nordic descent from their wholesome lives in the Midwest, make them emotionally dependent on them or physically dependent on their cocaine or heroin, then funnel them into New York City to work as prostitutes. I was wary of all black men, but particularly those in flashy clothes who muttered lewd comments about my "lookin' good, mama."

For a long time I succeeded in forgetting that unwelcomed first kiss. The taboo against associating with blacks was now firmly entrenched in my mind. I thought any white girl who dated a black boy was throwing herself away like a piece of garbage. She was crazy and needed a shrink. Who, in her right mind, would give up all her white friends and the love of her family for a black boy?

I took racial segregation for granted. It seemed only natural that blacks should stay with blacks and whites with whites. People were more comfortable among their own kind, and I was no exception. I did not miss Texas, did not miss the race riots, the "nigger jokes," the underwater assailants, the terror of being part of the intimidated minority at school. Though I had adopted liberal, democratic political views from my parents and believed in the ideal of racial equality, I saw nothing wrong in having only two or three blacks in my private high school of four hundred. I felt it was justified by the fact that only two percent of the population of Minnesota was black.

I did not become aware of the black population in Minneapolis until I was seventeen. After doing some Christmas shopping downtown one day, I paused in front of the Orpheum Theater on Hennepin Avenue to examine a poster portraying a young white man—or was he black? The poster read PRINCE—Live in Concert. I had vaguely heard of the twenty-one-year-old musician, knew this was his home town, and knew he had attended Central High, but I had never heard his music. I had no idea his latest hit album was called *Dirty Mind*.

Curious, I bought two tickets, one for myself and one for a friend of mine, a painfully shy and sheltered Jewish doctor's son who was cocaptain with me on the Blake cross-country ski team. The concert was like nothing I had imagined. I looked around the crowded concert hall and realized that, as far as I could see, my friend and I were the only whites.

Prince strutted around the stage, nude except for boots and leopard-skin bikini bottoms, moving his narrow hips back and forth like a piston. His bare-chested guitar player wore skin-tight black leather pants. The crowd was shouting something in time to the music, and I strained to hear what it was. With amazement I realized they were shouting, "Head!" and that the entire song was about oral sex.

I could not comprehend the blatant passion, the explicit sexual vibrations emanating from the stage that ran like electricity through the sweating, clapping, chanting crowd. My Jewish friend gasped, blushed, and covered his face with his hands in embarrassment. He could hardly wait to get out of there. I, too, barely out of puberty, felt overwhelmed by the bold and bacchanal celebration of sex, by the primal beat and hip thrusts, by the chanting and moaning that filled the cavernous theater. That night I concluded that blacks burned with superhuman sexual urges that made them dangerous, threatening, and far more capable of rape, incest, and adultery than whites.

The image of the black rapist, influenced subtly by TV images of black violence, became embedded in my mind. Like many white women, I began to see black men as predators, capable of horrendous acts of crime and passion. Many white women become paranoid around black men after they have been mugged, held at gun point, attacked, or sexually threatened by one; others grow to fear them simply out of rumors, the whispered warnings of their mothers, spouses, or boyfriends, and social innuendoes. Try as we may to be open-minded, liberal, and accepting, I doubt there are many white women who can honestly say they have never felt uneasy or terrified at finding themselves alone in an elevator with a black man.

When I attended Brown University in the early 1980s, I never wondered why blacks sat on one side of the Ratty (the cafeteria) while whites sat on the other. I never considered taking a course in Afro-American studies; those, I thought, were for blacks. Only once did I set foot in the Third World Center, and I quickly retreated when I saw black faces look up and stare at me, as if demanding an explanation for my intrusion. I was intimidated by militant black fraternity members who marched single file around campus and had orders not to speak to whites. When I became interested in feminism and started using the library at the Sarah Doyle Women's Center, I did not question the absence of black women.

It surprised me that so many students were arguing, shouting, gesticulating, and generally getting themselves all worked up and angry over the debate raging on campus about Third World Week—a special orientation week for minority students held at Brown each fall before white students arrive on campus. Many white students argued that Third World Week was unnecessary and contributed to campus segregation by allowing minorities to make friends with each other before whites arrived. Blacks retorted that they needed the extra week to prepare themselves mentally and emotionally for life at a predominantly white institution. I did not take a stand one way or the other. I was convinced that whites would inevitably befriend whites and blacks would stick with blacks, regardless of Brown's orientation system. Segregation was too deeply ingrained in all of us, both black and white, to be removed by eliminating or lengthening something called Third World Week.

I had many friends, but none of them was black. When one of my best friends, Carol Abizaid, told me she was attracted to a black man, I was horrified. Carol was a beautiful young woman of seventeen when I met her, the daughter of an American woman and a Lebanese businessman who had met at Cornell University in Ithaca, New York. She had the looks and build of a high-class model. She was raised in a huge house in Beirut until she was fourteen, grew up amid the booms and blasts of bombs and machine guns, and was often protected by armed guards. She spoke English to her mother, Arabic to her father and his friends, French to the maids, and Spanish to several of her relatives. When I first saw her she was driving a jeep around the Brown campus with a black Labrador puppy in her lap and her long brownish blond hair flying in the wind.

We became close friends. She lived with me at my parents' home in Minnesota the summer after our freshman year. We roomed together sophomore year. The summer following our junior year, after I had spent a semester at the University of Budapest, I visited Carol in Paris, where she was living in the plush apartment of a vacationing couple. Carol wanted to be a professional dancer and was doing all the things such aspiring performers often do: She deprived herself of food, trained vigorously throughout the academic year, and took classes in Paris during the summer.

One day I was resting in the apartment after a tour of the Pompadou Art Center when Carol came home from dance class, threw herself onto the couch, gazed up at the ceiling and murmured, "He's gorgeous." She grinned.

"Who's gorgeous?" I asked.

"A black dancer in my class."

"Who is he?"

"I don't know his name, but he's exquisite. Huge, really built. I've never seen a finer specimen of manhood. You should see him move. You can see every muscle in his legs, arms, abdomen. . . . And he speaks perfect French."

I laughed and rolled my eyes. "You've got the hots for a black man? Come on, Carol. You must be kidding."

Carol had just broken up with the prototype all-American white male: an extremely handsome football player from Ohio with dark curly hair, a strong chin, and brown eyes capable of melting any woman's heart. He had been the star running back for the Brown team, had been drafted by the New England Patriots, left football after a knee injury, and became a professional model for the Ford Agency in New York. He wrote long and heartfelt letters to Carol in Paris begging her to come back to Providence early. My friend was beautiful, rich, and self-assured enough to have her pick of white men. Why in the world would she choose a black?

"He's really beautiful," Carol repeated, still gazing rapturously at the ceiling. "If you don't believe me, stop by the studio and watch our dance rehearsal."

Curiosity lured me to the dance studio. I walked through narrow streets in a section of Paris where stone buildings might have toppled over if they had not been so tightly wedged together, found the dance studio, and ascended a flight of dimly lit stairs. The smell of sweat and the rhythmic thudding of feet guided me to Carol's class. I watched her bend, stretch, and leap with dozens of other dancers in time to piano music as the teacher shouted directions in French.

I spotted the black dancer. He was indeed a perfect example of physical fitness and moved with remarkable grace, but I still did not understand how Carol could find him sexually attractive. The energy he exuded and his dark skin made him seem alien, intimidating, and untouchable. I could not imagine kissing those big African lips or touching that wiry hair. As Carol and I walked toward the Metro, I teased her mercilessly for having a crush on a black man.

A short discussion I had once had with my father had deepened my aversion to black-white mixed couples and made me think Carol's attraction to the dancer was perverse. One day in Minneapolis I asked my father about the mixed couples gathered at one end of Lake Calhoun. The black men were thin, wore flashy clothes, and drove large cars like Cadillacs and Lincoln Continentals, while the women were usually large peroxide blonds with big hips and double chins. My father told me the women were most likely prostitutes and the men were probably pimps or drug dealers.

This made me hope that Carol would forget her strange crush and return to "normal" once we got back to Providence. But upon her return to Brown, Carol became completely infatuated with a tall and muscular biracial student named Paul.

"Why do you find black men so attractive?" I asked.

"Because I admire blacks," Carol replied. "They have to struggle a lot harder than whites. They have more strength of character. They weren't fed from silver spoons all their lives like so many students here. But don't get me wrong—I don't feel sorry for them. A lot of whites go out with black people because they pity them and want to fix their lives for them. It puts the white partner in a position of superiority. It's racist. That's not what my relationship with Paul is about.

I feel I can relate to him because we both live in two different worlds. He's both black and white. I'm both American and Lebanese. I feel closer to people who have multicultural backgrounds. We share a bicultural experience, which is both a strength and a struggle."

I scrutinized Carol from a distance. In a matter of months her boyfriend, roommate, and friends were all black or biracial. She often loaned her Toyota to her friends, and since I was accustomed to waving whenever I saw her car approach, I found myself greeting a car filled with blacks I did not know. I wondered why she let people take advantage of her and her possessions. Carol and I had been very close our first three years at Brown, but her attraction to blacks drove a wedge between us. I thought she was just going through a phase and would soon come back to the white world, which was safe and free of conflict and oblivious to racial tensions. I thought she was dating a black just to get back at her mother, with whom she constantly argued.

As graduation neared I spent more time with Carol and her boyfriend Paul. As I got to know her roommate Ellen, a kind and sensitive young biracial woman, I understood how Carol could feel very connected to her. I admired Carol for bridging the gap between the races with such honesty of emotion. She stayed in Providence to do graduate work in African cultures and be with Paul, and I moved to New York to attend graduate school at Columbia.

My parents came to my Brown graduation in May 1984, and I took them to Carol's cocktail party. My father, using his psychologist's mind off duty, listened attentively to Carol's conversations with her mother and carefully watched her interact with Paul.

"I think I know why Carol is with a black man," he said to me. "She's angry at her mother for taking her away from her father in Beirut, and she's acting out that anger by dating a black man. It's her way of really irking her mother."

"Have you ever considered the possibility that Carol simply fell in love with Paul?"

My father merely smiled, apparently amused by my naïveté about such complex, subconscious, subliminal matters. "There are always hidden motives behind interracial relationships," he said.

After the graduation ceremony, as we drove to Massachusetts to spend a weekend with relatives near New Bedford, my father again brought up the topic of Carol and Paul, as if fascinated by the relationship. He had counseled mixed couples before, but the fact that Carol was such a close friend of mine may have shaken him up. He seemed to want to convince me that their attraction for each other was unnatural and driven by dark motives.

"Did you hear the way Carol's mother criticized her hair style?" he asked. "No wonder Carol's trying to get back at her."

"Look, Dad, you don't even know Paul. Maybe Carol sees in him all the qualities she would admire in any man, regardless of color." My own words surprised me. There I was defending a relationship that even I had considered strange and unnatural just a few months earlier.

But it was not until I met Mark that I truly began to understand what Carol had gone through. From the moment he sat down next to me in the International House cafeteria and began talking to the Belgian across from him about his struggles growing up under apartheid, I was captivated. As the months went by and Mark and I grew to know, trust, and respect each other, it seemed only natural to express our affection.

One night, two weeks after we began seeing each other, we decided to go out and celebrate the fact that fate had brought us together. We dined by candlelight in a seafood restaurant in Midtown called Pier 52 where a blind black jazz musician played piano, cracked jokes, and reminisced about life in Harlem during the 1920s.

Mark became silent and serious.

"What are you thinking?" I asked.

"Someday, if we're still together, I will marry you," he said. "I want so much to see you grow as a writer and to be with you, as a companion, forever."

I reacted to his words with a shy smile on the surface and a mixture of love and fear in my heart. Everything had happened so fast. I feared that I might someday hurt him if I could not muster the courage to marry across racial lines, and I also feared that if we married I might alienate my family. The other fear I had was of losing my identity somewhere along the road to his fame. Though he was a poor graduate student when we met, and was still, my instincts told me that he would become a great writer and an eloquent orator. He was a survivor. He had tenacity, ambition, and integrity. I had little doubt that he would succeed in life, especially because he believed in himself.

One Sunday morning Mark and I walked two blocks to Riverside Church to hear Reverend William Sloane Coffin preach about the injustices of legalized racism in South Africa and the need for sanctuary churches for Salvadoran and Guatemalan refugees. As we sat side by side in that cavernous church filled with stained glass and candles, Mark slowly entwined his pinky around mine. For the rest of the service I was happily aware of our embracing pinkies. Touching felt right, and I knew then that our love was nothing to be ashamed of.

That night we stayed up late watching the film *Nicholas and Alexandra* in Mark's tiny dorm room, sitting on his single bed and leaning against the wall. Just as the Russian revolution began and Trotsky and Lenin were arguing, my eyes grew heavy and I fell asleep on Mark's shoulder. When I awoke a few minutes later and asked what I had missed, Mark smiled at me in the near darkness, wrapped his arms around me, and we kissed.

I awoke with a start as the first gray fingers of dawn touched the window. In the dim light I saw Mark's face inches away from mine, nestled into the downy pillow. I stared with curiosity at his wide nose, his little ears, the tiny eyelashes that curled rather than lay straight, the contrast between his unblemished black skin and the white blanket draped across his shoulder. I felt warm and full of love.

Then doubts crept in. "What would my parents say if they saw me now, lying in the arms of a black man?" My parents were liberal Democrats who had voted for George McGovern in 1972, but would they understand this? My father, a graduate of Wesleyan and Yale Divinity School who felt no one was good enough for his little girl, had disliked each and every one of my boyfriends. If he did not like those white men I had dated, what would he think of this black man? Isn't it every white father's worst nightmare to find out his only daughter loves a Negro?

I crawled out of bed in a panic, pulled on my boots and sweater, combed my hair hastily with my fingers, and headed for the door. I hoped no one would be in the halls. Mark's room was on an all-male wing of the dorm, and rumors spread fast. The hinges creaked. Mark awoke.

"Hey, Sweets," he said lovingly. "Don't leave yet. It's too early."

"I have to go."

"But it was so cozy. Is anything wrong?"

"No, it's just that I . . . I have to go." I gave him a quick kiss and left.

The coast was clear. I dashed down the hall and had almost made it to the stairwell when the door of the men's john swung open and a fellow journalism student walked out wearing a bathrobe. He was startled to see me in the men's wing. I smiled in embarrassment and ran up four flights of stairs to my room, locked the door, and faced my sunny view of Midtown, my guitar, my dusty stereo, my stacks of mail, Russian assignments, magazine articles, typing paper.

I immediately missed Mark and became upset with myself. "Why do you care so much what Dad thinks of you?" I said angrily to my reflection in the mirror. "When will you free yourself of your mental enslavement to this patriarchal, bigoted society? Follow your heart and forget about the rest! Think of yourself for once. You've fallen in love with a man. If people disapprove, that's *their* problem."

Stating a resolution is much easier than abiding by it. I continued to act paranoid every time I visited Mark's room. I would poke my head out the door, glance quickly both ways, listen for the sound of footsteps, then scuttle down the hall to the women's wing as fast as my legs would carry me. I carried my shoes so I could steal silently down the corridor. I always reached the women's bathroom breathless.

"Don't you live on the tenth floor?" one woman asked.

"Yes, but I like this bathroom better," I said.

As I brushed my teeth she looked quizzically at my bathrobe, a brown and red men's robe that belonged to Mark.

Sometimes I would get exasperated with myself. "Who am I hiding from? My parents? Myself? A society that sees mixed couples as morally unfit to appear in public? It's all in my head. I'll say it now and I hope it sticks: I don't care what anyone else thinks!"

3

GOING PUBLIC

MARK'S VIEW

Walking through Manhattan side by side, Gail and I blended into the diverse crowd of pedestrians, who ranged in color from as dark as I to as light and fair as Gail. Moving down the jammed sidewalks of Fifth Avenue at rush hour, we were inconspicuous in a throng that had to walk eight abreast to keep from tumbling off the curb and into the steady, noisy stream of traffic and honking yellow taxicabs. People bumped into each other in their mad dash for a vacant cab or a late appointment.

The smell of hot dogs and pretzels, blended with the malodorous steam rising from manholes, stung our noses; the blare of honking horns and corner evangelists shouting into loudspeakers deafened our ears. In such confusion and cacophony, it was easy to get lost in the anonymity of a crowd and still retain our individuality, without once letting go of each other's hand.

The subway was a different story. In a crowded train rumbling, rattling, and racing through the bowels of Manhattan, I would cling to the center pole and Gail would wrap her arms around my waist and hold on for dear life. She seemed oblivious to the fact that we stood out, and held onto me with unself-conscious ease. I, on the other hand, was hyperaware of people staring at us. Some would lift their weary eyes, ponder us for a moment, then resume reading the sports pages of the *New York Post, The New York Times,* or the *Daily News.* Older women would lean their faces together, gossiping in whispers, looking disdainfully at us from time to time. Others had seen it all before and were too jaded by New York even to cast a curious glance at us.

One evening as Gail and I hurried arm in arm from Fifth Avenue toward Port Authority, we passed two young black men.

"Hey, look at him," one young man shouted to his friend. "He got hisself a white girl. She be damn good lookin' too."

Such comments upset and saddened me. They reminded me of the pervasive stereotype that all black men are, at least subconsciously, out to "get a white girl." What did those two young men know about our relationship? Nothing. All they saw was black man, white woman.

Our first major evening out in public was to attend the 1985 Front Page Dinner Dance thrown by the Newswomen's Club of New York. Because she usually wore jeans and owned a scanty wardrobe of formal wear, Gail had to go out at the last minute and buy a new dress and shoes in which to receive her $2,500 Anne O'Hare McCormick scholarship. The dinner, an extravagant affair held in the Empire State Ballroom of the Grand Hyatt Hotel, was followed by an award ceremony for top journalists from *Newsday, The New York Times, The New Yorker,* ABC News "Nightline," and "20/20." I was the only black in the ballroom except for those stacking the dirty plates and clearing the clutter from the tables, which gave me a disquieting feeling of being back in South Africa, where blacks toiled as servants while whites were lavishly entertained. What was I doing in such a place?

But I quickly remembered my reason for being there when I watched Gail ascend the steps onto the stage to receive her scholarship award. I felt proud: That was my "Sweets" up there. The president of the Newswomen's Club, Joan O'Sullivan of King Features, made a short speech about Gail's off-beat accomplishments: mastering Hungarian, German, and Russian; traveling alone to Budapest and talking her way into the university there; graduating from Brown; and writing for Minneapolis *City Pages.*

Few couples were dancing, but Gail, in her exuberant mood,

dragged me onto the dance floor. We must have looked strange, a black man and a white woman, dancing together in the middle of a high-ceilinged ballroom while the white faces of the American media's movers and shakers looked on. I had been the only black in a room filled with whites many times, but never when I was dancing with a white woman. Some people gaped at us, a few with bemused indifference. I did my best to forget them and to focus on Gail, her happiness at receiving the award, and our joy at sharing a special moment.

Whenever I traveled to Long Island to lecture on South Africa and apartheid before various groups, Gail would accompany me. During these trips, we would never let on that we were anything more than friends. We wanted to keep our relationship private and, therefore, kept it a secret. It was easier to pretend to be platonic friends than to deal with people's prejudices. When we spent the night at a white minister's home, we requested separate rooms, despite his wife's attempt to coax us into revealing the true nature of our relationship.

"You *do* want to stay in the same room, don't you?" she said insinuatingly. "It would be fine with *us*, you know. *We* understand."

We insisted we were just friends and wanted separate rooms. In the morning at breakfast the minister spoke to me, in a confidential and fatherly tone, about the problems mixed couples confront and how difficult it is to stay married.

"I had a good friend once, a black man like yourself," the minister said. "He wanted to marry a white woman. Oh, I assure you I warned him against it. But no, he wouldn't listen to me. He went ahead and married her. And you know what happened? They're divorced now. I knew it would happen all along." He looked hard at me, then at Gail, then back to me, as if to say, "Don't make the same mistake."

Spring arrived and the weather grew warm. Gail and I went for regular runs along the Hudson River through Riverside Park, past rotting benches, screeching seagulls stained by the polluted air, and graffiti-covered stone walls. Whenever the exercise and warm weather made me sweat, I would peel off my shirt to cool down. People often stared at us, but we never heard a negative comment. Many were simply curious. Almost nothing can shock a New Yorker, not even people with pink hair, black lipstick, painted faces, or safety pins in their cheeks.

I felt completely natural around Gail when we were alone together, but as soon as we stepped out the door I became acutely sensitive to the way people regarded us. It was difficult for me to regard our love as an aberration in social norms. Only when people stared did I remember how deeply race as an issue still permeated American society. At times it seemed that the only difference between white attitudes in South Africa and America was that white South Africans had made the mistake of institutionalizing their racism.

It seemed half the audience turned around whenever we sat down in a movie theater or concert hall. When we asked to be seated at an elegant restaurant on Fifty-second Street, the waiter led us to a bad table directly in front of the kitchen's swinging doors—there were a couple of empty tables in nicer locations—next to the only black couple in the restaurant. Gail was outraged and wanted to insist on better seating, but I was so accustomed to prejudice that I saw no point in arguing. We left without ordering.

"Racism makes me so mad," Gail said, still upset. "Why do people do this to each other?"

"I really don't know," I replied. "The best way to deal with racism is not to be obsessed by it. It can make you paranoid and even drive you mad. It gives racists satisfaction to know they're messing up your life. Life is simply too short to let bigots spoil its few moments of happiness with their venom."

"But shouldn't we fight to change people's attitudes?" she asked.

"Yes, we should," I said. "But let's be realistic. For some people racism is a way of life. It's deeply ingrained in their psyches. No amount of argument and reason will change attitudes based on ignorance and fear."

We fell silent for a while, and continued walking through the streets of Manhattan, looking for another place to dine. Suddenly Gail looked up and said, "Do you sometimes wish I were black?"

The question surprised me and made me somewhat defensive. "I fell in love with you as you are! Why in the world would I want you to be something you're not?"

"It would be easier for you, wouldn't it, if I were black?"

"Easier how?"

"I mean, we wouldn't be so odd and conspicuous as a couple. Therefore people wouldn't mind us."

"Why are you obsessed about what other people think?" I asked. "I thought you were the one who said nothing matters but the way we feel about one another."

"I did say that, and I meant it. But Mark, tell me the truth. Doesn't it bother you that I'm white?"

I denied that it did, but deep down I was troubled that people, especially blacks, misconstrued my reasons for dating a white. I knew that should I enter the limelight after the publication of *Kaffir Boy*, the issue would become magnified, especially as I might be regarded as some sort of spokesperson for the anti-apartheid struggle, a voice for the black community. What effect would my relationship with Gail have on my career as a writer? What sacrifices would it entail? Was I willing to make those sacrifices? Only time would tell.

The two friends I was eager for Gail to meet were Stew and Claudia, a mixed couple on Long Island with whom I lived for a summer. Stew, a black stockbroker for a major national firm, grew up in Winston-Salem, North Carolina. His wife, Claudia, an elementary school teacher from New England, was disowned by her parents for marrying Stew. They had two children whom I was sure Gail would adore.

I wanted the visit to be a surprise. As Gail and I rode the Long Island Railroad toward Bellport, she kept asking me questions about Stew and Claudia. I told her a little about each of them, but not enough to give away their races. I wanted her to meet my friends with fresh eyes and an open heart, and to assure her that we were not the only mixed couple on earth.

GAIL'S VIEW

That weekend visit to Stew and Claudia's home on Long Island was both enlightening and troubling. First of all, it gave me a glimpse into suburban married life, which made me, a young graduate student with a fear of commitment, imagine that I would suffocate in such an environment. Like many women of my generation, I had not escaped the influence of radical feminism and was convinced that marriage and a house in the suburbs were nothing more than a paralyzing trap that transforms even the most talented and energetic women into unrespected housewives and overworked mothers.

Since the day I finished Betty Friedan's book *The Feminine Mystique* my sophomore year at Brown, I vowed I would never let myself become one of those complacent women with the frozen smiles in the laundry detergent commercials who derive their happiness from seeing dirty socks turn white. I swore I would never make the same mistakes as my mother, a brilliant woman who graduated from Mount Holyoke College at twenty; taught for a year; married a minister; then gave up her career ambitions under social pressure to devote herself to the church, her children, and her husband's career. She ended up feeling trapped and depressed for almost two decades.

Perhaps getting involved with a black man was my way of stating to the world that I would never succumb to the stereotype of the suburban housewife dressed in pink with the fake smile on her face hugging her three blond children. Falling in love with Mark, a nonconformist who throughout life had swum against the tide, gave me the feeling of being different.

But when I met Stew and Claudia, I realized that even mixed couples settle down at some point and have a fairly normal and routine life of grocery shopping, feeding the kids, washing the cars, and mowing the lawn. It upset me to learn that even mixed couples, those rebels against society, cannot avoid the numbing effects of all-American family life, with its mortgage payments and church meetings and football games.

That weekend I turned twenty-three. I felt old all day long. I realized I had reached adulthood and that I should be very careful with my heart. I could not continue to fall in and out of love with men indefinitely. I felt I had to consider my relationship with Mark as potentially permanent or flee. I sensed Mark had partly taken me to Stew and Claudia's house to test me, to see how I would react to interracial marriage. If by the end of the weekend I felt life was too hard for mixed couples, I knew I would have to break up with Mark. It would not be fair to either of us to carry on a relationship that could not lead to marriage.

What disturbed me most about our visit was something Claudia said at dinner one night.

"A mixed couple is viewed as a black couple," she said.

I stared at her milky skin, thin nose, and almond-shaped eyes and wondered how on earth people could consider her black.

"What do you mean?" I asked.

"The white woman becomes black in the eyes of the community," she said, then went on to explain the trouble they had finding a real estate agent who would show them homes in white neighborhoods.

I stared at Stew and Claudia's children. Both the boy and girl, Sudi and Leta, had skin the color of café au lait, dark brown eyes, and curly black hair. To the outside world they were black; their mother's white skin would never change that. They would be as discriminated against and stereotyped as any black child in America.

The night was long and dark. I tossed and turned, deeply troubled. I struggled to understand how a white woman like Claudia could so willingly relinquish the love of her parents and give up her identity as a white person to become a black man's wife and the mother of two black children. Claudia had been cut off emotionally and financially from her parents when she married Stew, had sacrificed the approval of society to be with the man she loved. I admired her strength and hoped that someday I too could learn to love as deeply and selflessly as Claudia, but that night I knew I was wavering, tossed back and forth between my strong attachment to Mark and my ingrained desire to please my parents and do what was expected of me. My parents still did not know I was dating a black man.

As I lay awake watching Mark sleep, I realized, with a stab in my heart that took my breath away, that I wanted a baby with pink cheeks and blue eyes someday. I wanted what many of us want: a child that reminds us of ourselves as we once were. I always pictured my child having straight blond hair and big, bright eyes. I thought, *I want a baby who won't be labeled, categorized, or discriminated against. It would be selfish of me not to think of my child's future. Shouldn't I marry a white man for my baby's sake? It may be morally strengthening to battle societal stereotypes, but I want a baby with blue eyes.*

Gail, age four, with self-inflicted haircut.

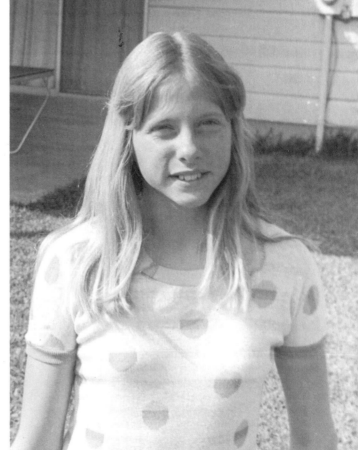

Gail, age twelve, in backyard of her family's home in Austin, Texas. (Dr. David J. Ernsberger)

Gail and her roommate, Carol Abizaid, as sophomores at Brown
University. *(Imre Kovacs)*

Gail, Bianca, Oprah, and Mark on the set of the
"Oprah Winfrey Show." *(Harpo, Inc.)*

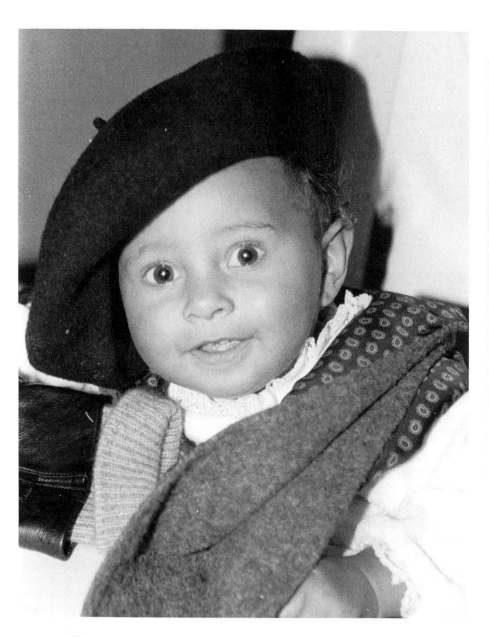

Bianca all spiffed up. *(Gail Mathabane)*

The public wedding on Long Island, August 1, 1987.
(Marty Van Lith)

Gail's grandfather (Grampa) holding newborn Bianca. *(Gail Mathabane)*

Diana, Linah, and George with their new niece. *(Gail Mathabane)*

Gail and Mark in the library of International House in New York, where they met. *(Gail Mathabane)*

The secret wedding at City Hall in Manhattan, February 27, 1987. *(Sandy)*

Mark with his parents during their 1990 U.S. visit.
(Gail Mathabane)

Bianca with Aunt Linah and Grandma. *(Gail Mathabane)*

Family reunion in Kernersville, North Carolina, Thanksgiving 1990. *From left to right:* Bianca; Mark; Mark's mother; Diana; Gail's mother; Mark's father; Gail; Linah; and Grampa. *(Gail Mathabane)*

Mark reunited with his father, Jackson, after a twelve-year separation. *(Gail Mathabane)*

M̲ark teaching his mother to read. *(Gail Mathabane)*

Bianca's first Christmas. *(Gail Mathabane)*

Gail's father playing with Bianca. (Gail Mathabane)

Diana with Bianca. (Gail Mathabane)

Our second child, Nathan Phillip, born January 20, 1991.
(Gail Mathabane)

Gail, her father, and Bianca. *(Mark Mathabane)*

Gail's mother and Bianca playing with Nathan.
(Gail Mathabane)

I fell asleep fantasizing about traveling through Finland and Russia, meeting strong, blond men with blue eyes. In another dream I stood in a group of tall blond Russian intellectuals on the steps of the University of Moscow.

When I opened my eyes the next morning I saw Mark's dark handsome face kissing my lips and whispering, "Oh, Sweets, I love you." I threw my arms around him with more passion and vigor than ever and shut my eyes tight against his shoulder, trying desperately to force out all thoughts of race and society and blue eyes. I loved Mark, the human being, and that was all that mattered to me.

That afternoon Mark and I went for a walk on the beach, holding hands and feeling the warmth of the sun on our upturned faces. The waves rolled in rhythmically and crashed on the smooth, packed plane of sand. Ocean blended into sky and land like one immense orb. We were sitting on the sand, half-leaning against each other, when five-year-old Leta snuck up behind us and hummed the wedding march.

"I now pronounce you man and wife," she said in her girlish voice, grinning from ear to ear. "You may kiss the bride . . . on the lips!" Leta burst into giggles as Mark chased her around the beach trying to kiss her. "I'm not the bride!" she shrieked. "You're supposed to marry Gail! I wouldn't marry you for all the candy in the world!"

Mark caught Leta in a bear hug and gave her a kiss. She started screaming and crying so hard she hyperventilated, then sat up laughing with tear-filled eyes.

"She's pretty smart for a five-year-old," I said when Mark returned.

"That's nothing," Mark said. "When she first heard I had a girlfriend, she asked me, 'Does she have big boobs?'"

We burst out laughing. Leta came skipping gleefully down the beach to join us. Little did we know her playful marriage pronouncement would come true, and that two and a half years later she would be the flower girl at our wedding.

That evening Stew and Claudia threw a party for Mark and invited numerous friends: writers, peace activists, Unitarians, teachers. Mark sat on a sofa between me and best-selling romance novelist Phyllis Whitney, a small and sprightly woman in her eighties who gazed up at the young African with admiration. In the living room the five guests listened with rapt attention to Mark expounding his views on politics and life. I turned my attention to the eyes transfixed on him.

At such moments, I sensed that Mark was too overpowering for me, too much the focus of attention, too strong and talkative and persuasive. I wondered if my own identity, still developing and tentative, could flourish beside his. I sometimes felt a need to be away from him in order to grow.

After the crowd dispersed and we were alone together, I watched Mark read beside me, his head nodding sleepily and his short curly eyelashes shutting his tired eyes, and thought how much I loved him, though I loved in an envious, competitive, adoring, worshiping way, constantly wracked with doubts about our future as an interracial couple.

I did not understand the complexities of interracial love, because I was, for the most part, unaware of what it meant to be black in America. Like most whites, I rarely had to concern myself with race issues. My knowledge of civil rights and the 1960s had taught me that racial tensions could explode into riots and bloodshed, and talking to frustrated and embittered blacks in Harlem and black teenage mothers in the South Bronx had enlightened me further, but I still could not grasp what it truly meant to be discriminated against or oppressed simply because of one's skin color and the texture of one's hair.

In an attempt to think and feel, if only briefly, like a black person, I began reading the works of black writers: Alice Walker, Zora Neale Hurston, James Baldwin, Richard Wright, and Claude Brown. A certain line in Baldwin's *The Fire Next Time* struck me: "He was defeated long before he died because at the bottom of his heart, he really believed what white people said about him." It was then I realized that color consciousness is deeply rooted not only in whites, but in blacks as well. When you are treated all your life as an inferior being, it is easy to believe you are indeed inferior.

As I walked across the Columbia campus in the early spring of 1985 I began encountering groups of people gathered in tight circles, deeply involved in heated discussions, around card tables labeled Coalition for a Free South Africa. Their tables attracted considerable attention, and soon I saw a large number of students, both black and white, wearing the colors of the African National Congress and pins reading Free Mandela. I sensed they were up to something.

On April 3, 1985, on the seventeenth anniversary of the assassination of Martin Luther King, Jr., I saw a huge group of students gathering on the steps of Hamilton Hall, the main administration building. It was around eleven o'clock on a crisp, sunny spring morning. Out of curiosity I slipped through the crowd to see what was happening. Students had just finished wrapping a silver-link chain around the door handles. The building was barricaded for the first time since the student protests of 1968.

"What's this all about?" I asked a young man clad in faded jeans and wearing a huge Free South Africa button.

"We want Columbia to stop supporting apartheid," he said. "This university has thirty-three million dollars worth of stocks invested in companies that do business in South Africa. We're not unlocking this building until they dump those stocks. Some of the people here are on a hunger strike. They haven't eaten in two weeks. If you support us, boycott your classes. We're not leaving these steps until President Sovran listens to us."

For weeks they camped out on the steps, made tents to protect themselves from the rain, kept warm in cold weather by staying in their sleeping bags all day. The massive divestment protest lasted all month, received national media coverage, and sparked similar protests at universities across the country.

Our professors at the journalism school warned us from getting involved in the protest.

"A good journalist has to be objective," one of the deans said sententiously. We were assembled in the World Room for a special meeting, and he spoke from behind a podium. We could hear the protesters chanting at the rally below the window. "In a political controversy, you cannot advocate only one side," he said. "You must present a balanced view. You have to be professionals. You should weigh the statements made by the trustees against the slogans those students are shouting in that uproar out there."

Most of us were too curious and excited to heed the dean's warning, and knowing how Mark had suffered made me determined to do whatever I could to help stop apartheid. Whenever we J-school students could, we would cross the campus to Hamilton Hall and join in with the others as they chanted, "Apartheid kills, Columbia pays the bills" and "South Africa's stocks have got to go."

Six members of the Coalition for a Free South Africa were fasting to protest the university's investments. Two of them, both white, were in my Russian class. They stopped attending class, but I saw them every day on the steps of the administration building, growing thinner and more gaunt each day. Eventually they had to be hospitalized for dehydration.

Rumors spread that the administration threatened to deport any South African exchange students participating in the protest, so Mark kept a cautious distance from the rally. I attended for both of us. I was amazed by the large turnout of whites. Watching blacks and whites work together to fight injustice made me feel hopeful that racism might someday be defeated, not only in South Africa, but in this country as well.

By May graduation, the protest had lost its steam and still the university had not divested. Several months later, Columbia finally withdrew its holdings in companies that do business in South Africa, but the administration denied that its decision had anything to do with the student protests.

The protest made me think more deeply about the oppression of blacks, and in doing so, I thought about what it means to be a woman in America. Just as it bothers a black person to be seen only as a Negro rather than as a human being with dignity and pride, it bothered me when men saw me only as a female, as a sexual object for their fantasies. Knowing that many men read porno magazines, I often felt vulnerable when a strange man stared at me. But I never felt that way with Mark. I knew that he saw me as an individual first, not as a female or as a white woman.

In fact, Mark was repulsed and astounded by the emphasis Americans placed on sex. In his culture, lovemaking was natural and spontaneous, not associated with sin and scandal and fitness and baby oil and hot tubs and fraternities and Freud. It was part of love, but it was not a major component. It was a fact of life, but it was not an obsession. It had not been analyzed, studied, surveyed, written about, and mutilated into a mechanical act as it had been in America. It had not been advocated and promoted and overemphasized by a sexual liberation movement, therapists, sexologists, stimulating videos, and sexy television programs and ads or pulsating popular music with lewd lyrics. It was one of life's most precious mysteries—a mystery that was best left unexplained.

My strong desire to become a foreign correspondent led me to apply to Reuters News Service, based in London. Soon after I applied, a fellow journalism student from Texas congratulated me on getting the internship.

"What do you mean?" I said. "All I did was apply. There are thousands of applicants and they'll only select a few."

"I know," Jody replied. "But people are saying that if anyone at Columbia has one chance in hell to get into Reuters, it will be you."

All my hopes for the future were wrapped up in that one application to Reuters. When the letter from Reuters arrived, it was thin. They did not need me.

"Why are you so troubled?" Mark asked. "I don't know why you even applied to Reuters."

"I want to work abroad," I said. "I've studied German and Hungarian and Russian for so long. I want to use them!"

"But if you had joined Reuters, you would never have had time to write. You don't need a boss. All you have to do is choose a long-term goal and divert all your energy toward achieving it. One needs only two things: confidence and self-motivation. With those you can do anything you choose. You've already told me you want to become a writer. Why don't you focus on your writing?"

I smiled at his advice, not understanding how one could focus on writing without first having an income.

"Look at that!" Mark said, pointing to my two-foot stack of typed and bound journals I had kept since I was thirteen. "Look how much you've written already. All you have to do is harness that energy, discipline it."

His encouragement made me cry. None of my previous boyfriends had believed in me as much as Mark did.

"I care for you too deeply to see you this unhappy," Mark said, lightly rubbing my arms and looking at me with concerned, sad eyes. "I've never felt so precious to anyone besides you outside my immediate family. Of course, I'll miss you if you find a job abroad. But we could write to one another. If it's what you really want, I'd never stand in your way."

In early May 1985 I left New York for West Germany, where I was to be an intern at *Die Neue Presse* newspaper in Hannover. When I showed Mark my letter of acceptance, he was delighted that I had the opportunity to do what I wanted: travel to Europe, practice my foreign languages, and get journalism experience. It amazed me that his love was so unselfish that he was not afraid to let me go.

On the plane flying over the Atlantic Ocean, I gazed into the darkness, but saw only the image of my face reflected in the small window pane—a face expressing deep sadness. All I had to remind me of Mark was a black-and-white photograph I had developed and printed in the I-House darkroom. He was standing on the roof of the dorm on the first warm day of spring, bare chested, wearing a camouflage army hat. His longshot application for a green card as a writer was pending and I wondered if he would still be in the country when I returned.

Those first two weeks in Germany before I received a letter from him were filled with regret at having left New York. I missed my soul mate. During the first week the nine other American journalists and I were kept busy touring government buildings in Bonn, meeting reporters and editors, and reading German newspapers. The language around me had a new and exciting ring to it, the bakeries and shops were quaint and welcoming, and most of the Germans I met were well educated, philosophical, politically aware, and fond of conversation.

It was only at night, when I lay in the darkness thinking of Mark and feeling terribly alone in a foreign world, that I would ask myself if I had done the right thing, if I truly wanted to spend my life moving from place to place, clinging to nothing but my career and leaping at every chance to advance it, breaking off relationships whenever they grew too constraining. Suddenly all the maxims I had learned while coming of age in America—Love them and leave them, Live life to the max, Indulge, Love the one you're with, Live for the moment, Be free and unfettered—grated on my ears like a pack of senseless formulas designed to produce the most intense feelings of misery and emptiness.

One morning when I passed a newsstand in Hamburg, I spotted the cover of a *Spiegel* magazine that read, "*Rassen Krieg in Süd Afrika*—Race War in South Africa." I immediately bought a copy and learned what had happened: The South African government had declared martial law. The country was closed to foreign journalists. Children were being rounded up and detained without trial. I feared for the safety of Mark's family and wondered how Mark was taking the news. I wanted to be there for him. Was he still in America?

As soon as I had a chance I sat down and wrote him a long, heartfelt letter. I didn't care anymore that we were different colors. I loved him and wanted to commit myself to our relationship. I signed my letter *Na ku randa ngopfu,* his native language for "I love you very much."

Three weeks later I received the following reply, and felt excited and jittery as I withdrew it from its envelope.

Gail, my dearest,

I miss you terribly. Your trip to Germany has left my soul destitute of serenity and confidence. Never have I felt such a wretch emotionally. The first week without you was a nightmarish phantasmagoria. One moment—from reading, say, a good novel or poem, or listening to an uplifting classical music record—my heart and mind would be drunk with joy and hope and a sense of control and a love for life, all of which often lead young people to believe they can never die; the next—from thinking of you and longing to touch you and kiss you, to hear the wisdom of your mind and heart—I would be plunged into the deepest gloom and despair.

As the second week rolled around, reality still appeared discordant, like a punctured African drum, and meaningless, like the suffering of children. It was pure torture to contemplate the miles and miles of ocean and land, the hot months made of tedious days and minutes and seconds, that separate us.

One thing I did learn from those lonely days and nights of sunken spirits is that I'm madly in love with you. So much in love that it terrifies me. You possess me wholly, you know me deeper than I know myself, I hide nothing away from you. You know the taste of every drop of my bleeding heart—bleeding because of man's inhumanity to man. Think of me as I think of you, for inspiration against life's trials and tribulations.

P.S. My immigration situation looks promising.

We wrote to each other regularly: ten-page letters full of longing. The time apart strengthened our relationship. Through letters we could communicate on more profound levels, exploring our feelings and seeking to describe our thoughts on writing and literature with greater precision. We sent each other lengthy quotes from the books we had read, excerpts of poems, long descriptions of our thoughts and dreams. I carried the photograph of him with me everywhere. I did not feel complete without it. The aching hollowness in my chest did not go away no matter where I was or how many people were around me. Our correspondence inspired me so much I began writing short stories and, later, a novel. As I reflected on the months I had spent living in Budapest, in an old apartment overlooking the Danube, I came up with a plot for a novel about two Hungarian lovers fleeing the east bloc in search of artistic freedom.

When I was well into the first chapter, I wrote in a letter to Mark: "It seems the only way to escape the hectic rush and tense routine of life is to be creative. The only way to gain a feeling of control over the chaos of our lives is to express our inner selves."

Confident in our relationship, I threw myself into my work, submerged myself in German culture, read books in German, reported stories with seasoned journalists on the newspaper's staff, traveled to conferences with the other nine interns scattered all over Germany, and made trips to Stuttgart, Heidelberg, Berlin, and Vienna.

When I was not traveling, I lived with a German family in the farming village of Börssum, south of Hannover near Hildesheim. I did not hang my treasured photograph of Mark on the wall but kept it hidden. I did not think my host family would understand. They were conservatives who supported Chancellor Helmut Kohl's ruling party and believed that Turkish workers should be deported back to Turkey, in the same manner many whites in this country believed blacks should be sent back to Africa. The father had been a leader in the Hitler Youth when he was young. Like most Germans, they had lived in fear of Nazi informers and felt compelled to hang portraits of Hitler all over their house and greet neighbors with "Heil, Hitler!" The grandmother, who lived on the second floor, had lost her husband when the American troops landed in Normandy and barely said a word to me the whole three months I was there.

When the last day of my internship came, I took the train to Frankfurt and excitedly boarded a plane for New York. Flying back across the Atlantic, I reread some of Mark's letters to me and wondered how we would combat the prejudices many people have toward interracial couples. Above all I wondered how my father would react if I ever mustered enough courage to tell him about Mark.

"How are things, darling?" Mark had written. "I got the letter in which you hinted that you might be willing to have us share an apartment in New York. I'm delighted."

At this I cringed, for I had changed my mind and decided to live with my brother Paul and sister-in-law, Debbie, on the Upper East Side. I was afraid of rushing things with Mark, and I wanted each of us to have enough space to maintain a healthy sense of independence. Most of all, my conscience had plagued me after I agreed to live with him. I could not fight the fact that I was a minister's daughter and that, deep down, I believed living together out of wedlock was somehow wrong. I continued reading: "I hope that your father (what a complex man!) will understand and give you his blessing."

I closed my eyes and imagined my father's probable reaction to the news that I was living with my boyfriend, who happened to be black. Would he rant, rave, question, pry, fume, apply pressure in all the right areas to make me leave Mark forever? I thought of my mother, who had once refused even to spend the night at a home in which the man and woman were not legally married.

I recalled my father's reaction when he met Carol's biracial boyfriend at a cocktail party during the weekend of Brown's 1984 graduation. He seemed to think interracial love should be addressed by textbooks on abnormal psychology. He was so absorbed in his career as a psychologist that his conversations were peppered with words like *schizophrenia, manic, incestuous tendencies, latent homosexuality, biofeedback, repressed anger,* and *psychotic behavior.* He and my brothers, who are also psychologists, seemed to speak a foreign language.

I gazed out the airplane window, picked up the letter from Mark, and read on.

"It is about time your father reconciled himself to the fact that he can never mold you after his own heart. You are a grown woman now, free to make your own decisions and choices and bear all responsibility. Though I have no doubt your father means well, he has his own life to live, and you have yours. I do not mind if your father chooses to hate me implacably; some day he will come to understand the depth of our feelings for each other, and understand too the spiritual, emotional and creative bond that has made our souls one, and made us such perfect complements of each other."

I smiled at Mark's optimism. I was not at all as confident that my father would accept my falling in love with an African. I was still not strong enough to follow my heart's desire, not courageous enough to live with Mark and risk the censure of my parents and relatives. Mark believed I was.

"One of the reasons I love you so much," he wrote, "is that you're a fighter for your rights as a woman, equal to, and as capable as, any man. Your attitude reminds me of my mother. That is why being with you has made me grow in so many ways. My mother was the first feminist to have a profound influence upon me. Your uncompromising defense of your womanhood is one reason I believe in you as a writer."

"Oh, Johannes, my love," I murmured as the plane touched down at Kennedy Airport, using Mark's middle name, the name he went by in his youth. "I've let you down. I wish I had your courage."

LOVE UNDER PRESSURE

4

When Gail returned from Germany I sensed that our relationship was poised to enter a difficult phase in which our feelings toward each other would be severely tested. Would our love survive the test?

I heard someone knocking on the door of my basement Staten Island apartment one sultry morning in August. I had just moved into a two-room apartment, sparsely furnished with a rickety kitchen table, two chairs with torn cushions, the cheapest bed I could find, and disorganized piles of books. The apartment was dark and dismal, crawled with mice and roaches, and cost more than half my monthly budget of nine hundred dollars. But it was home. Finally I had a place of my own where I could read and write and think without interruption.

The day before I had received Gail's letter telling me she had decided to live with her brother instead of me. This perplexing change had caught me off guard. Was she finally backing off? Had she met someone else? Distraught and confused, I was in the middle of attempting to write a coherent reply to her letter when I heard the knocking. I turned off my typewriter and, looking like a Rastafarian with my uncombed hair and wearing a Free South Africa T-shirt and rumpled running shorts, I went to the door, expecting perhaps a door-to-door salesman or the landlord.

Gail stood there, tan and smiling in shorts, a leopard-skin print top, Yugoslavian sandals, and long dangling earrings made of seashells. Suddenly I felt almost afraid to hold the woman I had longed to see. I squinted in the harsh summer sunlight and simply said, "Hello, Sweets."

She rushed into my arms and we held each other tight for several minutes, too overcome to speak.

"Did you get my letter?" Gail asked.

"Yesterday," I replied. "That's why I'm surprised you're here. I thought it was over."

"Over?" She cried. "How could it be over?"

"I thought that since you didn't want to live with me . . . I thought . . . well . . ."

"Just because I can't live with you right now doesn't mean I don't love you."

At hearing those words I embraced her once more, again without speaking. We stepped inside the apartment, made breakfast, and talked for hours. She asked me endless questions about the state of emergency in South Africa, how my family was doing, how the editing of *Kaffir Boy* was going, how I had survived the summer heat. In turn I quizzed her on her travels and the novel she had begun. We talked on and on. Finally exhausted, we sat on a couch by the window, wrapped ourselves in a blanket, fell silent, and listened to the falling rain and the footsteps of strangers passing my windows in the night. It was completely dark but for a single candle.

The morning light seeped through the blinds. It was the first morning of a fall that would pass like a dream, as if we were enveloped in a haze that the outside world could not penetrate. Gail and I created a mutual inner world that challenged and inspired us. The only time I felt fully human, understood, and accepted in all my idealism was when Gail and I were in that dark Staten Island apartment, reading and talking and laughing. We had neither steady jobs nor much money, but we did not feel we needed any more than was necessary to survive. The only thing we had of value was each other.

We typed side by side, read aloud to each other, dreamed together. We often became so excited by our ideas that we would rush about in search of pen and notebook, eager to capture thoughts on short stories, twists in plot, character development, setting up a disciplined reading and writing schedule, themes in Richard Wright's books, the greater social significance of art, or the individual rebelling against the suffocating demands of custom and authority. We traveled by ferry and subway to the midtown Manhattan library across from MOMA where we checked out recordings of Shakespeare, Dunbar, Langston Hughes, Milton, classical music, and Russian poetry.

Every day I worked on the *Kaffir Boy* manuscript, and Gail, on her growing first novel. We dined each night by candlelight while listening to folk music by Simon and Garfunkel, Joan Baez, and Mahalia Jackson. Three times a week we jogged ten miles up Victory Boulevard and around Silver Lake Park. Saturdays we lugged our laundry down the street to the laundromat and Sundays we walked three miles to the grocery store and back, carrying the bulging brown bags on our heads in the same way African women carry jugs of water from the river. Neither of us had a car, and for weeks I had no phone, until my editor and agent insisted I spend part of my advance to get one installed.

Whenever I had to go into the real world, that is, to meet with my editors at Macmillan, Gail would accompany me and wait outside the towering building, leaning against the wall reading nineteenth-century French novels or books about Indian women in *dehras* speaking Punjabi. When I returned I would find her sitting on her knapsack outside the lobby of the publishing house, engrossed in her reading and oblivious to the constant stream of formally dressed men and women flowing through the revolving doors of the major New York firm.

As far as her parents knew, Gail lived at her brother's apartment on the Upper East Side, but actually she spent most of her time with me. As pressure grew for her to help her brother Paul and sister-in-law, Deb, pay the rent and buy groceries, and as her Protestant work ethic began accusing her of being indolent, she started hunting for steady jobs. After a short stint as an intern at *Health* magazine, she landed a job translating, writing, and editing German news stories for the Manhattan-based branch of the German embassy. They paid her a decent wage for a twenty-hour workweek and gave her great benefits. She felt she had imposed too long on her brother and his wife and was eager to find a place of her own.

When Gail called me and said she had found an apartment to rent, I was disappointed. I worried about her safety in a city as large and dangerous as New York and would have felt more at ease if she shared my place. Besides, it would have been less expensive if we split the rent. But I did not want to stand in the way of her independence.

"I'll help you move," I said.

When I saw the room she had rented I was shocked. It was on the first floor of a dilapidated house in the slum section of Stapleton, a Staten Island neighborhood of roaming gangs and abandoned buildings used as crack houses. She had a view of the junkyard across the street, strewn with rubble and tangled bedsprings, and of rows of gutted and boarded-up buildings. Exposed electric wires hung from the ceiling. The doors and windows were flimsy and did not lock. The floors were caked with filth. There were gaping holes in the walls.

The whole apartment reeked of stale tobacco smoke. The white emaciated live-in landlord down the hall, with whom she had to share a kitchen and bath, was a chain smoker. The house, which had been abandoned and boarded up for months, turned out to have been a favorite hangout for drug dealers. Graffiti was scrawled in the closet. When Gail asked why the glass shelves had been removed from the bathroom cabinet, the landlord told her the former tenants had used them to divvy up cocaine.

"What has come over you?" I asked Gail as soon as I had recovered from my speechlessness. "How can you live in this horrible place? Don't you have any self-respect? Even the homeless wouldn't touch this dump."

"It's the only place I could afford," she said. "It's only two hundred dollars a month."

"Why don't you sleep on a subway grate?" I asked. "That would be free, and it would be a lot better than this."

She looked disappointed, then said, "I liked it because I would be near you."

"Being near me is not the issue. You would have to walk through a war zone to get to my place from here. I came to America to get out of the ghetto, not to move back into one. I hope you don't think I'm going to visit you here."

Gail and I sat down. I told her that she deserved better, that it was one thing to be independent and another to recklessly endanger one's life.

"I would never stop worrying about you knowing you lived in this hovel," I said. "Especially since it reminds me of my family's shack back in Alexandra. With these differences: We didn't have to deal with drugs, and our neighborhood, though poor and squalid, had some soul. American ghettos are soulless, inhuman."

Alone in my apartment that night I couldn't sleep. I had nightmares of Gail being raped, forced to take drugs. I had half a mind to wake up and go fetch her.

The next morning I heard a knock at my door. It was Gail, looking defeated and tired. Happy to see her safe, I took her by the hand and led her inside. There was an awkward silence before she said, "I know I'm being bullheaded. You're right. I don't think I can live there. I couldn't sleep all night."

"I couldn't either."

"The noise kept me awake," she said. "An old Buick cruised back and forth dragging its muffler; stray dogs barked as they dug through the junkyard; the faucet kept dripping into that stained sink; derelicts outside my window kept laughing and shouting and breaking bottles; the street lamp shot a blinding beam of light straight into my eyes through the uncurtained window."

I begged Gail not to return to that dreadful place. I prepared her a sandwich; she had not eaten since the day before.

"For some reason I thought having a place of my own was more important than anything, even my safety," she said. "I guess there are certain limits to a woman's independence."

I set the sandwich down in front of her and sat down beside her. "I think you have to stop and ask yourself what you are doing to yourself and why. What are you trying to prove? And to whom?"

Gail ate in silence, deep in thought. Finally she said, "I'm so afraid of living with you." She looked up at me with tears welling in her eyes. "I'm terrified of what my parents will say when they find out. I mean, they don't even know about you yet. I told my brothers not to reveal anything to Mom or Dad about you, and they haven't. I haven't mustered the courage to tell them."

"You'll have to find the courage, Gail," I said, "if you believe in our relationship."

Gail started crying.

"What's wrong?" I asked.

I love you very much," she said. "But I also love my family. My heart tells me I should move in with you. It also tells me that I have to confront my family soon, for the sake of our relationship."

For three weeks we were happy and secure in our small apartment. Several times Gail attempted to write a letter to her parents informing them of our relationship but she always ended by tearing them up. Though I believed in our relationship, this was her battle: If she believed we were meant for each other, she would muster the courage to do it, and face the consequences.

Finally Gail decided to tell her parents in person. At Thanksgiving she flew home to Minneapolis. When she returned to Staten Island, I could tell something was wrong. Her mood had changed. She resumed searching for her own apartment and announced she would move out January first.

Gail's parents flew to New York City for Christmas, but I timed my annual visit to Hilton Head Island, where I visited Stan Smith and his wife, Margie, so that I would be out of town when her parents arrived. I was not ready to meet them. Their opposition to our relationship was clear. And Gail had chosen to heed their advice. I saw no future for the two of us as long as she did what was expected of her, rather than what she truly felt and believed.

Gail shared the third floor of a brownstone building in Park Slope, Brooklyn, with a twenty-seven-year-old graduate student named Michal, a petite woman from Chicago who owned a smug and corpulent cat called Charles. Though Gail was in an adjacent borough, she seemed hundreds of miles away, wrapped up in her job, in free-lance articles, in new female friends. I could feel us drifting apart.

That dreaded feeling was confirmed when I met Gail's mother, Debbie Ernsberger. She had flown to New York in March for a solo visit. Not long after we were introduced, Gail, her mother, and I were riding the subway. In the jostling crowd, Gail's mother leaned toward me and asked, "So, what is your immigration status?"

The directness of her inquiry put me on guard. Why did she want to know? Had her husband, Gail's father, requested that she ask this? Suddenly I felt the sole purpose for Debbie's visit was to investigate the nature of our relationship. The question made me suspect that Gail's mother, and particularly her father, regarded me with great suspicion. They seemed afraid some African was out to marry their daughter so he could get himself a green card.

"My application for a work permit is still being processed by the I.N.S.," I said.

"Do you think you'll get it?" Gail's mother asked.

"I don't know," I said. "It's a long shot. They have stringent requirements now. I'm hopeful though. It's my only alternative."

Gail's mother looked at me and said, "I wish you luck."

"Thanks."

For days after Gail's mother returned to Minneapolis I was downcast. My relationship with Gail appeared to have no future. Rather than pretend that her parents would approve, especially after that train conversation with her mother, I started preparing for the worst. I stopped calling Gail.

It's better that it end now, I thought to myself. *Why continue a relationship in the face of such opposition? It wouldn't be fair to ask Gail to choose between you and her family.*

In the midst of my brooding over the possibility and consequences of Gail and I breaking up, I learned that two of my brothers-in-law, the husbands of my sisters Florah and Maria, had been murdered by a policeman one afternoon as they sat outside our shack in Alexandra. A motive for the dastardly killings was never found. I became distraught. I thought of my little niece Angeline and nephew Given, still in diapers. How would my widowed sisters cope alone? Who would protect and support their little ones? I blamed myself. Perhaps, I thought, my activism against apartheid had led to their untimely deaths. Just a week ago I had published in *Newsday* an article critical of President Botha's much-heralded "Rubicon" speech. Maybe these deaths were only a warning of what might happen if I continued to write and speak out against apartheid.

Following the tribal custom of my family, I mourned by shaving my head until I was as bald as Yul Brynner. It was a time-honored way of expressing grief and solidarity with the dead. The tighter my heart strings bound me to my homeland, the farther away I felt from America, its frenzied life, its empty materialism.

When Gail called to find out why I had not called lately, one misunderstanding led to another. We could no longer bridge the gulf between our cultures and our races. When I met her at the Strand Bookstore to talk, she was shocked and repulsed by my shaved head, amazed by how much of a hermit I had become. I felt she would never fully understand, no matter how much she loved me. I remained alone in my shell, torn by pain and guilt for being safe in America while my family suffered and mourned.

I had half a mind to leave America, to return home, but I knew that to do so would be tantamount to signing my own death warrant. The Pretoria regime had made it known that I was its enemy, someone it would dearly love to grab in its claws because I was doing damage to its image by the words, the truth, I revealed in what I wrote and spoke. My passport had already been revoked; the mysterious threatening phone calls hadn't ceased.

As the publication date of *Kaffir Boy* drew near, I became more and more convinced that I should let the flame die between Gail and me. I should devote all my energies to the anti-apartheid struggle. The only way I could expiate the deaths of my brothers-in-law was to do my utmost to bring about the complete destruction of the evil system that had caused their untimely deaths, to help galvanize Western public opinion against apartheid. A serious relationship now, especially with a white woman, would only complicate things.

Kaffir Boy finally came out and I left on a grueling two-week publicity tour without even saying good-bye to Gail.

GAIL'S VIEW

It is very difficult to keep a relationship alive when the souls of both partners are in turmoil. While Mark was mourning the loss of his brothers-in-law, I was lamenting the tragic loss of a best friend.

Two weeks before Mark left on his publicity tour, my close friend Naomi Vogel died in an auto accident on an interstate while driving from Wesleyan to New York to visit me and her boyfriend, Andrew Hollander. A toolbox slipped out of the truck in front of her, she swerved to avoid it, and the car broke through the guard rail and tumbled end to end into a ravine. She was killed instantly.

I had met Naomi at the University of Budapest in the spring of 1983, at a time when I was so lonely and overwhelmed with having to speak and think in Hungarian that it was a relief to meet another American. The year following our adventurous sojourn in Hungary, we had traveled back and forth between Brown and Wesleyan to visit each other. When I was in Germany I visited her in Heidelberg, where she was spending a semester abroad. Less than a month before her death she had spent a week at my place in Brooklyn, and we had stayed up past midnight many times sipping Hungarian wine and reminiscing boisterously over our days together in Budapest.

When Naomi's boyfriend Andrew called me at work to tell me about the auto accident, I thought he was joking. I laughed. When he repeated the grim news, I was incredulous. When his words finally sank in, I wept uncontrollably. As days wore on I became more and more pensive. I listened to Pachelbel over and over again, for Naomi had put on the album during her last visit. I stared vacantly at the wall, with tear-filled eyes, wondering why God had chosen Naomi instead of me. I wondered if Naomi could see me or hear me. She visited me in dreams and told me she was not really dead. Every day was cold, rainy, and dreary.

I could feel Mark distancing himself from me, and it hurt. I felt I had no one to turn to. My novel, the one I had written with such enthusiasm and confidence, was being rejected by publishers who saw no commercial value in a literary work about the search for artistic freedom set in foreign lands. Naomi had read the manuscript and loved it. My descriptions of Budapest and Hungarians, of Eastern European culture, reminded her of our days there. But now she was no longer around to encourage me with her bursts of enthusiastic praise and laughter.

I did not know exactly why Mark had pulled away from me, but I sensed it had something to do with my parents and his commitment to the struggle against apartheid. I had tried my best to make my parents accept Mark without having met him but I made little headway. I longed for those few weeks when Mark and I had lived together on Staten Island, after he had rescued me from the Stapleton slum.

During those brief weeks in November when we lived together, I would return each evening from the suffocating money-making hustle of Manhattan and enter the basement apartment, whose atmosphere Mark kept congenial with elaborate vegetarian dinners; wonderful folk music from Africa and America; and interminable discussions of politics, life, and creativity.

Mark's companionship had brought peace to my soul and a measure of security to my life. For the first time since I began living in New York, I felt safe, despite the fact that we lived in a crime-ridden and dangerous section of Staten Island. The ferry terminal was home to mental patients, drunkards, and other homeless persons who were sometimes hostile and threatening. But they never bothered me when Mark was near. On one occasion Mark grabbed the wrist of a man who had surreptitiously unzipped my purse and was reaching for my wallet. Another time he calmed me when I thought my end had come. The trunk of the unmarked cab we had taken would not open, so the black driver hopped out, pulled out a switchblade knife, and, as I tried to catch my breath and convince myself I was not really about to die, he used the knife to open the trunk.

I had grown accustomed to living in a predominantly black neighborhood. When I entered the nearest beauty parlor and requested a trim, the three black hairdressers stared at me in surprise. It seemed none of them had ever cut a white person's hair before, but one eventually volunteered. As she snipped away with the circumspection of a brain surgeon, I gazed at posters advertising Soft Sheen, curl activators, Murray's Hair-Glo, Vita-Gro, and fade creams. My haircut was terribly lopsided, but it was definitely a unique cut, so I gave her a tip and left well pleased.

Being in love with Mark had filled me with an adoration for black children. I would stare at little girls on the ferry, admiring their tightly woven braids decorated with colorful beads, the way their white clothes contrasted with their eager faces, their exuberant spirits and their energy.

"Look, Mama!" one child cried, pointing to the Statue of Liberty through the crimson evening mist. "It's the liberty lady!"

At ease in both the black and white worlds, I had felt confident that our relationship would last. Though Mark devoted his life to the fight against apartheid, constantly worried about his family and sought ways to help them, there were moments when he could let go of his guilt and laugh.

The only disruption of our happiness was the nagging knowledge that I had not yet found the courage to tell my parents about Mark. Telling them over the phone seemed inadequate, so I decided to fly home to Minneapolis and have a heart-to-heart talk with them. During the four nights before my flight, I was awakened several times by the image of my father's angry face.

It was late November 1985, the air was crisp and clear, and the wind gusted across the flat plains of southern Minnesota. My father, wearing a thick coat with broad shoulders, loose galoshes, and a ridiculous hat, picked me up at the airport and drove me directly to a Presbyterian Church in the suburbs for the Thanksgiving service. During the drive he told me he was still active in the ministry and deeply believed in God.

I gazed out the window as we drove past the neat yards and huge houses of Edina, and wondered if he intended to use religion to force me to change my mind about Mark. As a minister's daughter religion had always exerted a powerful influence on me. I began regretting having come home. The suburbs of Minneapolis reminded me of the provincialism and narrow-mindedness of Gopher Prairie in Sinclair Lewis's *Main Street*.

My father was born and raised in Minneapolis, and damn proud of it, so I made no unkind remarks about the Midwest. I had enormous respect for my father and had always been much closer to him than to my mother. But now that I had made a life for myself in New York, had lived in Hungary and Germany, and had fallen in love with an African, the closeness we once shared had begun to wane.

The church had vaulted ceilings, a booming organ, a satin-robed choir, and majestic stained glass windows that made one instantly feel meek and sinful upon entering. As I stood beside my father, singing from the hymnal he held rigidly before me, my hopes for telling him about Mark seemed doomed. I expected a religious browbeating, laced with snide comments about "shacking up"—his favorite expression for living together. I looked about me at the faces of the all-white congregation; I saw smiles and expressions of placid contentment. I told my father everyone looked too happy.

"You've been living in New York too long," Dad replied. "When are you coming home to the Midwest, where the women are strong, the men are good-looking, and the children are all above average?"

he said, quoting his favorite lines from Garrison Keillor's "Prairie Home Companion" radio show.

We drove to our split-level home on Xerxes Avenue, a few blocks south of Lake Calhoun. Everything was familiar except for a new couch and new paintings: the large living room with the gold-framed fireplace, the stereo cabinet, the piano room that my father sometimes used as a counseling office, the Flying Scot sailboat in the backyard, the skis and camping equipment in the garage. Upstairs in my old bedroom, filled with high-school athletic trophies and textbooks from Brown, I paced back and forth, rehearsing what I would say.

Mom, Dad, I'm living with my black African boyfriend, I said to myself. *No, no! That will never do. I don't want to give them heart attacks.* I tried again, but the news always sounded shocking, no matter how I worded it. I thought of my mother's mother, Susan Stork Scott, an active member of the Daughters of the American Revolution who was proud that her relative John Hopkins sailed to America on the *Mayflower.* How would my mother's relatives, descendants of pilgrims and Protestant ministers, react to the possibility that the purity of their English and Scottish line of descent might be "stained" by Negro blood? After all, they had given my mother a hard time just for marrying a German.

In my nervous despair, I believed my parents might disown me for being in love with a black.

"Don't tell your parents," a friend from Brown had said to me one evening as she leaned toward me over her cappuccino in Cafe Reggio in Greenwich Village. "You'd have to sacrifice your whole family. I should know—I had to. My father called me a whore for marrying 'down' to someone who was poor and non-Jewish."

I continued to pace, thinking of Prince Myshkin's honesty in Dostoyevsky's novel *The Idiot.* He had kept no secrets and was incapable of lying. I thought, *Isn't it better to be honest, and run the risk of evoking pain, grief, disappointment, and anger, than to live a life of secrets and half-truths, cowering in the shadows like a guilt-ridden criminal?*

Tell them now! I said to myself that evening. I was in the backseat of our Volkswagen Rabbit and my parents were in front. Slowly and carefully, I told them about the terrible room I had rented in Stapleton, how my friend Mark had worried about my safety, and how he had been gracious enough to invite me to move my things into his place in St. George. I held my breath and waited for their response.

My father was struck dumb.

"What is Mark's last name?" my mother asked, breaking a long and uncomfortable silence.

"Mathabane," I replied.

"What kind of a name is that?"

"South African."

"Is he of English or Afrikaner descent?" my mother asked.

Before I could reply, my father asked, "Is Mark an American citizen?"

"No."

"Does he have any plans to become one?"

"I don't know. That's his business, not mine."

I already knew my father's suspicions: A foreigner was out to trick his daughter into marriage so he could get a green card. From their questions, I could tell the possibility had not yet dawned on them that Mark might not be white.

"Why don't you go to a local church and find an old woman who will take in a boarder?" my father asked.

I choked on my reply. I realized he would never understand. I abruptly switched the topic.

The next morning I awoke determined to accomplish "Phase Two" of my plan to brief my parents on my personal life: tell them Mark is black. My mother was alone in the kitchen heating tea in the microwave.

"So, tell me more about Mark," she said with the curiosity every mother has toward her daughter's love life. "Where did he grow up?"

I described the ghetto of Alexandra, the shack his family lived in, his six siblings, and how his illiterate mother had cajoled him to go to school because she regarded an education as a powerful weapon of hope and a way out of a dead-end ghetto life. As I described Mark's mother, she asked nervously, "Oh, you mean, do you mean to tell me—Is his mother black?"

"Yes."

"And his father too?"

"Yes."

"*Both* of them?"

"Yes."

My mother's eyes widened with amazement but she quickly smoothed over her surprise and, speaking rapidly and nervously, told me that Winnie Mandela and Nadine Gordimer were to be awarded honorary degrees by her alma mater, Mount Holyoke College. She asked more questions about Mark. I told her how Mark had learned English through reading comic books, how he happened to pick up tennis, how he met Stan Smith at an international tennis tournament in Johannesburg where he was the only black player, and how Stan arranged for him to leave South Africa on a tennis scholarship.

"And Mark respects me for being a feminist," I said. "He says white women are seen as weak and submissive compared to black women, who are raised to be tough and assertive. He says I have to be strong and stand up for my rights as a woman, especially in a place like New York."

"That's so true," my mother said. "He sounds like a really nice guy. Do you have a picture of him?"

I bounded upstairs two at a time to fetch a color snapshot of Mark, taken as he raised his fist for emphasis during an anti-apartheid lecture.

"He's cute," my mother said.

Happily chatting, we finished our breakfast and my mother left to do errands. She returned two hours later with a stack of library books by Nadine Gordimer.

"Mom, what are those for?" I asked.

"I have to read up for the day I meet Mark," she said smiling.

I knew then that I had won my mother's sympathy. I joyfully threw my arms around her neck and laughed. Mom laughed too, and hugged me in return. Still embracing her I said, "I was afraid you wouldn't understand."

"Love is complex," she said. "Sometimes it doesn't need to be understood. It needs only to be accepted."

I spent the entire afternoon with my mother, talking, drinking tea, listening to records, and recalling shared memories. Both of us felt close and light-hearted, but as evening approached and the hour of my father's return from the office drew near, I grew tense.

"What do you think he'll do, Mom?" I asked. "I know he won't accept it as easily as you have."

"You're right," she said. "He couldn't sleep all night just knowing you were with a foreigner."

"Does he suspect Mark is black?"

"No, of course not. He'd have gone through the roof."

"Will you tell him?"

"It's your life, honey. You have to tell him."

"Will he disown me?"

"He loves you too much ever to do that, Gail. You're his only daughter and youngest child. He treasures you. He doesn't want to lose your love. Maybe that's why he's always disapproved of your boyfriends and told you they're not good enough for you. He loves you too much to let you go. He's afraid you'll get hurt."

I did not tell my father that evening, or the next. I almost told him one morning when we were shoveling two feet of snow off the driveway, then changed my mind. My father and I went to the Calhoun Beach Club together to lift weights and sit in the whirlpool, but neither of us brought up the topic of Mark. We went to some indoor tennis courts and played mixed doubles with another father-daughter pair. I was enjoying our time together and did not want to spoil it by bringing up a topic I knew made him uncomfortable. All he did was give me his advice: "Why don't you keep looking for a place of your own, honey?"

He probably already knows Mark is black, I thought to myself on the plane as I headed back to New York without having told him. *Now that Mom and my brothers know, it won't be long until he finds out.*

Every other day I went to my brother's apartment to type more chapters of my novel into his computer. I could tell my father had talked to Paul, for my brother started sounding more like my dad each day. He stood behind me at the computer. I could feel his presence as I tried to concentrate on the screen.

"So, are you looking for another place to live?" Paul asked.

"No," I replied.

Later his wife, Debbie, sat down beside me and said, "Gail, we both feel living together is a big deal. There needs to be a commitment, and we just don't get the feeling that you're ready to make such a big commitment. We feel protective toward you. We don't want to see you make a mistake or get hurt."

Was my father trying to apply pressure on me indirectly by getting Paul and Debbie to agree with him? At first it was easy for me to tell myself, *They just don't understand our relationship.* But with time I began to miss my solitude and independence. I was not ready to invest what little money I had in joint ventures with Mark—in buying a vacuum cleaner and dishes and a toaster oven and a down comforter.

The growing intensity of our commitment to each other made me panic. I was only twenty-three. I liked to meet my girlfriends for dinner in East Village cafés. I enjoyed going to parties in Soho and dances with Carol Abizaid and other friends from Brown. I felt an occasional need to flee from Mark's brooding concern with apartheid and injustice and indulge myself by having fun. Besides, I was not convinced I had the strength to stand up to the social pressures against interracial couples. I decided it would be best for me to search for a place of my own and let my commitment to Mark grow at a more gradual and natural pace, if it was meant to.

Carrying a tattered map of New York City in one hand and the *Village Voice* apartment share ads in the other, I searched for affordable rooms in Hoboken, Queens, and Brooklyn. At last I found a warm, sunny room in Park Slope to share with an honest, intelligent young woman named Michal.

My father was overjoyed to hear the news. He was particularly happy to hear that Michal was a graduate student at the same school he once attended—Union Theological Seminary. My brother Dan and his girlfriend, Lisa, helped me move. Mark looked morose as he helped us load my belongings—a tent, a sleeping bag, boxes of books and journals, a guitar, a pair of cross-country skis, and a box of artist supplies—into the trunk of Lisa's car.

As soon as I got settled into my new place I invited Mark to dinner. He made excuses not to come. Weeks went by, then months, and still he had not come to Brooklyn to see my new room or meet Michal. After my mother's visit to New York in March, during which she quizzed Mark about his immigration status and told me that Dad disapproved of our relationship, Mark became distant. After his brothers-in-law were murdered in Alexandra, he pulled away beyond reach. When he stopped calling me, I knew something was wrong. When I pressed him to tell me what was going on in his heart and mind, he told me it was pointless to continue our relationship.

"Gail, your father doesn't approve!" he said emphatically. "We can't go on pretending he does. You have to understand my position. Your father might do something drastic, like calling the I.N.S. and having me deported."

"He wouldn't do that," I said.

"Wouldn't he? I can't talk now. I have to go."

Mark started cutting the conversation short each time I called. Once he told me he could not talk to me and listen to the news at the same time. When he left for his promotional tour without calling to say good-bye, I knew he was determined to end our relationship.

In despair over losing Mark, I became angry at my father. *It's all his fault,* I thought to myself. All my misery and hurt over being abandoned by Mark was channeled into an uncontrollable rage against my father. One April night my anger became so intense that I could not sleep. I got up at four in the morning, switched on my desk lamp, sat down, and wrote my father the following letter:

April 20, 1986

Dad,

I'm writing regarding the lack of emotional support I receive from you. I don't feel as though you believe I will ever become a writer. In your "commandant" style you have always tried to mold me into what you wanted to show off to the neighbors: a doctor, a TV anchorwoman, anything but what *I* wanted to be. You have even tried to direct and manipulate my affections for men, as if I were a possession which you must entrust to a worthy owner. I'm not anyone's possession!

As for your latest move, sending Mom out here to ask Mark about his status in this country and to tell me that "Dad does not want to encourage Mark in any way," I have to respond the only way I can—in pure hate.

I'm sure you will be rubbing your hands in glee to find that since Mom's visit, Mark has distanced himself from me. Our relationship, which is of immense importance to both of us, is almost over. Why? First of all, he is hurt that you won't approve of him even though you have never met him. Secondly, he is afraid you will approach the media, tell them that a black South African is trying to use his daughter to gain citizenship, and that he will be kicked out of this country and be sent to prison or executed in his own.

Whether his fear is founded or not, it is very real to him. I know this news probably gives you great joy, but I'm going through hell, and decided to send you some of it.

GAIL

P.S. Of course I remember the times when you were a good father to me, and they make me cry. Perhaps because I wish it were always so.

A few days later, when I returned home from work, the phone rang. It was my father. He was crying.

"I love you so much," he said between breathless sobs, "but I feel like you don't even know me. I feel as if I were a stranger to my own daughter."

Tears sprang to my eyes.

"How could you think I'm not supportive of you as a writer?" he asked.

I tried to sound angry at first, but my feelings rushed up to squeeze the words lodged in my throat.

"What's wrong, honey?" he asked. "You sound all choked up."

"I've had a terrible month," I said. "I didn't mean to hurt you. I just had so much rage and pain inside I wanted to blame it on someone."

"That letter hurt me very deeply. I feel like there's a huge, red, gaping wound between us."

As we talked he began to realize that the angry letter had arisen from the depths of a profound depression that I had not even realized I was in.

"If you love Mark, go after him!" my father said. "I'll never stand in your way. I never wanted to interfere with your relationship with Mark. Mother was very impressed with him. She said he is another Gandhi. If you love him, go after him. GO AFTER HIM!!" His voice faded, he sounded emotionally exhausted. "Do you think your father is a racist? Me? What do you take me for?"

We talked for a while longer about Mark, about my novel, about my roommate and having my own room. Suddenly he asked, "Do you still hate me?"

"No," I said. "I love you very much."

We were both crying when we hung up. First I wept for having hurt my father so deeply. Then I wept over the fact that, now that we had my father's blessing, Mark was out of my life.

I survived the next week like a zombie, trying to come to grips with the fact that I was now alone. Every Thursday I went to my Russian tutor on Seventy-second Street, Inessa, who corrected my Russian essays and had me read to her from Pushkin. This week's essay was about my father and his suspicion that my foreign boyfriend just wanted American citizenship.

"Your boyfriend, he is Russian?" Inessa asked in broken English.

"No, South African."

"He is black?"

"Yes," I said.

"Then I think your father has right. I'm not a racist, but I think it is not good to have relations with these people. Look how he abandoned you when he found out your father's feelings. It means he only wanted citizenship. They may be good in the bed, but there are more important things."

I must have looked downcast, for Inessa continued, "But you are a very young girl. When I was your age in Moscow, I had many boyfriends. I went to the theater, to concerts, to films, but never to the bed. You must have self-respect. You could get a disease or get a baby. A man will give you money and say, 'Here, go get an abortion.' You are an educated girl from a good family. You must be selective."

"But I loved him," I said, feeling the tears rise.

"I don't think it was a real love," Inessa said firmly.

I left that tutoring session feeling vulnerable and sad, as if I had foolishly exposed my innermost self to someone who would never understand my true feelings.

One night when Michal was visiting her parents in Chicago, the doorbell rang. As usual, I opened the third-floor window, stuck my head into the night air, and tried to see who was on the stoop. Mark was standing there in his maroon Adidas sweat suit with the white stripes. He held a suitcase in each hand. My heart began to race.

"What are you doing here?" I yelled down to him.

"I got lost!" Mark replied, his wire-rim glasses glinting in the streetlight. He was smiling and laughing, obviously overjoyed to see me.

"Why do you have those bags?" I asked.

"I came straight from the airport."

I went downstairs to let him in. He stood in the doorway expecting a kiss. Disguising my delight with indifference, I picked up his bags and hauled them upstairs without even pausing to say hello. He had hurt me deeply, and I was not planning to let him off the hook lightly.

He talked a mile a minute about his publicity tour, which had taken him to all the major cities in America, then he began praising the oil painting I had been working on to take my mind off him.

"I had no idea you were such a fine artist," he said. "You should have been painting all along. You should be selling these. I like the colors. How did you get the proportions right? I had no idea . . ." He went on and on. "Can I put my juice in the refrigerator?"

"I don't think it would be worth the effort. You can't stay here tonight."

Mark looked hurt and pouted innocently.

"You can't just pull away and then reenter my life at will!" I said. "I've spent weeks trying to get over you, and now you come back as if nothing happened."

"My feelings for you haven't changed," he said.

"It's a fine time to tell me that now."

"While we were apart I realized that the book, the publicity tour, even my career as a writer are meaningless compared to the feelings that we share. Love, truth, simplicity, integrity—those make up the kernel of life. Everything else is worthless chaff."

"You wanted to break up with me. Is it because I'm white?"

"To be honest," he began, then hesitated. "To be honest I did think, for a while at least, that it would be better for both of us to marry within our race. I felt my life would be much simpler if I married a black woman. And yours too if you married white." He paused for a moment, awaiting a response, then continued, "I don't want to be accused of betraying the black race or of turning my back on the struggle in South Africa. But that was my head speaking, not my heart. I love you," he said, taking my hand and squeezing it. "We belong together, no matter how misunderstood we might be. Anyone who truly knows me will know I'm not betraying my people by loving you."

"I wish you had realized that before I wrote my father that letter," I said.

"What letter?"

I had kept a copy of the letter I sent my father, so I read it aloud in the angry tone in which it was written while Mark sat on the edge of a chair, head bowed, listening intently. When I looked up I detected tears in the corners of his eyes. He covered his face with his hands. I told him how my father had called, cried, and begged me to understand him. This made Mark weep even harder.

"My father told me that your fear of him is not paranoia," I said. "He says it's a real reaction to fears created by your cultural background. You've been conditioned to fear big white men."

"Hold me," Mark whispered.

I could not move. I was still too hurt to reach out to him. Before I reopened a wound that had begun to heal, I wanted some sort of guarantee that he would never again pull away from me. He threw his arms around me and squeezed me tight, burying his face between my neck and shoulder.

"I'm glad you finally confronted your father with your true feelings," Mark said, "but I wish it hadn't been so painful. I never thought you could write such a letter to your father. And I believe it's your love for me that made you write it."

We talked late into the night, and I told him about the pain and anguish I had felt in the weeks he had withdrawn from me. I explained why I felt like an emotional clam, afraid to emerge from my shell and risk being hurt again. In earlier relationships I had always done the breaking up. It was the first time a man had tried to break up with me, and it shook me to the core.

"You can sleep on the futon couch," I said, waving down the hall toward the living room.

"All right," he said. "I need to shower first."

When I returned to my room from the kitchen, I saw a damp towel hanging over my chair and found Mark under my covers, freshly showered.

"What do you think you're doing?" I said, trying to sound stern.

He grinned. "I got lost."

I laughed, shattering my facade. He knew I loved him and so did I. We talked and giggled and held each other until the room grew light. We could hear children calling to each other on their way to school. We finally fell asleep mid-morning. We ate breakfast at four in the afternoon.

5

OVERCOMING OBSTACLES

MARK'S VIEW

For several weeks after my return from the publicity tour, Gail and I were blissfully content. We reflected on the struggles we had been through and drew strength from them. We convinced each other that our relationship would endure, no matter how vilified or isolated or misunderstood we might become. We did our best to shun the frenzy of the outside world, its materialism, its rewards for conformity.

We saw everything as so much chaff, seldom leading to true happiness or growth of the soul, that part of ourselves we believed immortal. We vowed to resist, with all the strength our love could furnish us, the pressures and prejudices of such a world. Our spirits yearned to breathe free, to mingle with each other and with all that was True, Beautiful, and Good in life.

"Before, we were trying, without realizing it, to fit in," I said to Gail one evening as she sat across from me during a candlelight dinner at my Staten Island apartment. "We were attempting to satisfy society's impossible demands. We were obsessed about what people thought of us. You longed to please your family and I wanted to protect my public image. But we can't hope to change society if we suppress or hide or compromise what we deeply feel."

Gail looked up suddenly and asked, with a slightly worried

expression, "Do you think our relationship will withstand all the pressures?"

"Of course it will," I said. "We must make it work. It won't be easy. But our love is something worth fighting for, worth dying for."

Gail raised her wineglass and said, "I'll drink a toast to that." Our glasses clinked.

We slow danced around the kitchen to Fleetwood Mac, talking and laughing as we spun around the room.

"I've never felt this happy," Gail said. "My cheek muscles are sore from smiling. We don't need anybody or anything else, as long as we have each other."

For the first time in our relationship, we dared to hold hands and put our arms around each other in public. In the Museum of Natural History, while touring the prehistoric wing and examining the dinosaur skeletons, I kissed Gail in front of a staring brontosaurus. Stares and disapproving glances no longer fazed me.

But certain obstacles, both internal and external, kept cropping up. Gail had a hard time completely ignoring the opinions of out-siders, nor could she cease wondering what people were thinking when they stared at us. She became even more self-conscious after taking a tour of Forty-second Street with a group of women called Feminists Against Pornography. The tour was designed to educate women about pornography by taking them into adult book stores and sex shops, showing them the curtained booths where mini porno films were shown and pointing out the various categories of porn magazines. Gail was amazed at finding a whole rack of magazines devoted to "salt-'n'-pepper" pornography, showing blacks and whites in all sorts of crude and kinky positions. Some of the black men were depicted as slaves. The salt-'n'-pepper section was right beside the sex-with-children magazines.

"I can't believe people get their thrills from imagining all sorts of horrible things about interracial couples in bed," Gail said after describing to me what she had seen. "How awful! What kind of per-verse pleasure do they derive from it?"

"I really can't tell," I said. "Maybe their prejudices and the taboo against interracial love combine to conjure up all that trash."

"Do people actually see us that way?"

"There are lots of sick minds out there."

We frankly discussed our feelings whenever we encountered stereotypes against mixed couples in books, in the news, or in daily life. It was our way of supporting each other through emotionally trying situations, of reaffirming our commitment to each other despite the social pressures against us.

"Listen to this," Gail said, excitedly pacing my apartment with a copy of Frantz Fanon's *Black Skin, White Masks* in her hand. She read aloud from the chapter titled "The Man of Color and the White Woman."

" 'I wish to be acknowledged not as *black*, but as *white*,' " she read. " 'Now, who but a white woman can do this for me? By loving me she proves that I am worthy of white love. I am loved like a white man. I *am* a white man. When my restless hands caress those white breasts, they grasp white civilization and dignity and make them mine.' "

"What!" I exclaimed.

"Wait, there's more," she said. "'Enraged by degrading ostracism, mulattoes and Negroes have only one thought from the moment they land in Europe: to gratify their appetite for white women.' "

"That's ridiculous," I said. "Absolutely ridiculous."

Gail went on. " 'The majority of them tend to marry in Europe not so much out of love as for the satisfaction of being the master of a European woman. And a certain tang of proud revenge enters into this.' "

I was astounded by what I heard. "Why do people search for hidden motives when a black falls in love with someone white? No one tries to psychoanalyze why same-race couples fall in love. Yet there are endless theories and psychological studies to explain interracial love."

"And this chapter doesn't say anything about the feelings the woman may have for her man," Gail said. "She's just an object of innocence and purity to be despoiled by black hands. Women are human beings. They have complex emotions, they fall in love. They don't just sit around and wait to be conquered by a master." She looked down at the book. "It says here they used to castrate black men when caught with white women."

"In colonial Africa, sure," I said. "By the way, that was also done by the Klan down South."

"But why?" Gail asked. "What if they both loved each other?"

"That's the unanswered question of human history."

One warm day in May, as we sat on a blanket overlooking Staten Island's Silver Lake and eating a picnic lunch, I wondered what it would be like if Gail and I moved into one of the apartments above the park. Whenever I looked up, there she would be. And whenever she looked up, there I would be. We could gaze out the window each morning at the seagulls gathering on the banks and skimming the surface of the sparkling water.

For weeks I wanted to ask Gail to marry me, but I did not know how to say it without frightening her off. Her need for independence, her fear of commitment, and her love of solitude gave me the impression she was not yet ready to make any firm decisions about our future. Then there were her parents.

That spring Gail started going camping alone every other weekend. She would take her backpack, tent, and some food to Grand Central or Penn Station and catch a bus or train to Bear Mountain, the Catskills, or Montauk Point. She would return to the city after a weekend of hiking, reading in her tent by flashlight, and gazing into campfires looking healthy and fresh and alive. But her hours alone only served to strengthen her resolve to be on her own. I, on the other hand, yearned for more stability in our relationship.

Especially because I was becoming increasingly disillusioned with the stress of living in New York City. It was making me worry too much about money, distrust people, feel uptight most of the time, and harden my heart in order to rationalize the ubiquitous pain and misery of the homeless and the poor. My health was beginning to suffer from the pollution, the constant noise, the crowds.

I wanted to leave New York, and I wanted Gail, if she loved me, to come with me. If we were to get married, we would definitely not want our children raised in a place where they could not afford to be children: innocent, trusting. I had already been down South on a visit to High Point, North Carolina, and found the Piedmont area congenial, more humane than New York City, despite its lingering image among many Northerners as backward and racist.

How can you ask for a commitment from Gail when her heart is still torn between her love for you, her family, and her need for inde-

pendence? I asked myself. Yet I knew we had to choose a course and follow it, or our relationship would just flounder and cease to grow.

One afternoon Gail and I had just returned from a long run when the phone rang. It was my sister Florah calling from a neighbor's house in Alexandra, where most of my family had gathered to speak to me. They told me that a day ago the police had opened fire and hurled tear gas into a crowd of blacks gathered at a mass funeral for victims of a previous police massacre. Children were among those injured and detained but fortunately my siblings were among those who escaped. My father had fallen ill from some undiagnosed ailment that was thought to be tuberculosis. My mother got on the phone.

"Hello, my child," she said in Tsonga in her caressingly sweet voice.

"Hello, Mama."

"When are you getting married?"

I smiled and looked at Gail, who had taken off her running shoes and was stretching out.

"I don't know, Mama," I said in Tsonga. "Maybe in three years."

"Three years! But I want grandchildren right away!"

"Okay, one year," I said.

"So I have to wait that long before coming to America?" my mother said, sounding disappointed. "What's wrong? Don't you have enough money to pay *lobola*? How much do Gail's parents want?"

I laughed. "Mama, men don't have to pay for their brides in America."

"What, no *lobola*!" my mother exclaimed. "How do Gail's parents hope to get back the money they've spent raising such a beauty? If there's no *lobola* required, don't wait that long to get married. She may change her mind and leave you, you know."

I looked at Gail and laughed heartily. My mother knew from previous conversations that Gail was white, but not once did she make her color an issue. This hardly surprised me. Her judgment of people had always been based on one criterion: their character. As long as Gail was a good human being, was not lazy, did not smoke or drink, was respectful and compassionate, and loved me as much as I loved her, my mother unreservedly approved of our relationship. Each time I spoke to her on the phone she kept reminding me that there was no longer any "apartheid in marriage," by which she meant that the Prohibition of Mixed Marriages Act had been repealed.

Gail looked up. "Why do you keep looking at me and laughing? What is she saying?"

"She wants a big tribal wedding, and she wants it soon," I said. "And, oh, she also wants a tribe of grandchildren."

Gail groaned and rolled her eyes.

We had now been together for one and a half years. At the end of June, after hinting about living together for several weeks, I finally sprang my version of "the big question." Gail was working in her office at the German Information Center when I called. She had found out two weeks earlier that her parents were getting divorced, but I did not think their divorce would have much of an impact on our relationship. If anything, I thought, she might be more ready for some stability in her life.

I asked if she were ready to live with me.

"I can't make that decision right away," she said. "I need time."

"But we've had plenty of time," I said. "This should have been uppermost in our minds. I want to be able to say, 'This is my wife,' and I want you to be able to say, 'This is my husband,' and I want us to be able to say, 'This is our baby.'"

"Are you asking me to marry you?"

"Yes."

There was a pause, as if my words took her by surprise.

"Mark, I want you to know that I love you very much. But marriage is such a big step. You'll have to give me a little time. I'm only twenty-four."

"It's not age but maturity that counts."

"Still, I'd like to go home and talk to my parents about it. Not to ask for their advice and then obey them, but to discuss it openly with them. Besides, tonight is the last night they are staying under the same roof. I want to find out what has happened between them and if they can be reconciled."

Gail's request was reasonable. I supported her decision to fly to Minneapolis for the weekend. I did not want her to have to choose between me and her parents. I wanted us to have their blessing. Gail flew home the day the July 1986 issue of *People* magazine hit the newsstands. It contained an article about my growing up in a South

African ghetto and a few black-and-white photographs of me alone and with Stan Smith and his family. It was an odd feeling to pass a newsstand, pick up a copy of the magazine, and open it to find a large photo of me, naked to the waist and covered with sweat, holding a tennis racket and smiling shyly. It made me feel exposed but I was told by the editors of *People* that titillation sells magazines.

It was a long, hot, lonely Fourth of July weekend as I eagerly awaited Gail's return. It was impossible to get into Manhattan from Staten Island because the ferry was jammed with tourists taking snapshots of the tall ships brought into the harbor to celebrate the unveiling of the newly refurbished 100-year-old Statue of Liberty. Some madman pulled out a sword on the ferry that weekend and started slicing up tourists. I'm glad I decided to stay in St. George.

Tuesday came, then Wednesday, and still no word from Gail. Doubts began creeping into my mind. Why had she not called? How did her visit with her parents go? About a week later I received a letter from her.

July 7, 1986

Dear Mark,

You seemed to want a firm answer one way or the other as to whether our lives are converging or diverging. My reply is that they must diverge completely for at least five months if they are to converge at all. I need time, space, and solitude in which to think clearly, heal, and reflect. This is a very difficult time for me. Seeing my parents go through a divorce is frightening, bewildering, and anger-provoking. I know that I never want to go through such an experience. I never want to make the mistake of choosing the wrong man as my life partner. None of this is your fault, I know, but it affects me and subsequently our relationship. I have decided it would be best if we do not see, speak or write to each other until mid-December. I realize that I am taking a huge gamble—you may move to North Carolina and/or find another woman by then. But it is a risk I feel I must take if I am ever to love you without reservations and internal conflicts.

Sincerely,
GAIL

The letter shocked me. More shock and bewilderment awaited me when I learned that Gail had moved out of the apartment she shared with Michal. Neither her friends nor her brothers would reveal her new address or phone number. I could have called her at work, but I refrained. If she wanted to speak to me she would call. I felt new depths of pain. I could not imagine what could have made her abruptly sever all ties with me, especially when I knew how much she loved me.

I waited. There was nothing else I could do. Muggy July ended and sultry August began and still I held out hope. But by the end of August I could stand the city no longer. Every street and every museum and every café brought back memories of Gail that tormented and mocked me with their lucidity and force. Finally I decided to leave the city and memories of Gail behind. I hired an Iranian driver and loaded all my belongings into his truck. He drove me to High Point, North Carolina, where I had seen several apartments I liked.

My agent and publisher kept urging me to write a sequel to *Kaffir Boy*, but my mind was distracted. I could not force myself to be productive or attend to the simplest household tasks. I let bills lie unpaid on the table, and would then take a check to the telephone or utility company only after my phone or power had been cut off. I felt restless, aimless, gloomy. Life became insipid and meaningless. What used to give me pleasure no longer did. I would pick up a book, start reading it, then immediately drop it and reach for another, then another.

Always my thoughts were on Gail. I wondered what she was doing and whether she had met someone else. Whenever the Southerners who had helped me get settled in High Point politely asked if I had a girlfriend, I told them my heart was with a woman in New York. I kept Gail's picture in my wallet. I would not give up hope. I waited.

September arrived: no word from Gail. I *had* to see her. I flew to New York and stood outside the glass skyscraper on the corner of Third Avenue and Fifty-seventh Street, waiting for her to get off work. When she saw me she smiled and I could detect a sad yearning in her eyes, but she quickly forced a change in her expression and headed for the post office. I walked along beside her, telling her about my new place in High Point and how much she would love the South.

"I have to be at track practice at six thirty," she said brusquely. "I've joined the Astoria Track Club."

"Can't you skip that?" I said. "We'll have dinner."

"No, Mark. You don't understand."

"You've built quite a fortress around yourself. It's like the Berlin Wall. You're acting like such a stoic. Why are you trying to hide your true emotions?"

"I'm simply more skeptical of marriage," Gail said. "I mean, when you see the two people who brought you into this world split up, you feel rootless. At this point in my life I'm afraid of intimacy, I'm afraid of counting on another person to always be there."

"But marriage has nothing to do with dependence."

"Besides, you have such a strong personality. How can I ever stand up to it? My mother couldn't stand up to my father, and now they're divorcing."

"All right, it's true that I have a strong personality," I said. "But that's because of where I came from and what I had to fight. But you've fought your own battles as a woman! You're not like other women. You're a nonconformist, an individual. Or am I mistaken? Didn't you go to Budapest alone and live there for six months? Didn't you travel all over Europe and America alone? Don't you hike and camp alone for days at a time? Didn't you reject your father's choice of a career for you? Those things take strength, they build character. You're much stronger than you realize."

Gail averted her eyes and fell silent. Finally she said, "But what about the other difficulties?"

"Such as?"

"I hated the way we had to hide our relationship from others."

"I hated it too. But we had begun to change that. We were becoming ourselves. You remember how many times we pledged to live as we desired and not as society dictated."

"But it's so hard to fight society," Gail said. "I can't help it—I'm still dependent on the opinions and approval of others. It's difficult not to be."

"I understand that," I said. "But I know that with time, if we remain true to our convictions and to each other, enough people will come to accept us on our own terms. Remember the progress we had already made. We started by denying our relationship, then we tried hiding it from the public. But that's all changing. You know, some mixed couples continue to act like strangers to each other for fear of losing their jobs or meeting with public disapproval."

"You see?" she cried. "I don't want to live that kind of life."

"We won't. And neither should they!"

As we descended the grimy steps of the subway I tried to convince Gail that two people who truly love each other can overcome all obstacles. The subway was crowded. The stale, musty air was suffocating. People were pushing with all their might to get into the train before the doors closed on them.

"Oh, let's get out of here!" I said. "Let's have dinner somewhere."

"Here comes my train to Queens," Gail said.

The train screeched to a halt and the doors slid open. She looked at me, and I thought I detected a tear in her eye. She hesitated, obviously at war with her own emotions, then stepped onto the train just as the doors were closing. She vanished from sight. I returned to North Carolina with a heavy heart.

October arrived, bringing with it the smell of falling leaves and the rain-soaked earth. The trees outside my balcony, once green and dancing in the breeze, began to turn brown and wither. I furnished my apartment, learned to drive, and did a few lectures, but still my spirits were low.

One day Marion Salzman, a friend of Gail's from her days at Brown University, called me to ask if I were willing to give a speech at a private dinner in New York before a group of top investment bankers, including the president of Citicorp. They wanted to know the truth about black life in South Africa and my views on divestment and sanctions. Faintly hoping that Gail might attend, I accepted.

GAIL'S VIEW

When I flew to Minneapolis for the July Fourth weekend, I simply wanted to let my parents know how serious Mark and I had become about marriage and to find out the real reasons for their breaking up after thirty-five years of marriage, three grown children, and countless precious memories. I had no idea the divorce would turn my whole world upside down and make me suddenly fear making a commitment to the man I loved.

The news of their divorce stupefied me. It was June 1986 and I was at my grandfather's home, a rustic cottage in the White Mountains of northern New Hampshire, when my parents called. Grampa had prepared a sumptuous meal of glazed Cornish hens and the two of us were sharing a bottle of Hungarian wine, clinking glasses as we made silly toasts and swapped stories. Thunder boomed and lightning flashed across the mountains as Grampa told me, in vivid detail, about the day in 1927 he and his sweetheart Susan Stork got married. He was studying to be a minister at Union Theological Seminary and she was a Barnard College undergrad, a flapper who wore her hair bobbed. They knew their parents would disapprove of their marrying when they were still students and before Grampa was ordained as a minister, so they took the subway from 116th Street to City Hall and got married secretly. It reminded me of Romeo and Juliet stealing away to Friar Laurence's cell and getting married without either family's knowledge or consent. I wished that someday I might marry in such a romantic and private way.

Grampa had just finished telling me the emotionally riveting story when the phone rang. "Your parents have something they want to tell you," he said, handing me the phone.

After some hesitation, my mother said, "Your father and I have begun divorce proceedings."

Stunned silence.

"Is this the first you've heard of it?" Dad asked.

I struggled to get a grip on my emotions. I tried to sound rational. "We're all adults now and, therefore, friends, right?" I said slowly. "I guess that means I have to stop seeing you as parents and start seeing you as two individuals. People go through changes, and friends accept those changes."

"You sound as though you were thirty-four, not twenty-four," Dad said.

"I've grown up a lot in the past two years," I said. "I've known a lot of sorrow and a lot of pain."

There was not much more to say. No one had any good news. "I love you both," I said.

"We know you do, honey," my father replied.

I hung up and sat down on a kitchen stool feeling glum. Grampa and I discussed the divorce, then I went upstairs to bed. Sleep was long in coming, and I had shed tears before sleep finally stole away my despair and twisted it into confusing dreams. *Where is the love that transcends all misery and hardships?* I wondered. *How could they just walk away from each other after thirty-five years of marriage? Why?*

In an attempt to find the answers I went to Minneapolis. My mother picked me up from the airport, and when I told her about Mark's proposal, her reaction was not what I expected.

"Dad is very concerned about you," she said. "We both are. He thinks that if you marry Mark, the chances of divorce are high. And he asked, 'What are her chances of remarrying when she has black children?' "

"Why does he think we would divorce?"

"Because it's so common, and mixed couples have to endure extra pressures. He's counseled a few mixed couples and wasn't able to save the marriages. Besides, honey," she said, reaching across the front seat to touch my arm, "you should wait and be sure. You don't want to go through a divorce. It's a living hell."

What I saw and heard in the next few days convinced me of this fact. When I was with my mother I heard one side of the story; with my father I heard a completely different one. It was easy to sympathize with both of them, which confused me. They argued about money. They argued about where I should stay. One pressed me to reveal what the other had said. Each blamed the other. At times I went outside, feeling unwanted, and asked myself, *Why did I come home? They are divorcing. They have no time or emotional energy for me.*

"Your mother did her best, Gail," Dad said, sitting beside me on the couch with his arm around me. "She gave everything she could. I harbor no ill will toward her. She's a brilliant woman. It's just that we're so darn different, that's all."

I tried to talk to him about Mark, but I did not know how to broach the subject. Without a word I pulled the current *People* magazine out of my purse, opened it to the article on Mark, and handed it to my father. He stared at it for several minutes.

"He wants to marry me," I said.

My father closed his eyes, pinched the bridge of his nose, and broke into an unexpected, chest-deep sob. He was as emotional as he had been when he called me in New York after receiving my hate letter. This was not my father. He had changed completely. In place of the controlling patriarch was this sensitive fifty-five-year-old whose inner turmoil could boil to the surface in an instant.

I threw my arms around him. He held me tightly and sobbed even more vehemently.

"I'm so glad you came home, Gail," he said between breaths. "What a godsend you are to both of us at this time."

"But why are you crying?"

"Because Mark is such a prince, and you're such a princess. It's the first time you've gone out with someone who's a real class act—who's on your intellectual and creative level. He's a real prince. And one assumes that princes and princesses belong together. But that's not always true. There are other issues to consider and, oh"—he sobbed again—"it's so tragic."

"But *why* don't princes and princesses belong together?"

"Look at your mother," he said between gasps. "She's intelligent, well bred, sophisticated. And look at me—I'm a hardworking minister and psychologist with an Ivy League education. But we don't work together. That's what's tragic. We're cutting each other down instead of building each other up."

I wondered how my mother must have felt watching us embrace each other. I looked up. She was standing in the doorway, her brow knit and her eyes full of sorrow. Later, when I was alone with her, I stared at the *People* photograph of Mark, at his limbs and eyes and smiling lips.

"I don't think I'm strong enough to break up with him," I said.

"Why not?" my mother asked.

"I'm too much in love with him."

"But you can find a support group to help give you strength, can't you?" she asked.

"Have you ever tried to kill a love you've felt for someone?" I asked.

"No."

"It's hard to force your heart to listen to your head. All I'll have to do is hear his gentle voice and I'll melt."

"If you want to stay with him, go ahead," she replied. "But I've learned that staying together with the wrong man is a poor excuse for living."

The trauma of seeing a divorce unfold before my very eyes was enough to peak my fear of commitment. And the way my parents were pleading with me to slow down, pull back, and rethink my relationship with Mark gave me the feeling I needed some time to reflect and sort out my feelings.

To heighten my dilemma, it seemed that everywhere I looked in Minneapolis I saw a mixed couple. As I dined with my father in a restaurant one night, I could not take my eyes off the beautiful milk chocolate skin of a little girl sitting between her black father and white mother. She smiled with little baby teeth, her black hair hung in tight ringlets, and her charcoal eyes glittered. I missed Mark. I did my best to hold up my end of the conversation, but my deepest thoughts lay elsewhere.

At last I decided to wage an all-out war against my emotions. I swore I would smother my love for Mark before it consumed me entirely, leaving only a trace of my former self. I reasoned that if I could survive on my own for five months, without leaning on anyone for emotional support, then I just might be able to love Mark with no reservations, without the slightest worry about the odds society might stack against us as a mixed couple.

I moved to a dingy railroad apartment in Astoria, Queens, which I shared with an aspiring singer named Tammy and her cat, Reebok. I gave orders to my friends and brothers not to reveal my new address or phone number to Mark. I tried to convince myself and my relatives that I was fine, but I sorely missed Mark and felt miserable. Sometimes I asked myself why I was torturing both of us so much by insisting on this separation.

Night after night I had a recurring dream: Mark and I lay side by side on the deck of a boat, floating on a lake. He caressed my cheek; I said I had better go. "When will you return?" he asked. "In five months," I replied. He tried to prevent me from leaving, but I pulled away and dove into the water, terrified of my feelings for him. As I swam away I felt sorrowful, for I had left a large chunk of myself behind on that boat.

Summer passed and heavy rains ushered in the fall. I received an occasional note from Mark, and wrote him once, when he moved to

North Carolina, to tell him I missed him. I knew I was sending him mixed signals, but I could not help letting my true feelings slip out once in a while. In early October Mark surprised me by calling me from North Carolina.

I was at my part-time job doing word processing for a group of consulting scientists.

"I have a surprise for you," Mark said. "Can you guess what it is?"

"The Japanese are bombing Pearl Harbor."

"No, guess again."

"London Bridge is falling down."

"No."

"You're moving to France."

"Not in the near future."

"I give up."

"I'm going to arrange to have you fly down to North Carolina this weekend. I want you to see my new place."

I was silent. I did not know how to respond. My heart cried YES! but my head restrained me.

"Sweets? Are you there?"

"I can't."

"How about meeting me in Boston on my birthday?"

"No, it's the same thing. I don't want to see you," I said, but at the same time I wondered, *What am I so afraid of? Why am I running from his love?*

I heard nothing but silence, then a sort of whimper. "Oh, Gail. I love you so deeply. I really do. Do you know that?"

Tears welled in my eyes. I wanted to believe him so much. Part of me wanted to give up and revive our relationship, but something powerful—a fear of disappointing my father, a fear of being part of a mixed couple, a fear of getting married and then divorced—held me back.

"Hello, Gail? Are you there, darling?"

"Yes," I whispered, barely audible.

"Do you know how much I love you? Do you really know?"

I looked up as my boss came in from lunch and walked by my desk. "I really can't talk right now," I said.

"Don't go. You can't go yet. Please talk to me. How are you doing?

What are you feeling? Don't you feel anything at all for your little bushman?"

"I'm sorry it had to be you," I said.

"What do you mean?"

"I'm just sorry you had to be the man in my life when all this happened to me. I didn't want to hurt you."

"I've felt a lot of pain in my lifetime," Mark said. "It clarifies things, shows me what is real. And I've realized lately how deeply I love you. I left New York to give you space. You know that, don't you?"

I did not respond.

"But I couldn't get away from you, even down here. I carry your spirit in my heart."

"Mark, I have to go," I said, becoming aware of the office around me.

"Will you come to North Carolina?"

"I don't know. I'll write."

I hung up, flustered and confused. The office manager, Sandy, a very emotional and caring woman who had suffered through eight years as a heroin addict in the 1970s, tried to comfort me. When I told her it was Mark, her jaw dropped. She had been my confidante and knew the whole painful story of our tenuous relationship.

"I'm afraid no one will ever love me as much as he does," I said sadly.

"Gail! What are you *talking* about?!" Sandy cried. "Everyone who's met you has told me what a beautiful, intelligent, delightful person you are. Half the men in this building would jump at the chance to go out with you. But it's not only your physical attractiveness. It's what's *inside* that's most important."

"Thanks," I said, too miserable to let her kind words fully soak in.

My father called me the following Saturday, told me he was reading *Kaffir Boy*, then said he detected a certain sadness in my voice when he mentioned Mark's name.

"Sounds like you're still grieving, honey," he said.

It was the first time during the entire separation from Mark that my father showed any compassion for what I was feeling, for the pain I was putting myself through. I could feel a tear roll down my cheek.

"Why don't you date around?" he asked.

"I don't want to," I said, then paused. "Dad, I feel strange talking to you about my relationships."

"Yes, well, I guess that's my fault."

There was a silence.

"It's okay," I said.

"No, I don't think it is," he said. "I don't know why I felt so possessive, so . . ." He stopped talking and I could almost hear the crack of the emotional whip as he flogged himself for having been so overprotective and jealous. When I was a teenager he called me "Babe," or "Hey, Beautiful." He told me boys just want to "get in your pants."

"In your opinion no one was ever good enough for me, were they?" I asked.

"I don't know if *anyone* could have been," he said, sounding defeated.

I knew I needed to make peace with my father, the first man in my life, in order to have a fulfilling adult relationship with a man. I needed to get rid of any deep-rooted anger I might harbor against him, admire his strengths, and understand and forgive his weaknesses.

In October I began to see Carol Abizaid twice a week, for she was teaching a dance class in Soho I was taking. She could not understand why I was pushing Mark away when she knew how much I still loved him. Carol was falling in love with a French-speaking black man named Robert, a dancer who had grown up an orphan in West Africa. There was only one problem: Robert had a wife. Carol seemed distracted during dance class, and after we had finished she borrowed a quarter from me and went to make a phone call.

In the locker room I spotted Ellen, Carol's gorgeous biracial roommate, and asked, "What do you think of Carol's falling in love with a married man? I think she's setting herself up for a lot of pain."

"Well, she's a grown woman," Ellen said, bending down to strip off her leg warmers. "I guess all we can do is be there for her when she feels down. He tells her certain things, and she believes him, so I guess we have to respect her feelings."

"She's really falling seriously in love, isn't she?"

"*Fallen*—past tense. I haven't seen her like this since we were at Brown and she fell for Paul. She's far gone."

But even the fact that Carol, one of my dearest friends, dated black men and seemed to feel comfortable with that did not make me feel at ease with the prospect of interracial marriage. The stronger my love for Mark grew, the more I feared marriage and commitment. At times I wished I could fall blindly and irrevocably in love with a white man, as if that would solve everything. But in my heart I knew I would never meet another man like Mark in all the billions of this world.

That autumn I spent endless hours in Cafe Dante in Greenwich Village, sipping cappuccino and scribbling feverishly in my journal, trying to compose short story plots, writing notes for a second novel. The manuscript of my first novel was with Kim Witherspoon, a fellow Brown graduate who had just become a literary agent specializing in young fiction writers. She had submitted my manuscript to six major houses and promoted me over lunch meetings with book editors. It was Kim who told me that Mark was lecturing in Midtown. I had dropped by her office on Broadway to see her.

"You *will* come to Mark's speech with us, won't you?" Kim said, standing up from her desk and pulling on her long black coat. "Marion is waiting downstairs in a cab."

I felt torn. I yearned to see Mark, yet I was afraid of what it might lead to. My heart, which was constantly at war with my head, finally triumphed and I found myself in a cab between Marion and Kim, bouncing down Park Avenue on our way to the New York Men's Club.

I spotted Mark, politely nodding to an elderly gentleman, across a crowded room filled with investment bankers in black suits who conversed in low and distinguished voices. His eyes widened in amazement when he saw me. In seconds he was beside me.

"I can't believe you came," he whispered. "You look lovely."

We were called in to dinner and seated around a long U-shaped table. I sat at the farthest end, separated from Mark by the length of the entire room, but even at that distance he looked more handsome and self-assured than I remembered. As he spoke about black life under apartheid, about the imperative need to pressure the Pretoria regime to change, his jaw seemed more square and forceful than ever, his words more eloquent and powerful than I'd ever heard. The bankers dared not set a teacup on a saucer for fear of disturbing the silence of Mark's dramatic pauses.

"You'd better leave," my head whispered to me. "This is dangerous. You still love him too much to be here."

"What's wrong with love?" my heart retorted. "Why should I suppress my feelings? What for? To please whom?"

"But he's black, and you'll have mulatto babies," my head replied. "You'll be ostracized from society. No one will invite you to their homes. Your mother will say, 'I told you so,' and your father will *say* he approves in order to keep your affection, but he'll privately hate Mark."

"Do I have to spend my whole life *hiding* from the man I love?"

"Not your whole life. Just long enough to stop loving him."

"You're coldhearted."

"I'm Gail's mind. *You're* her heart."

Finally I could take it no longer. I was torn in half. The bond between us was so strong that I could feel Mark's gravitational pull from across the room.

"I have to go," I whispered to Kim.

"You're really afraid to be left alone with him, aren't you?" Kim asked.

I nodded. We left before Mark's speech was finished and headed down the spiraling marble steps.

"It must be difficult to break up with such an incredible man," Kim said. "I mean, he's not just a person, he's a *cause*. It must be hard to separate the two. And he's not just talking about apartheid, he's talking about being *human*."

I knew immediately from the look in her eyes that Mark's full impact had hit her. It was the same impact that had first held me, and still held me, in his power. As I was leaving I saw Mark, in a crisp dark suit and tie, quickly descending the stairs after me. I frantically tried to push open the door, but it stuck. I saw Mark's eyes widen, his mouth open. The door burst open and I dashed outside, looked both ways, then ran down Sixty-ninth Street toward Lexington Avenue. I did not feel safe from the whirl of my emotions until the doors of the bus had closed, and even then I could not believe I had left the man I loved standing on those steps, aghast.

The next day Mark called me at work at the scientists' association and invited me to lunch. I accepted before my head could object, and I took Sandy along as a chaperone. But when Sandy had to leave early to get back to the office, I found myself alone with Mark, walking down Forty-second Street.

"So where do we go from here, Gail?" Mark asked. "What is to become of us?"

We stopped in front of the office building where I worked. My fears took control. I said I had to go, that our relationship would never work.

"Why, Gail? Why don't you think it can work? Let's give it another try. I know it will work out. I've learned a lot in these past three and a half months."

Thoughts of my parents and relatives loomed in my mind. My head said, "You have to be strong, Gail. It was a mistake to see him."

"Is this good-bye then . . . forever?" he asked.

"Yes, this is good-bye." I ran inside the building. He followed me.

"Do you want me to forget you?"

"Yes."

"I can never forget you, Gail."

"It would never work."

"Then please, give me one final farewell kiss."

"That would only make it harder," I said. But inside my heart was breaking. I wanted to throw my arms around him, I wanted to take him home with me, I wanted to talk about writing and traveling and make plans to visit him in North Carolina and shout, "To *hell* with the world! I don't care what anyone thinks of us! I don't care that I'm white and he's black! I have to follow my feelings!"

But I remained stoic, even when I saw tears welling in Mark's eyes. I turned toward the elevator to hide my own tears from him.

"Let's try again," he said.

"No, no, no!" I cried, then rushed past him and into the elevator.

"Good-bye, Gail," he said softly as the elevator doors slid shut.

Sandy was in the office when I arrived but our boss was not yet back from lunch. I burst into tears and Sandy did her best to comfort me. She put her arm around me.

"Oh, Gail! I can see why this must be hard for you. He's the nicest man I've ever met."

My heart was so heavy I could not bear it. I had no desire to go out and battle the New York crowds, no desire to do anything but wrap my arms around Mark. But he was gone, on his way to the airport to head back to North Carolina, probably gone from my life forever. I felt I was to blame. I was too stubborn. I began crying, hysterically. My face was red, my eyes swollen. I hyperventilated from sobbing so hard.

"Oh, kid," Sandy said. "You got it that bad, don't you? Can't you call him? Can't you reach him somehow?"

I called Ellie Spiegel, the programs director at International House on 122nd and Riverside. I knew Mark had spent the night at her home across the George Washington Bridge in Leonia. She said she was not sure whether Mark had left yet or not.

When I stepped onto the streets of New York at five o'clock, I said to myself, "I *must* see him! I'll go to Leonia. Perhaps he's still there." I was irrational with grief as I boarded the A train and headed north through Manhattan. I spent my last dollar on bus fare to cross the bridge.

"I don't care what anyone says anymore," I said to myself as tears slid down my cheeks. "My heart has won, and I'm glad. If he has left for North Carolina, then Fate meant for us to be apart. If not, then we belong together."

Ellie, a gray-haired and pert woman, was on the front porch getting the mail as I came up the tree-lined walk.

"Hello, I'm still looking for Mark," I called to her.

"Oh, come in, Gail. Let me see if his things are upstairs."

I stood at the foot of the stairs, almost reeling with suspense. "Oh, please, dear God," I whispered. "Let his bags be there. Oh, please!"

"His bags are still there," Ellie said, coming down the stairs. "I think he's staying until . . . oh, dear! What's the matter?"

"Oh, nothing," I said, blinking back tears of joy. "It's just that . . . well, it's kind of personal but I think you should know. Mark and I fell in love while we were at International House. My parents disapproved, at least my father did, and I broke up with Mark in July under all kinds of pressure. It's so hard to be a mixed couple in this world."

"Oh, you poor girl," she said, throwing her arms around me. We stood there hugging for a moment.

Ellie, her husband, Hans, and I were halfway through dinner when the phone finally rang around nine o'clock. Ellie answered it. "Oh, hello Mark, where *are* you?" She nodded toward me excitedly and winked. "Yes, I'll pick you up outside the terminal. You're just in time for dinner."

As she ran to get her coat, I said, "Don't tell him I'm here."

Ten minutes later Mark walked into the dining room, took one look at me, and broke into a grin. "Oh, Ellie!" he said, "You should have told me!"

"I was under instructions," she said.

"Oh, what a surprise!" He was beaming and made no attempt to hide his joy.

When he went upstairs to wash up for dinner, I went up after him. We wrapped our arms around each other tightly. Our lips met for the first time in nearly four months.

"Oh, Gail. I love you so much," he whispered.

"And I love you."

"I was so miserable. I've been wandering around Manhattan in a stupor of depression. But now . . ." He could do nothing more than smile.

We went downstairs and joined the dinner conversation, while under the table his toes massaged my stocking feet. As soon as we could get away we went for a walk around the neighborhood in our socks, holding hands and discussing the tumultuous four months we had spent apart. The night was warm and tender and compassionate as we whispered back and forth. And I asked myself, *Why did you fight your love for him for so long? Accept yourself as you are, Gail. Accept the fact that you're in love with a black South African.*

We spent the weekend in North Carolina, just the two of us, deep in discussion, walking hand in hand through the woods, picnicking by a lake, sharing an umbrella in the pouring rain. The leaves overhead made a canopy of crimson and gold as we ran down a trail through the forest. We talked excitedly about writing a book that would encourage mixed couples to choose love and disregard the world around them. My feelings for him were so real, so genuine. I now saw that all my desperate struggles to break away from him had been artificial, based on a fear of what others would think, say, do.

Back in New York, I was heading up the stairs to the office I shared with Sandy two days a week, when a young executive in a starched white shirt and tie spotted me. Ryan worked in an office one floor below me and had been hinting for months that we date.

"You look unusually happy today," Ryan said.

"I do?" I laughed.

"Yes! You're exuberant. You're radiating light."

"I am?"

"Well, what happened this weekend?"

I felt like shouting, "I got back together with my boyfriend and we love each other like crazy!" But instead I simply smiled and said, "This is my usual exuberant self. You usually see me on Fridays when I can't wait to go home."

"You get like that without drugs?" he asked.

I laughed. It amazed me that drugs had made cocaine addicts like Ryan forget the experience of real joy. The building crawled with coke heads, supplied by the elevator operators who would stop the car between floors to make the exchanges. The sound of sniffling filled the bathrooms. I worried that Sandy, who had resisted the temptation of heroin for years and was still taking methadone through a drug rehab program, might be pressured back into snorting or shooting up by the addicts who came to work with bloodshot eyes and chain-saw smiles.

When I entered the office, Sandy was alone with the elevator operator. I suspected they had just completed an exchange, for they quickly switched their conversation when I entered. I looked to Sandy for an explanation, but she just smiled and asked me if I had found Mark before he left for North Carolina.

"We're back together again," I said, unable to contain my joy.

"He must be happier than a pig in shit!" she cried. "And he deserves to be, too!"

My friend Carol, too, was delighted that Mark and I were back together again. She could tell just by looking at me.

"I finally decided that all the external pressures mean nothing compared to what I feel inside," I whispered to her in the darkness of a movie theater where we were watching a Spike Lee film.

"Yeah! Forget what other people think!"

"And what my parents are going through shouldn't have to affect my life so much."

"Hooray! Gail's being a rebel!" Carol cried, making several heads turn to glare at us in the dark theater.

But my family and many of my friends, who had encouraged my

independence, were shocked and then disappointed to learn I had suddenly changed my mind about Mark. They felt I had turned against them, and I knew I had set them up to feel that way. My father called my apartment when I was away, and, learning from my roommate Tammy that I was with Mark in North Carolina, immediately called my mother and brothers to alert them. I dreaded trying to explain to them the painful and joyous twists of emotion that led to my decision, but I knew that for once in my life, I had made a choice, alone, that it was my own, and that it made me happy.

The dreaded call from my father finally came.

"So, you're back together with Mark again. What does this mean? Are you going to move to North Carolina?"

"No, not yet. He has his life and I have mine. For now, we'll visit each other and talk on the phone."

"Are you still free to date other men?"

"I suppose so, but I don't feel like it."

There was a long silence.

"Well, I don't know what to say," he said.

"Don't say anything. I'm not asking for your opinion."

"Okay." He paused, then started talking about my mother, casting her in a negative light. I bristled.

"Did you ever love Mom?" I asked.

He reflected for a moment, then said, "We were fond of each other. We were companions."

"You married her for appearance' sake, didn't you? She was good wife material for an aspiring minister. Am I right?"

"Yes," he said. "We made a good-looking pair. I didn't realize the importance of love in a relationship."

"I feel like you expect me to go out and find some socially acceptable mate, even if I don't love him."

"No, I don't. I wouldn't wish that on anybody."

"Mark and I love each other, even though we may get strange looks walking down the street. In society's eyes, we're not a perfect match. But at least I've learned to choose love over social acceptability."

My father was silent. I knew I had won my case. The struggle to overcome my need to be guided, led, controlled, taught, and protected had been long and difficult, but I finally felt I was out there on my own, a free woman, at last.

My mother, after recovering from her surprise at our reunion, accepted my invitation to spend Thanksgiving in North Carolina with Mark and me. She flew down from Minneapolis for a weekend of hiking in the woods, walking beside Oak Hollow Lake, feasting on turkey, and dining at a Moravian Inn at Salem College in Winston-Salem. As the three of us wandered through a High Point furniture store, we passed through a room filled with baby cribs.

"Pay special attention to this room, Sweets," Mark said.

My mother laughed, finding Mark's comment charming. I blushed in embarrassment. Having a baby was the furthest thing from my mind. I had no idea that less than three years later we would purchase a crib from the very same store.

6

GETTING MARRIED

MARK'S VIEW

Gail lived in an all-white neighborhood in Queens, inhabited mostly by Eastern Europeans and Italians accustomed to poking their heads between faded curtains and shouting down to their children playing baseball in the middle of the street. The block was one solid building, divided only by walls and floors into railroad apartments. Sagging clotheslines crisscrossed the courtyard outside the kitchen window, where her roommate's cat, Reebok, sat for hours watching birds.

Leaving the subway at the corner of Steinway and Broadway in Astoria, on my way to Gail's place, I'd walk several blocks past gangs of white youths who glared at me suspiciously. I sensed this was whites-only territory. Occasionally I was followed for a block or so but luckily was never harassed. A few months later, in another section of Queens called Howard Beach, a gang of white teenagers chased a black man onto a highway and to his death.

Gail's "apartment" was the living room, without privacy. Her roommate, Tammy, passed through it whenever she needed to use the kitchen or bath. Whenever I was there, Tammy and her boyfriend, Billy, tried staying out of our way, but conflicts invariably arose.

"It's rather crowded in this apartment, isn't it?" Gail said one morning to Tammy, who immediately flew into a rage.

"It's strange that *you* should say that! *You* weren't inconvenienced at all until your black boyfriend came along! Do you know what *we* have to do to accommodate you two lovebirds? Billy has to go outside to pee and I pee into a trash can. Yet this is *my* apartment."

By December Gail and her friend Carol Abizaid were looking for an apartment to share in Brooklyn, a place large enough and private enough to allow visits from Carol's West African boyfriend, Robert, and me. They found a sunny, five-room place with hardwood floors and freshly painted white walls on the second floor of a beauty parlor on Flatbush Avenue near Prospect Park. It belonged to a sweet, understanding woman from Trinidad named Cecilia, who also owned the beauty parlor. Gail and Carol moved in a few days after New Year's 1987.

I was glad Gail was now living with a trusted friend. The only inconveniences were the mice denizened behind the refrigerator, the barking and growling of Windy, Carol's black Labrador, in the middle of the night, the clanking heating pipe by the head of Gail's bed that awoke us at six on cold mornings, and the constant flow of traffic and screaming sirens on Flatbush Avenue.

It was a predominantly black neighborhood, accented by a handful of white yuppies living in recently renovated brownstones toward the Slope. With such a cultural mix in the neighborhood, we were just another couple each time we walked down Flatbush Avenue to the park on Sunday afternoons.

A third roommate moved in with Gail and Carol. Mandy was black, a dancer, and a native of Brooklyn.

"I've never lived with two white girls before," Mandy told Gail and Carol. "But I guess you two aren't really all that white, I mean, you both got black boyfriends."

Her room was separated from Gail's by nothing but a large piece of plywood that sealed the opening between the two rooms. On some weekends there were six of us, three women and their three black boyfriends. Behind the plywood from Mandy's room came the *thump-thump* of rap music and boogie funk.

Down the hall we would hear Carol and Robert arguing. His

English was not half as fluent as his French, so they had difficulty communicating each time a conflict arose. When his anger completely took over, Robert could be heard repeating a belligerent "Fuck you!" But Carol loved him with passionate devotion. He was light-skinned and handsome, was adored by many young women, had a shy and pleasing smile, and had just opened his own business. Beyond these aspects of his life, Carol knew very little except that he had grown up as an orphan and been abused as a child. He seldom answered questions about his wife, but he hinted to Carol that he would soon leave her.

I found myself contrasting my relationship with Gail with that of Carol and Robert. Carol believed that marrying Robert would put an end to her emotional turmoil and doubts. She would be his wife, not his mistress. She would be able to call him on the phone and not have to hang up if his wife answered. She would see him more than once or twice a week. They would build a life together and become closer each day. She clung to these uncertain hopes and refused to let them die, no matter how many lies Robert told her. Carol's mother and father urged her to break off the relationship but she angrily refused.

One morning in the kitchen, Carol turned to Gail and said, "Robert and I are getting married today."

"Really?" Gail said with surprise.

"His divorce was finalized yesterday. We have to marry right away, for his green card. He says we'll have a public wedding later."

Carol came home that night alone, carrying a bottle of champagne and calling for a celebration. But the bottle remained unopened and she spent her wedding night watching television alone in her room.

"What was it like?" Gail asked the next day.

"It was sort of anticlimactic. Not that I expected much anyway," Carol said. She then described the marriage bureau at City Hall, thronging with people, mostly foreigners, waiting to get married. She described how she had felt faint at the weirdness of it all when the preacher read the lines, "Do you, Carol Abizaid, take this man to be your lawfully wedded husband?" And how she had given Robert a "serious" kiss when the City Clerk said, "You may kiss the bride."

Carol fell silent and stirred soup on the stove.

"Has anything changed?" Gail asked.

"Nothing's changed," she said, staring into the pan, expressionless. "He still lives with his ex-wife. We'll see each other once or twice a week. Things won't change until she goes back to West Africa."

"When will that be?"

"Soon." She continued staring vacantly into the pan. "At least, that's what he told me."

"Did he give you a ring?"

"No. But I didn't expect one."

Gail stared at her for a moment, confused by the strangeness of Carol's relationship. Finally she said, "Wow, you're a married woman. You're a Mrs. Somebody."

"Shut up! Now don't you start teasing me!" Carol said, then managed a faint laugh.

The next day Robert's ex-wife called Carol and thanked her for marrying Robert. "That was a big favor you did," she said. "We really appreciate it. Now he can get his green card."

This phone call upset Carol, but Robert explained to her that he had to tell his wife certain white lies to get her to agree to the divorce.

Carol told no one about the marriage, perhaps hoping that someday, when Robert "grows up," they would live together and plan an actual wedding. In the meantime, she spent many of her nights alone, waiting for Robert to call and crying herself to sleep when he did not.

Gail and I tried to include Carol in our conversations and invited her to join us for home-cooked dinners of baked chicken, rice pilaf, and special sauces, but the intimacy and contentment between Gail and me seemed only to exacerbate Carol's misery and loneliness. She later confessed she was terribly envious of us.

Weekends at my apartment in North Carolina were much more relaxed. We would cuddle under an afghan before the fire, dine by candlelight while discussing Dickens and the French revolution; talk about the importance of keeping a journal, having convictions, and speaking one's mind; skip rocks across a lake; take floral-scented baths after working out on Nautilus machines; and listen to Paul Simon's *Graceland* album and to Bob Marley.

We would wander aimlessly through the grocery store, oblivious to the stares, shocked expressions, and raised eyebrows of elderly Southern belles and disapproving Confederate gents. I rarely called her Gail anymore. To me she was always "Sweets," a nickname that never failed to draw a smile from her lips.

Neither of us welcomed the arrival of Monday mornings. Mondays meant that one of us would have to go to the airport and return home. Long-distance relationships are difficult, especially when days of intense closeness are interrupted by weeks of being alone. We were ready to marry, but Gail was not yet ready to leave New York, her friends, and brothers in the city or her job as an editor, and I was afraid she might feel unhappy and isolated if she did so.

One Monday morning in Brooklyn, I canceled my flight back to North Carolina. I postponed it a day, then two more, then a week. I could not tear myself away, especially as it was the week of Gail's twenty-fifth birthday, and she did not want me to leave either.

One February afternoon as Gail and I strolled through Central Park, among joggers, cyclists, and patches of melting snow, we started talking seriously about marriage. She squeezed my hand and said, "Let's just do it."

"What do you mean?" I asked.

"We're always talking about getting married. Why don't we just go ahead and do it?"

"How?"

"Like my grandfather and Grandma Sue did, back in the 1920s when they took the subway from Columbia down to City Hall. Wouldn't that be a great way to marry?"

"But that's how Carol and Robert got married, and they're miserable. I've hardly seen Robert over at your apartment since the wedding."

"Their relationship is the problem, not where they married," she said. "I've always thought of my grandparents' marriage as being romantic, unconventional. Just think of it: It would be just the two of us. And that's what it's all about, after all, isn't it? It's a promise between two people, not a social event. I was sitting in my office today, making a list of guests to invite to our wedding. Then I stopped and tore it up. I don't want anyone else to be there, just the two of us."

I was surprised but pleased by her sudden readiness. After all we had been through, it was hard to believe we had finally reached that level of confidence and trust to decide to make the final commitment, despite the obstacles that still lay ahead.

"Are you sure you want such a quiet wedding?"

"You wouldn't mind, would you?" she asked.

"No, not really. Since I can't afford to bring my family to America, and since they probably could not get passports anyway, I guess it wouldn't matter if we don't have a big wedding. But what about *your* family? Won't they feel left out?"

"We can send them announcements, after the fact."

"Gail, what's the real meaning behind this? Are you afraid to tell your family we're getting married? Do you want a fait accompli so they can't pressure you into changing your mind?"

My remarks disturbed her. She averted her face, walked a bit faster, and stared across a windswept field toward Central Park South. Then she turned to me and said, "Yes, that's exactly what I'm afraid of. I've let my father push me this way and that for too long. I want to go ahead and make a decision alone for once. I love you. And I'm never going to let anyone manipulate my feelings for you any longer. My father calls once in a while to express his 'concern' about me, as if I were throwing away my life by loving you. He's been sending me books. One of them was *Women Who Love Too Much* and the other was *Women Who Love Men Who Hate Women*."

"Why would he send such books?"

"He read *Kaffir Boy*, probably with a red pen in one hand, searching for your behavioral patterns and trying to psychoanalyze your childhood. He thinks that anyone raised in such a brutal environment will inevitably become brutal, and that anyone with a father like yours will definitely become a controlling tyrant. I didn't let him finish. I hung up on him and then screamed at the phone, 'Bastard!' "

"But why would he think I hate women? My book flows with praise and admiration for my mother and grandmother. Women have shaped my character and made me grow in ways I never could have. Most important they taught me how to survive the horrors of apartheid with my soul intact. It is their values and example that helped me overcome my anger and hatred."

"I don't know. I think he's just trying whatever he can to make me question my relationship with you."

"Don't let it bother you," I said, drawing her toward me by the hand. She was trembling. "Let go of your anger. He'll grow to understand. He hasn't even met me yet. And we don't need to rush into anything. I don't want you to have to choose between me and your family. I don't want you to marry me out of fear that someone might convince you to stop loving me."

"It's not out of fear," she said. "I'm sure of my feelings for you. I just want to protect those feelings from the pressures of the outside world. I want it to be just the two of us. At least for a while. You see, everyone in my family seems to know what's best for me, and I know I feed their malleable image of me with my words, my timid smiles, my hesitations, my silences. I have to be bold in making my own decisions. The future seems so vague and a bit frightening. I've been so afraid of making the wrong choice that I've made no decisions at all. I want to change that."

GAIL'S VIEW

The subway ground to a screeching halt and the doors jolted open. We were spewed onto the platform at City Hall in an oozing stream of harried commuters. We ascended the pee-stained, littered steps slowly, clasping each other's hands with the desperation of children clinging to their mothers' skirts in a milling crowd of strangers.

City Hall loomed over our heads as we stepped up to the revolving doors, hesitant, peering through the glass. I spotted a sign that read: "Marriage Licenses."

"To the left, up those stairs," I said.

Mark's hand felt warm and moist in mine as we made our way to the second floor and walked down the corridor, our footsteps echoing on the polished linoleum. He was dressed in his best suit and shined brown shoes; I wore slacks and a blazer.

As we waited in line for a marriage license application, I reflected on a phone conversation I had with my grandfather four days earlier. Eager for the opinion of someone older and wiser, I had called him at his home in New Hampshire. I started by talking to him about my strained relationship with my father. I did not talk about Mark, so my grandfather assumed the major trouble between my father and me was my reaction to the divorce.

"Look, kid," he said. "He divorced my daughter and I don't plan to renew my relationship with him. But *you've got* to renew your relationship with him. He's your father!"

"I don't know how to go about it," I said.

"He hasn't handled his problems very well," Grampa said, "and he's dealt with them at the expense of my daughter, and you. I feel resentment, sure. It's a disappointment, a lifetime shock. The relationship between your mother and father can't be healed, but *your* relationship with him *can* be salvaged. I pray for him every night, not because I'm a great Christian, but because I hope he finds whatever it is he's looking for.

"I wish your father well," Grampa continued. "And you should do more than wish him well. Don't try to correct him. Live your own life. And in living it, try not to hurt the lives of others. I think your father's a bastard, but that's all right. I don't support his decision, but I won't limit him one bit. You've got a tough road ahead of you, kid. Internally. We're talking about feelings, and there's no microwave for that stuff. It has to develop slowly."

"It'll take time."

"More than time, it will take effort. On your part as well as his. But c'mon, kid," he said. "I'll tell you what marriage is really all about. I thanked God every night I lay in bed next to Sue. And I said, 'May it always be like this!' Not only when things were good, but every night, even during the bad times. That's what marriage is all about."

He paused, and I reflected sadly on the fact that he had lost his wife, Sue, to cancer when I was still a small child. As we talked about marriage in general, I brought up the topic of interracial marriage, which is what I desperately wanted his advice on. A retired minister who had been President Richard Nixon's pastor in Washington, D.C., my grandfather had married mixed couples in the nation's capital when it was still illegal in many states. He seemed to comprehend immediately that I was talking about marrying Mark. My mother had told him a great deal about Mark.

"You've got to find out what the reasons are for each of you to be together," Grampa said. "I think you should back into it, march toward it, and go sideways all at the same time. It's complicated.

You've got to make sure you're not marrying for a cause or to prove something to someone else."

"I guess I should just follow my feelings and not worry about other people," I said.

"No, that's not the solution either. You're not only marrying one person, you're marrying a set. Unless you expect to live in isolation. Sue and I got married quietly, but we also knew we wouldn't mind having a big public wedding later. My friends were her friends. But you can't very well marry interracially and keep it a secret," he said, laughing.

I had not mentioned anything about a secret marriage, and it made me wonder whether he was predicting one. And here I was with Mark, filling out marriage license applications, most likely in the same room Grampa and Sue did about sixty years earlier.

Besides calling my grandfather, I had also gone to the New York Public Library to do research on mixed couples. The main questions in my mind were: Do interracial marriages last? Are they common? How do mixed couples feel about their marriages?

I did not find much, and most of what I found was negative. So-called experts on interracial relationships had a plethora of absurd theories and explanations about white woman–black man marriages. The woman was too fat and ugly to get a white man, was acting out against a racist parent, had already been ostracized by white society, or had such low self-esteem that she felt like trash that belonged in a black ghetto.

The black man was denying his skin color and attempting to be white. He was trying to avenge himself against white oppression by defiling a white woman. The children of such mixed up marriages suffered the cruel fate of being caught, trapped between two worlds, rejected by both races, traumatized by a perpetual identity crisis. Anger and disgust made me slam shut each book I read. Where was the human story? Why were mixed couples constantly analyzed? When will they finally talk openly about who they really are and what they truly feel?

Mark and I waited on hard wooden chairs amid smooching couples for our names to be called. It was a jovial atmosphere, full of love, hope, and shy joy, though the office was rundown and cluttered and most of the exhausted-looking employees were probably underpaid and overworked.

At the window we had to raise our right hands and pledge that all the information provided was true. Then they sent us away with our typed license, littered with typos, and told us to come back on Monday for the actual wedding ceremony.

Mark teased me as we wandered through Chinatown, calling me "wifey" and "Mrs. Mathabane." It was all rather surreal and humorous, but it was also a nice, warm, stabilizing feeling. *I just turned twenty-five, and I'm about to be married,* I thought to myself. *How strange.* In college my friends had predicted I'd be the last one of us to let myself get snared. This made me the first, besides Carol, and she did not consider herself married in the true sense of the word.

That night, as Mark and I sat in my room in Brooklyn eating Ben & Jerry's ice cream and discussing Boris Pasternak's poetry, we could hear Carol and Robert arguing down the hall.

"He's jealous of her male friends," I whispered in explanation.

"That's not it," Mark said. "He's trying to drive her away."

We were silent for a while, listening to the angry shouts. I felt sorry for Carol. She always did everything she could for Robert, who was ungrateful and inconsiderate in return. He never lifted a finger to help her in the kitchen, he accused her of staring at other guys on the street, he showed up hours late without calling, he wheedled her into borrowing thousands of dollars from her mother to finance his suspicious business ventures. Carol had been giving selflessly up to that point, but she was reaching her limit.

One night Robert called Carol and accidentally asked for Maureen, one of his many lovers. Carol flew into a rage, then, feeling helpless, hung up and wept bitterly. All Robert's girlfriends, except Carol, were black. It had finally dawned on Carol that Robert, a militant black, was having serious problems dealing with his relationship with a white woman. Whenever Carol referred to herself as white, he would angrily insist she was Lebanese, and Third World like himself. But he had a hard time deluding himself, so he spent less and less time with her.

Monday arrived. Carol, who had agreed to be our witness, was unable to meet us at City Hall, so I turned to the only other person who knew our secret: my coworker Sandy, from my part-time job. I hadn't seen Sandy in several weeks. Mark and I waited in a room on the second floor of City Hall, holding hands and nervously waiting for her. She was already half an hour late. I felt vulnerable and embarrassed proclaiming my love for Mark in such a formal and public way. Blushes constantly swept my face. Most of the people around us were speaking Spanish or some other foreign language; some had photographers, bouquets, and families; one even had a veil. For five dollars, it wasn't a bad place to get married.

Our name was about to be called and Sandy was still nowhere to be seen. I panicked. We needed a witness, quick. I approached a group of young men and women sitting on a row of chairs.

"Excuse me," I said politely. "But our witness didn't show up. Would one of you mind being our witness?"

"I will," a young woman replied.

"Do you need a husband too?" asked the young man seated next to her.

At that moment Sandy burst into the room, wearing a tight black sweater, tight red pants, and purple lipstick. She seemed rushed and panicky. I feared she was high on something, especially as she now dressed and acted as if she had slid back to her old life as a street-walker and addict. Our names were called. Sandy followed us into a dim chapel where we stood before the City Clerk. I showed Sandy how to focus my manual camera.

"Hurry up!" the clerk snapped. "Do you know how many other people are out there waiting to get married?"

I ran and took my place beside Mark. There was no introduction, no organ, no choir, no sermon. He got right to the point. After asking the empty room if anyone had any objections to this marriage, he said, "Do you, Mark Mathabane, take this woman . . ."

I watched Mark as he said, "I do," then turned to listen to the clerk say, "Do you, Gail Ernsberger, take this man . . ."

Sandy ran around taking photos from all angles. The ring she had loaned Mark to give me got stuck on my knuckle, and as I wrenched it on the rest of the way, I heard the words, "You are now officially man and wife. You may kiss the bride."

"Oh, wait, wait! Hold that kiss!" Sandy cried, snapping away.

After the clerk had wished us well and complimented Sandy on her camera work, the three of us stumbled out into the hall. A black woman smiled and said, "Congratulations!"

I was in a daze as we descended the spiral steps. Sandy wished us well, kissed us both, and disappeared as suddenly as she had arrived.

"Are you sure you don't need a husband?" the young man yelled to me as we left City Hall.

That afternoon, as we lay reading side by side in my Flatbush Avenue apartment, Mark said softly, "It's begun to rain. Do you hear the tires whirring on the pavement?"

I nodded. We were enjoying our first lazy afternoon as husband and wife. He reached over and stroked my back lightly, unconsciously, still concentrating on his book by John Dewey.

I felt different, somehow, unexpectedly. I told Mark so as we sat across the table from each other, having our wedding feast by candlelight. The whole time I sat there, spinning the borrowed gold band around my finger, I felt very much in love, rooted, calm. The bubbles in the champagne were too much for us, so we added orange juice. Unaccustomed to too much alcohol, the champagne knocked us both out. We fell asleep on our wedding night fully clothed in a happy embrace, on top of the covers.

In the morning Mark's first words were, "I forgot to brush my teeth!"

Nothing ever turns out the way you expect it to. As a girl I had imagined a tall white groom, people throwing rice, a black limousine with streamers, and a three-week honeymoon on a tropical island. I cannot say I missed any of that, because this wedding was more real, private, honest, and based on love, not show.

The shop windows on Forty-second Street are filled with diamond rings and wedding bands. We stared at them one by one, shook our heads at the exorbitant prices, as we moved slowly down the street with our arms around each other. Finally we entered a jewelry store and asked for service. I felt vulnerable, as if we were shopping for condoms, not wedding rings. Marriage, in my mind, was like publicizing your sexuality, which the church and my upbringing had taught me was dirty, vile, low-down, and unacceptable. Mark bought me a diamond ring—the diamond was so tiny one needed a microscope to see it. I bought him a gold band. Both were under one hundred dollars.

"Do you think I should send out wedding announcements?" I asked Mark as we left the jewelry store.

"Not yet. Let's savor the privacy of our marriage a little longer. We don't want to shock people. We have to think of a way to tell them gracefully. We might even have a public wedding. Maybe, if we ever get some money, I can bring my family over for the wedding."

This suggestion sounded so absurdly far-fetched that I simply smiled. How in the world would we ever get that kind of money? And why would the white South African regime issue passports to an impoverished black family it does not even regard as citizens in the land of their birth?

Because I was in no hurry to upset my family and friends, I let the marriage remain a secret. Being legally married prepared me mentally for confronting life as a mixed couple and standing up to the opposition of family members, which I knew was inevitable. I was the youngest of all my cousins, the youngest child in my family, and the only girl. Everyone was used to guiding and protecting me. It would take a lot of strength to stand up to all those people who cared about me, had watched me grow, and felt they knew me more than I knew myself.

Carol congratulated me on the marriage but couldn't understand why I wanted to keep the news a secret when Mark and I had such a solid relationship. She had kept her marriage a secret from her parents and friends only because she didn't know where her troubled relationship with Robert would lead.

"Why don't you just tell people you're married," she said.

"The idea of saying I'm married makes me uncomfortable," I said. "I'm afraid of what people would think."

"But you married because you love the man!"

"Yes, of course."

"What then are you afraid of?" Carol asked.

I was afraid of my father. I could not even imagine telling him that I was married, let alone to a black man. He had never even met Mark. Yet he was flying to New York to visit me and my brothers in one week. I realized it was an issue of honesty. How would I feel if I found myself in the position of having to lie? Wouldn't it be easier to be honest, proud of the marriage, proud of my husband? The only thing I needed was courage.

My mother called, asked how Mark and I were doing, and, as if the words came of their own accord, I said, "We're engaged!"

Mark turned toward me, his eyes and mouth opened wide in amazement.

"Oh, congratulations!" she said excitedly. "Let me speak to Mark!"

I handed the phone to Mark, who cleared his throat nervously, pressed the receiver to his ear, and greeted my mother. She went on and on about how happy she was for us.

Before long various family members knew of the engagement and called to congratulate us. I was taken aback by their positive response. Maybe I had been mistaken in my judgment of my family. But there was still my father. I still hadn't heard his reaction to the news of our "engagement."

Carol's father, a wealthy Lebanese Christian, flew to New York from Beirut to visit her. Carol's older sisters were all married, and Carol had always been her father's favorite daughter. Carol, her father, and Robert went out to dinner, then father and daughter returned alone to our Flatbush Avenue apartment. The door to Carol's room was open, and I could hear her father gently explain to her that she must lead her own life, separate from Robert's, and become self-reliant.

"How can you sit here and tell me this?" she cried. "I trust one person in this world, and that's Robert. Now you're telling me not to trust him! But I do, and I will! It's true I had no interest in business before I met him, but it's something I'm willing to try, and it's as much my thing now as it is his. But now because you've said these things to me I'm going to look at him twice, I'll begin to doubt him."

"I didn't say you had to doubt him," her father said gently.

"Yes you did! And you know how much influence you have over me. I rely on you more than Cindy or Allison or Linda does. They're all married and have husbands to turn to. But I turn to *you* for support."

"And I give that support gladly," he said softly.

"I know! I'm not questioning that. But you have a lot of influence over me, and it's not fair for you to use it this way. If you told Cindy to divorce her husband, she would do it in a second!"

"I never told Cindy to divorce her husband."

"No, you didn't. But I'm just telling you that what you say influences me—influences all of us . . ." She wept when despair cracked her voice. "I've invested a lot in my relationship with Robert, and now you're telling me to throw it all away and not trust him simply because of his wife. I don't *care* about his wife!"

I pulled on my coat and boots, grabbed my shoulder bag, and

let myself out of the apartment quietly, wondering if what I had overheard was a dress-rehearsal for my own confrontation with my father over Mark. My father was arriving in New York in a week. He still didn't know that Mark and I had announced our "engagement."

7

MEETING THE FAMILY

MARK'S VIEW

I rode the subway to Central Park, where I would meet Gail, her brothers, and her father. Her father. I tensed at the thought. How would this complex man receive me? What were his true feelings about my love for his daughter?

Was his tearful response to Gail's letter genuine, or was there latent racism in him, carefully masked by his intelligence and urbanity?

But Gail had had lunch with him the day before and told him of our engagement and showed him the ring. He had responded not angrily and suspiciously, but with congratulations and he seemed ready, enthusiastic, to meet and to accept me as a future son-in-law.

I could understand how, looking at our relationship from the outside, from a psychologist's point of view, Gail's father could have doubted its staying power, especially against deeply rooted prejudices. He knew the depth of racism in white society. He knew that the attitudes of many Americans had changed very little from those that thirty years ago condoned segregation and the dehumanization of blacks. Yes, the laws and institutions had changed, but few hearts had changed with them.

At times it seemed to me the attitudes of many whites in America were little different from the attitudes of most whites in South Africa. White Americans were simply more adept at hiding their true feelings. Crude, apartheid-style racism was not their preferred weapon of keeping the black man down. It was in the subtle kind of racism, often hidden by a veneer of liberalism and tolerance, at which they excelled.

This type of racism was more insidious because not only did it continue to deny blacks equal opportunity in housing, in the workplace, in schools, and before the law but it had blacks constantly wondering how many of their problems were due to racism and how many to their own failings.

If black and white Americans had not yet learned how to get along, how to respect cultural differences, how to talk to each other rather than always about each other, what chance did mixed couples and their children have of being accepted, let alone understood?

It was easy to see how both sides in the racial conflict could turn their venomous arrows of hate and anger and fear at us. After all, we were a reminder of the ideal of racial harmony they had abandoned; we were a reminder of how much work still had to be done, on both sides, before racial concord could truly exist. But also, and most important, we were a reminder that it could be done. That Americans, despite their racial and cultural differences, can find common ground, can treat each other with respect if not with love. Though Gail and I were husband and wife, at the bottom of our relationship there lay a genuine friendship founded on mutual trust and respect for each other as individuals. And reciprocated trust and respect are prerequisites for racial harmony.

During the two years Gail and I had been together, we had, like most couples, experienced ups and downs, games of tug of war—I would pull away, then she would pull away. But the odyssey and ordeals had taught us much, had made us grow. Now that we were married, and accepted the responsibilities that accompanied our union, we had begun moving about naturally, sure of our feelings for each other. We moved forward together, rather than pulling in opposite directions. I hoped her family would notice these important changes and give us their unqualified blessing.

Two weeks earlier Gail had received from her father a copy of a sermon on desegregation he had delivered at a church in Saginaw,

Michigan, in 1961. The gist of the sermon was that white Christians should let blacks move into their all-white neighborhoods. Whites should not worry about their children marrying blacks, he argued, because it seldom happens that a girl marries "the boy next door." Gail and her brother Dan puzzled over their father's motive in sending it. Gail's father had a history of being criticized for being too liberal and pro-black in his sermons.

It was a warm, blue, and beautiful weekend in early March 1986. The Ernsbergers had arranged to meet at the Museum of Natural History, but in typical Ernsberger fashion, this entailed one-and-a-half-hour waits at three separate entrances.

At last Gail found me wandering about the cavernous entrance hall. She took me by the hand and led me down the broad stone steps to meet her father. The moment he saw me he threw his arms wide open and embraced me. I was flabbergasted. I glanced at Gail; tears of joy filled her eyes.

Years later Gail asked her father about his changed attitude toward me. Dr. Ernsberger replied that there had been "no change whatsoever. At least, no conscious change."

"My earlier reservations had nothing to do with accepting Mark as a future son-in-law," he said. "It's just that like any father, I wanted my little girl to have the most hassle-free, stress-free existence. I wanted her to have the best possible start out of the blocks."

"Why did you think I'd have all sorts of problems if I married Mark?"

"I specialize in marital therapy, babe, I should know," he replied. "I've counseled mixed couples before. Being an interracial couple adds external stress to a marriage, and marriage, by nature, has a lot of stress already built into it. Coming out of a failed marriage myself, I'm very aware of the stresses and strains involved in any marital relationship. Then there are additional strains between the couple and the environing society. The stress placed on mixed couples in a racist society is considerable, at times intolerable. And when a couple becomes socially isolated, that really creates stress."

"Then why did you embrace Mark?"

"It was a spontaneous act of admiration. I had some worries and concerns at first, but that doesn't mean your father is a bigot. Why shouldn't I have embraced my future son-in-law?"

Gail's father, brothers, and I left the brilliant sunshine and entered the museum. We began at the African cultures wing. I explained the significance and symbolism of various ceremonial masks and artifacts. Throughout the museum visit Dr. Ernsberger kept watching Gail and me, as if studying how we interacted. His occasional remarks suggested that he was well satisfied with what he saw. At one point I furtively and quickly removed my gold wedding band: Gail and I were, after all, not yet "married."

The highlight of the weekend was Sunday brunch overlooking the water at South Street Seaport. Gail, her father, her two brothers, Paul's wife, Debbie, Dan's girlfriend, Lisa, and I splurged on a gourmet, all-you-can-eat, free-champagne brunch in a breezy room flooded with light. A black woman played romantic tunes on a grand piano and sang in the background. We were all relaxed and smiling as we made champagne toasts.

"To Gail and Mark," her father said, raising his tall narrow glass.

"Hear, hear," the others said amid clinking glasses and again congratulated us on our engagement.

Following brunch the seven of us strolled lazily through the crowds of southern Manhattan and rode the Staten Island Ferry across the bay. A thousand memories flooded my mind as I thought of those months I lived on Staten Island, those months of struggle and emotional turmoil. Then I looked up and saw the woman I had shared it all with, the woman who was now my wife, and I smiled.

Now that I felt welcomed by Gail's parents and her brothers, I fervently wished she could someday meet my own dear family. It would complete the circle of our marriage.

GAIL'S VIEW

In late June 1987 the phone rang in my Brooklyn apartment. Stumbling out of bed, I groped for the receiver and managed a hoarse "Hello?"

"Sweets? I have a surprise for you. Can you be at JFK Saturday morning around ten?"

"Yes, but what for?"

"My family is arriving from South Africa."

"What!"

"Yes, darling, they're on their way," Mark said. "It's all arranged. Oprah Winfrey is paying for their airline tickets and putting them up at the Sheraton in Midtown for a few days."

"How did Oprah get involved in all this?" I asked.

"It all happened so fast," Mark said. "She was walking down some street one evening with her boyfriend and saw *Kaffir Boy* displayed in the window. She bought it, read it, and was deeply moved. She then began a nationwide hunt for me. At last she found me here in High Point. We talked for over an hour. She asked about the family and I told her that I hadn't seen them in nine years and wanted dearly for them to visit America. Oprah was eager to help and she arranged and paid for everything. What a wonderful soul she is."

I could hardly believe my ears. It was not only the coincidence of everything and the mention of Oprah's name that surprised me. What astounded me most was that Mark's mythical family would soon become reality. I could not imagine Mark surrounded by his mother, grandmother, and siblings. To me he had been a solitary intellectual, a loner in an American world of bewildering extremes and contradictions that had severely tested the down-to-earth values his family had instilled in him. Sometimes it seemed his closest friends were dead writers: Gibbons, Wright, Dickens, Shakespeare, Hughes, Shelley, Du Bois, Keats, Tennyson.

To me his family members were characters in *Kaffir Boy*. There was a long-suffering and courageous mother; a dignified, queenly matriarch named Granny, resplendent in colorful African garb and bracelets; a younger sister named Florah who had lived through the same hunger and terrors Mark had; and a brother George whom Mark nearly smothered to death in an attempt to keep him quiet during a police invasion of their ghetto neighborhood.

The youngest two, Linah and Diana, had been so small when their eldest brother left South Africa at age eighteen that even Mark had only a vague idea of what his own sisters would be like.

"You must be excited to see them," I said. "It's been nine years. I can't believe I'll finally get to meet your mother."

"I'll probably want to spend some time alone with them at first," he said. "You understand, don't you?"

"Of course," I said. But, deep down, I had already begun to fear that I might lose Mark to a group of loving strangers I had not yet met. Up to that point, I felt that I alone, besides Stan and Margie Smith, had been his family in America. Now his real family was coming—full of love and eagerness to see him and hold him again. Perhaps, I thought anxiously, he will never again need me as powerfully as he did when it was just the two of us against the world.

I went to the airport on the JFK Express train. It was Saturday. I wore a casual blouse and matching skirt and fastened my hair, now grown long, with a barrette.

Once in the airport, it was not difficult to spot Mark, Oprah, and her boyfriend Stedman Graham. The ABC network crew surrounded them, shining bright spotlights on the double doors leading out of customs, pointing a large microphone at Mark, then at Oprah, then at Mark again. Oprah's presence created quite a commotion, and travelers pushed through the crowd to snap photos of her.

Ellie Spiegel, the director of programs at International House, arrived with her husband, Hans, to witness the grand event.

"Have you met Oprah yet?" Ellie asked me.

"Oh, no, of course not," I said. I had been hiding in the back of the crowd behind a pillar. Even Mark was not aware of my arrival. I wanted to stay out of the way as much as possible. This was Mark's big event, not mine. And I certainly did not want to draw any attention to myself, especially because I am white and Mark is black.

Before I could express any of these trepidations to Ellie, she had dashed through the crowd and was tugging at Oprah's arm.

"Hi, Oprah," Ellie said with her usual zest. "Have you met Mark's fiancée?"

"Fiancée!" Oprah exclaimed. "No, is she here?"

I looked for a way to escape, but Ellie took my hand and pulled me through the crowd toward Oprah. I saw Oprah's large brown eyes grow even larger when she spotted me. Stedman glanced at me and seemed to stiffen. I almost died of embarrassment.

Before Oprah and I could exchange more than a hello, a cry of excitement arose from the crowd and Mark's family emerged from customs wearing acrylic knit caps. I quickly withdrew to my original place behind the pillar to watch, unobserved. I could not believe how small and malnourished they all looked as they walked up the ramp on thin legs. George's hair was yellowed at the ends, probably from a lack of protein.

Granny, Mark's mother, Florah, George, Linah, and Diana all descended on Mark in a pack, wrapping all twelve arms around him. Watching him hug his mother touched me deeply and I could not keep myself from smiling and laughing and crying along with them.

Oprah snapped photos of the reunion as ABC reporters jockeyed for position, interviewing those who could speak English—George and Florah. As I stood watching the melee, Florah surged toward me, having recognized me from a photograph Mark had sent them. She cried, "Are you Gail?"

I nodded slightly, and was hugged with more vigor than I had ever been in my life. She turned and called to Mark's mother in Tsonga, who gave a cry of delight, rushed toward me, and planted a kiss solidly on my lips. Florah and Mark's mother, whom I quickly learned to call *Mhani* (Tsonga for "Mother"), took both my hands and escorted me out of the airport along with the rest of the throng.

Oprah threw her arm around Granny, who was walking slightly ahead of us, and said, "Hey, Granny! I'm Oprah." Granny nodded, bewildered by the loving gesture from a total stranger who was speaking to her in an unintelligible language.

Mark's mother was determined to get me into the limousine with them, but it was already crowded with Mathabanes and I knew Mark wanted to be alone with his family. I said good-bye to everyone and turned to head back to Brooklyn.

"How are you getting into the city?" Oprah asked.

"The same way I arrived," I said, embarrassed to say, "By subway."

"You can ride with us," she said.

"No, that's all right. Mark wants to be alone with his family."

"Well, you're part of the family now," she insisted. "Come on, hop in."

As I stepped into the long black limo I wondered, *Am I really part of this huge family? Can I, a white woman, ever truly become integrated into a tight-knit African clan whose language and customs I don't yet fully understand?* I did not yet realize how much mutual admiration, trust, and affection can be communicated without words.

I sat beside Debbie DiMaio, the producer of the "Oprah Winfrey Show," and across from Oprah and Stedman, who did not remove his sunglasses, though the limo had tinted windows. Oprah asked me questions about myself and about Mark's family as we rode. Stedman did not say a word the whole trip, even when Oprah teased him to take off his sunglasses. He refused. I never saw his eyes. I found it strange that he was so uncommunicative, that he kept his face rigid the entire ride into Manhattan, no matter how many times Oprah tried to make him laugh by cracking jokes. She even kicked off her shoes and threw her legs playfully across his lap, but still he did not smile. I had the awful feeling that his solemn mood had something to do with the fact that I, Mark's fiancée, was white. Two years later I learned the reason for his silence, but to reveal that now would be to get ahead of the story.

As the limousine raced down the highway toward Manhattan, Oprah lowered the window and snapped photos of the limousine in the next lane. Through a half-opened window I caught a glimpse of Mark in the backseat, surrounded by his siblings, his head thrown back in laughter and a smile on his face broader than I had ever seen it. I felt a pang in my chest. *Why had I never before seen him so happy?*

Mark seemed an entirely different person. He was no longer the guilt-ridden and brooding loner I had known. A dramatic change had taken place within him, and I felt more than ever that I was losing him to these laughing, loving Africans, who made him happier than I ever could.

When the limousine arrived in front of the Sheraton, Mark was busy ushering his family into the hotel through the revolving doors. Granny almost got trapped in one: she had never used such doors before. Knowing that Mark wanted to be alone with them, I slipped away unnoticed, descended into the subway, and waited for the Number 2 Express to take me home to Brooklyn.

That night I watched the reunion on the local news, then crawled into bed, feeling terribly alone. I tried to convince myself that Mark loved his family differently from the way he loved me, that I was still as important to him as they were, but I gave up in despair and fell asleep fearing our relationship would never be the same, fearing he would never again need my love as he once did.

"I'm not surprised you feel that way," Carol said when I shared my feelings with her. "You're going to have to live with certain things for the rest of your life—certain aspects of African culture that are entirely different from American culture. One of those things is big families that are very close and take care of each other."

I listened attentively to her, for she had done graduate work at Brown in anthropology and had studied Middle Eastern and African cultures closely. Having grown up in Lebanon, she had lived and breathed Arab culture, which in many ways is similar to African culture. Her Lebanese father had always been more devoted to his country and his mother than he was to his American wife. Carol's mother realized this when he refused to leave Lebanon, even when the lives of his wife and children were endangered by constant bombing and gunfire in Beirut. Carol's mother packed up her six children in 1979 and moved back to the United States. Carol's father stayed in Lebanon.

"How can you expect me to leave my mother and family?" he asked.

"If, after twenty-two years of marriage, your children and I are not your family, then I guess our definitions of 'family' will never be the same," Carol's mother replied angrily.

"Mark's mother will always be more important to him than you," Carol told me. "He owes her his life. Sons treat their mothers with a type of respect that borders on awe and reverence. You can't compete with that. You'll just have to accept it. Now that his family is here, everything will be different. It may never again be just the two of you. I bet you anything some of his family members will stay in America. What do they have to go back to?"

I listened to her words with a heavy heart and wondered if Mark and I would ever again be as close as we were when it was just the two of us.

Two days later Mark came to Brooklyn, alone, late at night, to stay with me. He seemed farther away than ever. He would try to kiss me, then burst out laughing and relate yet another tale about his family's adventures in department stores, elevators, escalators. He fell asleep, chuckling to himself, filled with warm thoughts of his family—a family he hadn't seen since he left South Africa nearly a decade ago—while I sat up in bed, watching him drift away.

In the morning I tried to discuss with him my feelings of being pushed aside, but when I said I feared his family had supplanted me, he became very defensive.

"How can you feel that way toward people who love you?" he said.

"Love me? But they don't even know me! We can't even speak to each other."

"It doesn't matter. They love you! Unconditionally."

This statement startled me. Could it be true? Or was Mark simply attempting to mollify me?

We descended the narrow staircase to Flatbush Avenue, squeezed ourselves into a crowded subway car, and were soon entering the Sheraton in Midtown. While Mark went off to talk to George, I was left in a hotel room with Granny, Mhani, Florah, Diana, and Linah. They were speaking in rapid Tsonga, getting dressed, rearranging their suitcases. I sat in a chair in the corner, feeling out of place. Mark's mother patted the bed beside her and beckoned for me to "Come, sit."

I sat down beside her. Florah made a list of common words for me in Tsonga so I might learn to understand at least a little of their conversation. Linah and Diana sat on the bed watching me with their large, dark eyes, eager to know me.

Mark and I took his family for a walk in Central Park. As we left the hotel, a black woman ran up to us and cried, "Are you the African family I saw on TV last night? You are! Oh, I'm so happy you're together again!" She hugged Mark, George, Florah, Linah, and Diana. She hesitated when she got to me, then said, "Oh, I don't care if you're white!" and she threw her arms around me as well. I felt it was one of the nicest things any black woman had ever said to me.

During our walk Linah and Diana laughed at the different shapes and sizes of women's legs. In South Africa it is a tribal custom for women to dress modestly, so they had never seen grown women in shorts. Diana was accustomed to walking barefoot, so she had difficulty keeping her shoes on. We had to keep checking her feet, and once had to send her back up to the hotel room when we discovered she was barefoot in a fancy restaurant.

Linah and Diana stared in horror at the salad placed on the table before them. "How come it's not cooked?" they wanted to know. Back home, with their scanty diet, they had never had the luxury of eating salads. The only vegetables they ate and could afford were boiled greens called *murogo*. During hard times, poignantly described in *Kaffir Boy*, the family even drank boiled cattle blood as soup, and ate prickly worms called *sonjas* along with the staple, *pap* (cooked porridge).

The next day Mark and his family flew to North Carolina, and I remained in New York to continue my job as an editor at the German Information Center. His mother and sisters simply could not understand why, in a free country like America, two people who love each other have to be separated. They thought it was only in South Africa, where black workers must leave their homes to seek jobs as migrant workers in distant gold and diamond mines, that couples and families are torn asunder.

Mark called me when he was at his wits' end. "Everyone keeps asking me, 'Where's *skwiza*? Where's *skwiza*?' " he said. (*Skwiza* is an affectionate term for "sister-in-law.") "I'm getting jealous. They didn't come to America to see me. They came to see you! All they can talk about is you and the wedding. Please come down this weekend. They're all eager to see you, and . . . so am I."

That weekend I experienced more love than I had ever known in my life; not only from Mark, but also from his family. Just as my own family was falling apart, sparked by my parents' divorce and the fact that we children were now grown and going our separate ways, I found this new family—a tight-knit and loving group of people with deeply genuine emotions, no facade, and nothing to hide; with immense patience, compassion, and infinite understanding. They accepted me without the slightest reservation, without giving a moment's thought to my race, color, or social class. To them I was simply human. I now understood the powerful forces that had shaped Mark's character, especially his open-mindedness and lack of bitterness and hate.

Florah, Linah, Diana, and I spent hours in the apartment complex's swimming pool, laughing, and splashing, playing keep away with a pink plastic ball while Granny and Mhani watched from the deck. I had noticed over the months I had been visiting Mark that most of the white sunbathers, who lounged about the pool taking only occasional dips to cool down, would abruptly leave whenever one or more blacks entered the pool. It seemed some sort of unspoken rule.

"You see what I mean by white attitudes not having changed much," Mark said to me one time. "And yet these same people who can't stand swimming alongside blacks will self-righteously condemn apartheid. It is interesting that when they point two fingers of a hand at white South Africans for being racist, three fingers are pointing straight at them."

As I entered the pool with Mark's sisters, I always felt the eyes of white strangers on me, filled with what I imagined was curious disdain or disgust, as they grabbed their towels and left.

But I tried not to let such things bother me. I was part of a new family now. Linah and Diana both hugged me and hung all over me. The whole family began calling me "Sweets" in imitation of Mark.

One night we ate a Southern dinner of biscuits and beans and fried chicken at the home of a black woman named Edmonious, who had befriended Mark's mother and Granny. As we sat in the living room after the meal, discussing racial tensions in the North versus the South, I was aware that I was the only white in a room filled with blacks. But I felt, to my amazement, completely at home. Diana was fast asleep with her head in my lap and Florah was leaning against me.

Every morning Granny would greet me with a long, drawn-out "*Kunjani?*" ("How are you, my dear?") And I would reply with an equally slow, "*Nikone Kokwana.*" ("Fine, my beloved Grandma.") Hearing me speak Tsonga would send Granny into paroxysms of laughter; she would clap her hands together, making her bracelets clink and clang, then heave a deep sigh of contentment after her laughing had subsided.

Mark's mother, when she was not playing cards with Granny or reminiscing about her life, would sit on the living room floor studying an ABC book. "A—apple," she would say proudly. She listened attentively to English conversations, and by the end of her three-month visit she could speak English tolerably well. Her dearest wish as a child had been to attend school, but as a girl, she was dissuaded from such a pursuit. Women at that time were regarded largely as the possessions of their future husbands and, therefore, not worth educating. When I realized that she used the word *she* to refer to anything from *he, she, it,* and *you* to *they* and *these,* I was able to get her meaning.

"She's toooooo big," Mhani told me, pointing to a box I just brought into the room. It took me a few minutes to understand that she meant, "That's a very big box."

"She's washing," she said to me, handing me some dirty clothes when I was loading the washer. She meant, "These need to be washed." Her pidgin English, however, masked an astounding intelligence. I was awed by how much she knew of life, especially about human nature and emotions. Mark credited her mesmerizing storytelling with inspiring him as a writer. "The way she weaves a story and infuses it with all the elements of tragedy, comedy, history, philosophy, and morals rivals anything I have read by Shakespeare, Homer, and Plato," he once said.

The family laughed and teased me about the approaching wedding. Linah and Diana serenaded me with a song in Tsonga about how sisters-in-law cook and clean and wash for the husband's entire family. After much insistence on my part, Florah translated the song for me.

"Is that song designed to praise sisters-in-law or degrade them?" I asked.

George burst out laughing.

"It's a terrible song," Florah said. "No woman wants to do all that work."

Granny came out of the bedroom carrying a traditional tribal wedding dress and tied it around my waist. It looked like a big bush of colorful yarn and sat on my hips like an innertube. Then Granny wrapped a huge piece of colorful cloth around me so I looked like an enormous bell.

George was dying of laughter. "She says you must wear that on your wedding day!"

I danced around a bit, making the big bushy dress jiggle. Granny clapped her hands in delight and exclaimed in Tsonga that I reminded her of herself as a young woman on her wedding day.

When we were together in Mark's apartment, I felt like one of the family. But when we went out in public, especially in the South, I often felt uncomfortable. One Sunday morning we went to services at an all-black AME Zion Church in High Point. When the minister called Mark into the pulpit and asked the Mathabane family to please stand, everyone rose except me. I sat in the rigid pew petrified, never having been the sole white in such a large crowd of blacks before. I thought they would soon sing "We Shall Overcome" while glaring at me.

"Come on, Sweets, get up!" Florah whispered, hauling me by the arm into a standing position. We stood there in a row, being introduced one by one.

"That's my mother, Magdeline," Mark said. "Next to her is my sister Florah, and next to her is my fiancée, Gail."

I felt dozens of black faces register looks of shock. I felt my face flush crimson. I could not wait to sit down. The service dragged on for two hours and I almost passed out from hunger, heat, and boredom. The music was a motley mixture of Mozart and gospel, and the minister delivered a sermon on marriage.

"You shouldn't marry for looks," the minister bellowed from the pulpit, beads of sweat glistening on his forehead. "Looks can't cook a meal."

"Amen," the black women around me murmured.

"Looks can't clean the house!"

"Praise God," they muttered, fanning themselves with their bulletins.

"Looks can't do the dishes!"

It depressed me that the only prerequisites for marrying, as cited by the minister, were good looks and domestic abilities. "What about love?" I whispered to Mark. "He said nothing about love."

"That's reality," Mark replied. "Many people don't have the luxury of falling in love. They have to think of necessities, of survival."

At long last the service was over and we were invited downstairs to a reception in honor of the Mathabane family, where we were fed fried chicken, black-eyed peas, cornbread, squash casserole, collard greens, and peach cobbler—traditional Southern soul food.

The wife of a prominent black businessman walked up to me and said, "I hear you're from New York. Have you ever been to the South?"

I made a polite reply, but in her question I heard another: "Don't you know it's rather unusual down here for a white girl to marry one of our boys?"

As my last day of work and the day of the official wedding approached, I tried to erase from my mind all thoughts of black and white opposition to interracial relationships. I wanted it to be a beautiful wedding, a celebration of the love that different cultures and races can have for each other. I did not want to reflect on why the KKK lynched black men accused of raping white women or on black militants' opposition to one of "their men being snared by a white Circe" or on mixed couples being victimized by the growing racial polarization of Northern cities.

Like most brides-to-be, I spent a great deal of my time trying to coordinate all the arrangements for the flowers, wedding invitations, music, catering, church bulletins, ceremony details, bridal registry, reception hall decorations, plates, and utensils. I had my mother's wedding dress altered to fit me better and searched for a veil.

Sometimes it struck me as absurd that women have to preoccupy themselves with so many ridiculous details just to get married. What made it all seem aggravatingly superfluous was the fact that we were already married. I much preferred the quiet, intimate way we first married to this big to-do. But I also knew that in the eyes of society, we would not be considered truly married unless there was a wedding, and I must admit, a part of me did not want to miss out on any of life's official rites of passage.

There was only one thing more difficult than planning the wedding, and that was handling calls from "concerned" relatives, people I had grown up among, respected, admired, and loved. One relative got right to the point.

"Gail, just remember, it's never too late to call off the wedding," she said in a confidential tone. "If you have any doubts, any at all, you can call the whole thing off. Even if it's two minutes before the wedding is to begin, you can just say, 'I'm not coming.' Don't think you have to go through with it just because it's all arranged."

When I assured her I was not going to call it off, she seemed a bit disappointed.

One of my cousins called, twice in one week, to vent his strong opposition to my impending marriage to a black South African. These calls hurt me deeply, because I had been very close to my cousin. When I was eight I had even convinced myself I was in love with him. Throughout college we confided in each other about our love lives and hopes for the future, went sailboarding together on the Atlantic Ocean, and visited each other in Boston and Providence.

But now my cousin spoke in such a loud and aggressive tone I had to hold the phone away from my ear.

"Mark went through some horrific experiences at the hands of white people," he said. "He must have a deep, latent rage against everyone white. His book is very angry. I just hope his anger doesn't erupt against you."

"He's never laid a hand on me," I said. "And if he did, I'd leave instantly." I was shocked at the very suggestion that Mark would ever use violence against me. I felt my cousin's "concerns" were unfounded and rather racist. My cousin, an Ivy League graduate who lived in Boston, was admirably tall, handsome, and blond with a classic WASPness about him. *He's probably afraid of blacks and doesn't know any*, I told myself. *You should try to allay his fears.*

"What happens after Mark becomes a citizen?" he demanded. "Might he dump you? Is his family going to stay here? Where will you fit in with all those Africans? He's doing well now, but what happens when the money runs out? How's he going to support his whole family and you? How will your views of him change when you're the main breadwinner and you're supporting him and his family?"

The questions came in a barrage, and he hardly listened to my answers before jumping to the next.

"I'm concerned mostly about the fact that he's South African, from a totally different country, and that his father was totally dominant and controlling," he said. "He must be *so* angry at whites. And now that he has a white woman under his control—"

"Hey, wait a minute!" I cried angrily. "Wait, hold on! I'm not under anybody's control."

"Yeah, all right, but he's from a patriarchal society and has an incredibly strong will."

"And he saw his mother and grandmother stand up to that male dominance and win. He admires strong women. He's not looking for someone to control. Far from it. He's looking for a friend, a woman who is her own person, whom he can respect, trust, and love."

I felt beaten down by the conversation. I said I was tired and had to go to bed. I could have refused to answer his questions, hung up, told him to mind his own business, or simply made an excuse to get away from the phone, but I decided to stand firm right in the firing line, and as he hurled his concerns at me, I did my best to shoot them down one by one. I wanted to prove to him that I wasn't afraid to answer his questions, that I wasn't avoiding serious issues, that I fully understood what I was getting into by marrying a black foreigner. I only hoped he got my message and would learn to accept my decision.

"This is a difficult but strengthening process," I wrote that night in my journal. "I'm glad I did not turn and run from talking to him. I want my family to understand me, and the only way to do that is by communicating with them."

But my dreams that night were filled with images of black-white clashes, race riots, my escape down a long twisted chute into another world, my mother, my father, Mark. I was trying to go somewhere, find someone to talk to, to listen to me, but my attempts were in vain. I tossed and turned, torn apart by vivid dreams of endless fights and arguments. It was mid-July, hot and humid. My fan creaked as it rotated back and forth, pushing warm air over my sticky body. Sirens, horns, and the constant roar of traffic below my window kept sleep at bay.

That night was the beginning of the two-week period before the wedding during which I did not have a single night's sleep. I was a walking zombie by day, a restless insomniac by night. My dreams were alternately wild, majestic, beautiful, confusing, grand, strange, and surreal. I dreamed of parading triumphantly down the aisle leaning on my father's arm, of saying my vows in a blur of joyful tears as I gazed into Mark's dark and startled eyes, of dancing to my favorite songs in my mother's satin wedding dress as beads of sweat slid between my breasts, of seeing the smiling faces of my family and friends.

The minister who was to marry us, Reverend A. Wayne Benson of Middle Island Presbyterian Church, insisted that Mark and I go through premarital counseling with him. This was difficult, as Mark was in North Carolina, but we made it to one session. Sitting calmly side by side in front of the minister in a small book-lined office, we were quizzed about our expectations, fears, and hopes in relation to marriage. The whole time I kept thinking, *Should I tell him? This is*

*ridiculous. Who ever heard of premarital counseling for people who
are already married?*

One week before the wedding, I could keep our secret from the
minister no longer. I went to the church and told him he did not have
to bother with securing a marriage license for us.

"What do you mean?" Rev. Benson asked.

I told him, in a roundabout and hesitant way, about my reluc-
tance to face my family's opposition head-on and our decision to go
down to City Hall quietly.

"You mean, you're married?" he said with a start.

"Yes."

"Oh, well," he said, leaning back in his swivel chair and chuckling to himself. "This changes things a bit."

"But I don't want anyone to know," I said, leaning forward. "It
would spoil the wedding. You see, I wasn't ready for a public wedding then, but now I am."

"I won't tell a soul," he said. "I'll give your father a church wedding certificate, but it won't be an official one registered with the
state, since you already have one of those." He smiled knowingly.

I thanked him profusely.

A few days before the wedding my mother called from Minneapolis just to tell me she was proud of me and loved me very
much.

"Oh . . . thanks," I said, a bit overwhelmed. "But, why are you so
proud of me?"

"You're so grown up. You've planned this whole wedding by
yourself. You're so organized and efficient and, most of all, you're
able to do what you feel is right."

"Thanks," I said, feeling a warm glow within me. "And I love you,
too."

Over the next few days several people told me they admired my
courage and were proud of me. In spite of the negative stereotypes
about white women who date and marry black men, I realized that
most of my friends, family, and acquaintances truly admired me for
what I was doing, for my courage in marrying interracially. And yes,
it did take courage for me to marry a black man, just as it took a lot
of courage for Mark to marry a white woman, but we knew the bond
between us was strong and true.

I did not sleep at all the night before the wedding. I was in a hotel room with Florah, whose shower cap crinkled on the pillow beside mine each time she moved, and my mother, who occasionally snored and knocked the phone off the nightstand in her sleep.

The next morning, surrounded by my bridesmaids at breakfast, I could not keep my leg from bouncing up and down in nervous agitation. Joanne Matzen, my maid of honor, kept putting her hand on my leg to keep it from shaking. As I walked down the aisle beside my father, my bouquet vibrated and I tried in vain to control my trembling. I felt a sea of faces turned toward me. Were they smiling? Who had decided to come? Which relatives had boycotted in protest?

One of my bridesmaids, Brita Heimarck, played flute for us, our friend Phyllis Reed sang a tune she had written lyrics for, my father stepped into the pulpit and gave us his blessing to be "fruitful," and Rev. Benson led us in our vows. As I looked into Mark's gentle eyes, clasping his hand and promising to love him in sickness and in health, for rich or for poor, my trembling ceased and the onlookers faded from my consciousness. I felt it was just the two of us standing there, whispering promises into the hollow emptiness of an echoing cathedral.

Through my tear-filled eyes the wedding guests appeared to be one huge mass of smiling humanity as I walked down the aisle arm in arm with Mark. It was not until we were standing in the reception line that I was able to look around me. What I saw overwhelmed me: every single one of my relatives, except those who had sent gifts and notes of apology, had come to the wedding—that is, all but one uncle.

My cousin, the one who had plagued me with his concerns over the phone, threw his arms around me, hugged me tight, and whispered in my ear, "You look beautiful." Later he apologized to both me and Mark for the phone calls, said that he had overcome his reservations and wished us happiness. Those words, coming from someone who grew up with me and who had to struggle so desperately with his own prejudices and fears in order to accept my decision, meant a great deal to me. It showed me that the prejudice of some people is not inborn but the result of ignorance and unfounded fears.

The reception was held at the Bellport Unitarian Fellowship, a small white building overlooking Great South Bay, which was a bright and shimmering blue, studded by white caps. The hours passed quickly, speeded on by animated conversation, an array of food, tall glasses of champagne, and heartfelt toasts, dancing and laughing, hugs and smiles, the cutting of the wedding cake, the throwing of rice, and the tossing of the bridal bouquet. My cousin Debbie caught the bouquet but Diana tore it out of her hand.

Carol, who was one of my bridesmaids, whispered in my ear from time to time exactly what I was supposed to do and when.

"You freeze the top layer of the cake and eat it in one year—on your anniversary," she whispered.

I grimaced. "You mean eat this a whole year later?"

Later she whispered urgently, "You and Mark need to leave right away."

We hurried out of the church under a shower of rice. I had rice in my ears, rice sliding down my back, rice in my bra. As Mark and I drove off, in a car loaded with wedding gifts and wrapped in pink and white streamers, I turned to get one last look at all those beloved people who were cheering the two of us on, who not only accepted us and our love, but who genuinely celebrated it.

Why was I so afraid to have a public wedding? I asked myself. *Look at them, waving and wishing us happiness. Perhaps there's little to fear as long as you follow your heart and stand by your convictions.*

Mark and I spent two very rainy but wonderful days of our honeymoon at the American Hotel in Sag Harbor, then rejoined his family and headed down to Hilton Head, South Carolina, to visit Stan Smith and his family.

Leaving my friends and coworkers at the German Information Center was difficult, but the worst part of leaving New York was saying good-bye to Carol and leaving the apartment we shared. Carol was still embroiled in her painful relationship with Robert, which ended a year later in a divorce as secretive and quiet as their wedding had been. I regretted that I would no longer be there to support her on the days his constant absence and numerous affairs particularly depressed her. She helped Mark and me carry boxes loaded with my belongings downstairs to the rented van on Flatbush Avenue and, wishing us the best, gave me one last long hug good-bye.

Despite leaving my friends and job, part of me rejoiced at leaving New York. As I lost some of my Midwestern naïveté and became more acutely aware of the dangers and pressures of living in a large city as a single woman, I had begun to feel harried. At times my fear of rape rose to such a pitch that I wished my breasts and hips and blond hair would all disappear and that I could become invisible. I would cringe, shudder, and walk faster across Central Park or down Flatbush Avenue, my head bent and eyes averted, whenever I heard men murmur from a park bench or from the shadows, "Hey, baby, you lookin' damn *good*, you make me wanna . . ."

A few days later we were on Hilton Head Island. In all my wildest childhood dreams I had never expected to go on a honeymoon with seven South Africans. But there we were, all eight of us, stepping onto an exclusive but crowded beach on one of Hilton Head's many plantations.

The beach looked like a scene out of any grade-B summer film: teenagers playing volleyball and Frisbee, Coppertone-covered bodies clad in skimpy bikinis baking and burning in the sun, motley towels strewn across the hot sand, couples strolling along the shore as waves crashed and swirled around their ankles, seagulls screeching and fighting over bread crumbs, transistor radios blaring.

As we walked across the beach I was acutely aware that there were no blacks in sight except Mark and his family. People stared at us intently, probably wondering how so many blacks, some dressed in African tribal garb, had managed to gain access to their exclusive vacation site and what I, a blond American in a blue bikini, was doing with them. Were they my servants? After all, most blacks on Hilton Head were servants of one sort or another.

Granny stared about her in dismay. She probably wondered how so many women could get away with wearing so little, and why whites, who usually seem so proud of their light skin color, were trying so hard to turn her color. She wrapped her long African print *mucheka* closer about her legs and headed for the shade of an umbrella. She was immediately confronted by a muscular lifeguard with white cream smeared on his sunburned nose.

"You have to pay to rent one of those," he said.

"How much?" Mark asked.

"Ten bucks. But these ones aren't for rent. You can take one of those," he said, pointing to the last row of umbrella chairs nestled close to the sand dunes, far from the water, with broken handles and missing slats.

"What about this one?" Mark said, pointing to the one on which Granny was resting.

"These are reserved," he said.

We spent several hours at the beach that afternoon, and no one came to claim the "reserved" chairs, which were in much better condition than the ones Mark ended up renting near the sand dunes. My senses having become keen to the subtlest discrimination, I burned with anger and resentment, ashamed that members of my own race could behave so abominably to my new family, or to any blacks for that matter. But like Mark and his family, I was learning that such discrimination was too subtle and pervasive to fight. Granny, who, to appease an irate bus driver in South Africa, had once wiped the steps of an all-white bus onto which Mark had innocently clambered as a child, gathered her belongings in silence and moved to the last row of umbrella chairs.

The typical Southern atmosphere of Hilton Head made me more aware than ever that I, now a member of a black family, had forfeited my rights and privileges as a white person. I could no longer ignore the fact that racial prejudice exists. The predominantly white plantations—the retention of this name from a master-slave past seemed more than a coincidence—with their elegant ocean-front mansions and summer homes were worlds apart from the rundown shacks where the black natives of Hilton Head Island lived. Also, the smooth, clean beaches with golden sand were paradisiacal compared to the rocky beaches strewn with trash and broken glass, where blacks swam. To enter the white plantations and swim on their beaches one needed a permit. There was apartheid again, without the name.

By the end of our trip I was fed up with plantations and permits and eager to return home to North Carolina. Being checked by guards in booths every time we went anywhere reminded me of the months I spent in Budapest in 1983, when it was still under Communist rule, and reminded Mark of his days in South Africa, when he had to show his passbook on demand to the police and anytime he left the ghetto and entered the white world.

In late August Linah and Diana wept at the Piedmont International Airport in Greensboro when Florah, Granny, and their mother boarded a plane to return to South Africa. A few days later Linah and

Diana headed for Long Island to live with our friends Marty and Anita, a childless white couple who were eager to educate and support them. George moved into a room on the bottom floor of a large rambling house in High Point, belonging to a Christian ministry, while Mark and I packed for our move to Ithaca, New York, where Mark had accepted a teaching fellowship at Cornell University.

Mark, who had always been close to his family, had serious reservations about their being so scattered. He wanted to be there when they needed him in their difficult task of adapting to American society. But our financial situation made that difficult. Also, we had our own lives to live, our own careers to pursue.

The day we were supposed to leave for Ithaca, he changed his mind. His siblings needed him, he explained. It would be selfish and wrong for him to abandon them at this time.

"But what about us and our needs?" I said.

"Sweets," he said, "I know the sacrifices we'll be making. But I need your support in this. Please try to understand."

I gave the issue more thought. The rental truck was already loaded, we had already been to Ithaca and rented and paid for our new apartment, and the fellowship was important for Mark's career. But his family was more important. I relented.

We immediately began looking for another apartment in High Point. Mark called the English Department at Cornell University and explained his decision to the people who had offered him the fellowship. They were very understanding. We found a vacant townhouse after three days of looking and moved in.

After only one week of living together, just the two of us, as a typical newlywed couple, George had problems with his housemates and moved into our apartment. A week after Thanksgiving Linah and Diana left Long Island and moved in with us as well. The apartment, which had seemed enormous at first, now felt crowded.

"What's it like to have three grown children just a few months after you marry?" people would ask me. "It must be terribly hard on you."

"Poor girl," said another.

"If I were your mother, I'd be very angry," said a middle-aged white woman. "It's unfair for such a young woman, newly married, to have to assume such a heavy burden."

I cannot deny that it was, at first, difficult to give up my dreams and expectations of having my new husband all to myself, of feeling free to dance around and act silly together in privacy, of being able to run downstairs in the middle of the night for some juice without having to pull on a robe or worry about tripping over George, who slept on the fold-out couch in the family room.

Mark and I could no longer fall asleep together under an afghan on the living room floor while watching old black-and-white movies. No more romantic candlelight dinners with beading goblets of white wine. No more spontaneous tackling or surprise kisses.

Suddenly we were surrogate parents. I had to take on roles I'd never known. I became role model, teacher of English as a fifth language (after Tsonga, Venda, Zulu, and Sotho), homework tutor, house chef, and family accountant. To make the situation even more unusual, I was not only part of a mixed couple, I was now the only white member of a five-person family, a wife and "mother" of three. Of course, Mark shared in all responsibilities. Also, he not only supported the five of us but he also supported the rest of his family in South Africa. All this without a steady income but that of a free-lance writer and lecturer.

At times I would go into the woods behind our apartment complex, sit down to listen to the rustling leaves, and weep. Though I had no hard feelings against George, Linah, or Diana, it took a lot of time and effort for me to come to terms with the changes in my life, to realize that I had to give up certain expectations in exchange for new, and perhaps better, realities and sources of happiness and fulfillment.

For as long as I could remember, way back to my childhood in Ohio, I had always had a room of my own, privacy, independence, and a great deal of freedom and security. I was the youngest child, so I never learned to reprimand, teach, or guide a younger sibling. Taking on so many adult responsibilities, and so suddenly, made me fantasize about packing up a few necessary items and hitchhiking to Alaska or Sante Fe or California, wherever I could find peace in solitude and nature, set down new roots, and live a life of my own.

I recalled how much Frau Lange, the mother of the German family with whom I had lived outside Hannover in the summer of 1985, had envied my freedom to travel around Europe. The day I returned from a week in Vienna, she cried, *"Ach, Wien!"* and explained how she had longed all her life to see the famous city.

"Then why don't you go?" I asked, perplexed.

"Meine Pflichte! Meine Pflichte!" she cried despairingly. "My duties! My responsibilities!"

At the time I was twenty-three and single and could not imagine that any human being could be so tied down by circumstances that they could not fulfill their lifelong dream of seeing a city that was only six hundred miles away. I vowed I'd never let myself get so burdened with duties that I would not be free to travel and explore.

But an hour or so of reveling in such memories, or imagining future travels and adventures in foreign lands, inevitably ended as soon as I heard Mark's gentle voice or Diana's laughter or Linah's excited chatter emanating through the open windows, beckoning me to leave the dark woods and come into the warmth of a loving home.

Mark and I, twenty-seven and twenty-five, respectively, were in many ways still kids ourselves, often casting off our robes of parental authority and simply becoming big brother and big sister. In the spring Mark, George, Linah, Diana, and I would play baseball in a nearby field with a horde of neighborhood kids. We would pack up the grill, Frisbee, hamburgers, potato salad, and neighbors and have picnics at Jamestown Park. We played practical jokes on each other, like the time Linah fell asleep in a chair while reading and Mark tied her shoelaces together and turned her book upside down.

We laughed over the mistakes Linah and Diana made while struggling to learn English. For instance, Linah always talked about the "disgusting" questions they talked about in school, not knowing how to pronounce *discussion.* She often sang songs she heard on the radio, and went around the apartment singing, "Every time you go away, you take a piece of meat with you."

"No!" I exclaimed, laughing. "The words are 'You take a piece of *me* with you!'"

When Mark said grace before a meal, he often ended with, "And provide food for those who lack it." When it was Diana's turn to say grace one evening, she ended with, "And provide food for those who like it." She was bewildered by our laughter.

Linah and Diana sometimes ran into trouble when they used South African words to refer to American things: they used the word *cocks* for "soccer cleats" and *rubber* for "eraser."

When Diana asked her male history teacher for a rubber, he stared at her in shock and told her to sit down. She went back to her desk without the much-needed eraser. When Linah asked the soccer coach, "Don't we need cocks to play on the team?" he replied, "No, we have a girls' team too." Of course Mark's sisters had no idea their words had a double meaning, and they would ask me what their teachers meant.

"Never mind," I said, stifling my laughter. "Just call them erasers and soccer cleats from now on."

Diana, Linah, and George usually spoke to each other in Tsonga, and aware that I sometimes felt left out of the conversation, Mark would often translate for me. He was also teaching me the language. But translating from one language to another was usually not enough to close the vast gulf that separated my white middle-class background from their lives in South Africa. One Saturday morning when I entered the kitchen I found Mark making omelets for everyone and reminiscing with his siblings about life in Alexandra. I caught snatches of what they were saying because, though most of it was in Tsonga, they threw in enough English words for me to follow.

"Remember that fat man who wanted to marry our sister Merriam?" Linah said. "He would get Dad drunk instead of paying *lobola*. Each time Dad went over to his house to drink, the fat man was getting closer and closer to paying off the *lobola* and getting Merriam for his wife. Boy, Merriam was *so* mad when she found out! It turned out the fat man already had two wives. Merriam screamed at Daddy, 'What do you take me for?!'"

They laughed uproariously, interrupting each other in an attempt to relate yet another story.

"What happened to that studious boy who lived near the bus stop on Fourteenth Avenue?" Mark asked. "The one with the older brother who was knifed in the *shebeen*?"

"He was run over by a truck," Diana replied. "He was helping it back up."

"Didn't the driver see him?" Mark asked.

"He did, but he was jealous of him because he made more money than he did, so he ran him over."

They talked about how Florah and Maria used to cheat at card games and gamble, how their mother was poisoned by a neighbor who was jealous that her children were all so intelligent and studying in America, how mean older boys used to rob children on their way to the store, how certain migrant workers would take new wives on coming to cities, leaving behind in the homelands large families starving and struggling, and how young men known as *Tsotsis* and *Comrades* harassed those who defied the school boycott and often killed each other in senseless disputes over girls, money, and turf.

Mark stopped the conversation and said, "Okay, Gail. Now that you've heard all about Alex, why don't you tell us all about *your* home town?"

I thought of the happy hours I spent in my sandbox outside our duplex in Green Hills, a suburb of Cincinnati. I thought of roller-skating down Brookhollow Lane in Springfield, Ohio, past mowed lawns and freshly painted homes and well-fed pets. I thought of the pleasant faces of the old ladies who smiled down at me on Sunday mornings at church, and the way my father would step into the pulpit in his long black robe, open a huge Bible, and clear his throat before delivering the day's sermon.

"There's not much to tell," I said. "At least, not compared to your stories."

While George, Linah, and Diana were at school, Mark and I would write, sharing the same cramped study, reading each other's work and making suggestions. I was working on my third and fourth novels simultaneously, while Mark worked on *Kaffir Boy in America*. We were at our computers by seven every morning and, pausing only for breakfast and lunch, would write until two or three in the afternoon, then go to the gym together to jump rope and lift weights. At night we read like maniacs, going through several books a month, underlining, writing down ideas, discussing them, just as we used to do on Staten Island.

We had plenty of time to ourselves, and we also had the satisfaction of knowing we were sharing our good fortune with Mark's siblings, who were trying their best to master English and do well in school. The violence and unrest in the black townships, which disrupted schooling and every other aspect of black life, would have made it impossible for them to get a decent education in South Africa. The more Mark and I helped them with their homework;

made them aware of the dangers of too much television and materialism; and reminded them of the importance of retaining the values of responsibility, respect, discipline, and hard work they had been taught back home, the better we felt.

Each day I realized the truth of the adage: It is in giving that we receive.

8

BIRTH OF A CHILD

MARK'S VIEW

Few events have enriched my life as much as fatherhood. From the instant I learned the surprising, joyous, and bewildering news that Gail was pregnant, I made the leap from being a friend and husband to the exhilarating position of a father-to-be.

There was an added dimension to the thrilling news. What Gail and I had long believed in theory—that humankind is one and the races are but individual members of a large family—became reality. Our child stood to inherit and to benefit from the best of all worlds and cultures because we the parents had worked hard at bridging the gap that separated people from each other on the biologically irrelevant basis of skin color.

With the birth of our firstborn a cycle was now complete. I had grown from a child, to a son, to a parent. I couldn't help but contrast my own experiences as a father with those of my own father, Jackson. Though in his own way he deeply cared for my mother, he was never present during the birth of any of his seven children. Tradition forbade it. Even had it not, his strange sense of manhood would have disdained being beside his wife during childbirth.

For my father and most tribal men of his time and culture, the process of childbearing was strictly a woman's affair. It was taboo for them to be present even in the house. They would be contaminated and their manhood would be weakened by the mysterious, almost magical experience. All the husband needed to know were the end results: Is it a boy or girl child, is it alive or dead?

The wife's emotional need for her husband's presence during the birth of a joint responsibility—her need for his love, his encouragement, and his support—could not be accommodated in a relationship where the husband was master of the house and "owner" of his wife and where society taught him to hide, suppress, and even deny his true feelings.

But as a child I set out to be different emotionally from my father. My heart yearned to feel, to love, to care, to cry, to laugh. I resisted and endured enormous pressure designed to teach me that boys and men never show their emotions. My father would sometimes beat me for crying when hurt. But his attempts to truncate me emotionally failed. I could not stop feeling. In my mind and heart to feel was to be human.

Each one of my mother's later pregnancies deeply affected me. I pitied each new child for coming into a world full of pain, hunger, suffering, injustice, and the early death of innocence. I pitied my mother for the risks, the pain, and the difficulties of each pregnancy. The lack of prenatal and postnatal care, the absence of basic sanitation in the ghetto in which we were quarantined, and her frequent flights from the police (even late in her pregnancies) to escape arrest, endangered not only her life but also that of the growing life within her.

It pained me to see her, when she was pregnant with her third child, set off at dawn, trudging barefoot through the township, begging for food or odd jobs. She even had to beg pennies from neighbors to buy diapers because my father, in a futile effort to drown the unimaginable pain and sorrow of his emasculated life, had squandered his meager ten-dollar-a-week wage on dice and alcohol.

When she became pregnant for the seventh time, I was distraught. Not only had previous difficult pregnancies taken their toll on her body (she was also a diabetic and didn't know it) but the family's poverty and miseries had worsened. Food was scarce. The two-room shack offered neither space nor privacy and my father was in and out of prison for such "crimes" as being unemployed and harboring illegal aliens in the form of his wife and children.

At school things were going badly for me. I was constantly being whipped and humiliated for lacking books, school fees, and proper uniforms. I had half a mind to quit school and find a menial job somewhere so I could ameliorate my mother's suffering. But she wouldn't hear of it. She insisted that I stay in school. "All will be well," she would say. "God will provide."

Barely two months after her seventh child, Diana, was born, my mother had the baby strapped to her back and returned to her laborious work cleaning the house and washing and ironing the laundry for a fifteen-member Indian family. She was paid three dollars a week.

My mother became seriously ill under the strain. The infant became afflicted with strange diseases caused by an inadequate diet. Miraculously both mother and child survived. I remember vowing to my mother that if I ever got married, I would never allow my wife to suffer as she had suffered. I would be by her side at all times, even during childbirth, taboo or no taboo.

"I know you will, my child," my mother said. "That's the right thing for a father and a husband to do. God will bless you for it all the days of your life."

When Gail first told me that she was pregnant, one of the thoughts that came to mind was the vow I made to my mother. It was a lovely spring day in May 1988, nine months after our public wedding. I had just returned home from a long run around Oak Hollow Lake. I pulled off my wet sweatshirt and bounded up the stairs to the small bedroom I shared with Gail. She was in a gray armchair, not reading or writing as usual, but just sitting and staring contemplatively at the budding trees outside our small window, twisting a strand of blond hair with her fingers.

"What's the matter?" I asked.

She glanced up at me with a worried look in her eyes. She let go her hair and clasped her hands tightly together, betraying her nervousness. She paused for a moment before whispering, "I'm pregnant."

"Really!" I exclaimed. "Are you sure? How did you find out?"

She pointed to a white box on the dresser that read, "Home Pregnancy Test Kit." I quickly picked up the box and read the instructions: a blue stick indicates pregnancy. The stick in Gail's hand was blue.

"Oh, Mark, I'm so scared," Gail said. "I know we don't have any health insurance and we're financially strapped. I know we weren't planning for a child so soon. Please don't be angry."

"Angry?" I cried, dropping the box and rushing toward her. "Me angry? How could I be angry? I'm thrilled! I'm so proud of you, Sweets. Remember, there's never a perfect time to have baby. Money or no money, this is our baby, our firstborn." I threw my arms around her, pulled her up from the chair, and we danced.

Though both Gail and I are pro-choice, we never once discussed having an abortion, despite our precarious financial condition and our fears that an unexpected pregnancy might drown our career ambitions in a sea of diapers and baby wipes.

Over the next several months I shared every strange phase of emotional and physical change Gail underwent. I was alternately in awe, fascinated, and bewildered. My life became transformed as I strove to understand and contribute to the joy Gail felt as a mother-to-be. Once so full of energy and eager to get up and write at seven each morning, Gail now slept until ten, dragging herself from the warm bedclothes only at the prompting of hunger pangs. I made her elaborate meals, only to see her sicken at the smell of food, become nauseous at the sight of fish or salad, push her plate away after forcing down only a few bites at dinner.

In the first two months she lost ten pounds. Worried that her weight loss would endanger her and the baby, I constantly begged her to eat—to no avail.

It was the summer of 1988: hot, humid, and muggy. In June, to have some room for the additional member of the family, we moved from our apartment in High Point to a farmhouse—our first real home—in Kernersville. It had a long front porch, sat on a huge lot filled with trees, perfect for a child to grow up loving the outdoors.

George, Linah, Diana, and I did the moving. Our belongings filled a U-Haul truck. I was unable to drive a stick shift; George tried and stripped several gears. Gail, despite my protestations, drove the rumbling truck the twenty miles up Highway 66 to Kernersville. "I may be pregnant," she said, "but I'm not an invalid."

Exhausted from our efforts, the five of us collapsed amid the piles of moving boxes and furniture, wolfed down a bucket of fried chicken, and fell asleep on hastily assembled beds.

As winter approached, Gail's stomach resembled an eggplant. The baby was fully formed and near term. Gail left her temporary job at RJR Nabisco in Winston-Salem. By now the slight rumblings within her belly had become vigorous kicks and punches. Several times a day I would pause to press my ear against the little creature and tap. My light knockings and words of greeting were always answered with a powerful punch to my head. Each night we read to the baby.

Gail and I attended childbirth classes in the basement of an old church in High Point. We were the only mixed couple and I was the only black. We were always the last ones to arrive, shuffling into the large, brightly lit room wearing winter jackets and clutching pillows. The female instructor would pause to smile at us as we made our way to the back of the room, past the two dozen or so couples seated in folding chairs.

Sometimes the husbands and wives were told to split up for group discussions. I found myself sitting in a circle of white Southern men. We were asked to come up with a list of emotions we felt at the prospect of becoming fathers.

"I feel excited," one said.

"I feel scared of the responsibility," said another.

"I feel so goddamned horny all the time I don't know what to do," said a third.

The men broke out laughing, nodding their heads in agreement. I made a comment about how close to Gail, and more respectful and proud of her, the pregnancy made me feel. Everyone stopped talking and stared at me with curiosity, either because my accent took them by surprise or because they were unaccustomed to hearing a black man express his opinion, especially about such an intimate matter. I'm certain some of the men felt I had no right to be there, or worse, but most of them were open-minded and regarded me only as a fellow daddy-to-be.

As the weeks went by I lost much of my self-consciousness. I would be down on the floor with the rest of the young fathers in the class, holding Gail's ankles, stuffing pillows under her at the appropriate places, counting aloud for her as she panted and breathed, telling her when to take her deep cleansing breath, and diligently studying the handouts we were given on relaxation techniques and different breathing rhythms.

I spent a good deal of time wondering what our child would look like. Would it have a big blond Afro and blue eyes? Or would it look more like I did as a child, with chocolate brown skin, nappy hair, and large brown eyes? How would Gail feel carrying around a biracial child? How would I feel carrying a child lighter than myself? What kinds of stares and comments would we get when we appeared in public with our baby?

GAIL'S VIEW

Ever since those troubled nights before our public wedding, when I tossed and turned in a restless sweat in my bed on Flatbush Avenue with my mind full of wild visions, I had dreamed many times of giving birth. In one dream I was whisked from the chapel in my white satin wedding dress to a delivery room across the hall, where I promptly gave birth to a small brown baby amid the shouts, hoorays, and champagne toasts of all our wedding guests.

And now, as I lay on the hammock strung between two towering trees beside our home in Kernersville, a mug of steaming Ovaltine balanced on my rounded belly, I recalled all the recent dreams I had had of childbirth. As if my subconscious mind could not decide whether my child would be black or white, I dreamed I bore a little panda bear: pitch black in parts and snow white in others. Besides a mother's natural curiosity to know whether she will have a boy or girl and whether it will have all ten fingers and toes, I was dying to know what strange combination of pigments and facial features was forming within me.

Whenever we spoke on the phone with Mark's family in South Africa, they were full of suggestions for what we should name our baby, which everyone assumed would be a boy. Mark's mother insisted we call him Lazarus, after the biblical character who arose from the dead. His sister Merriam urged us to call him Remembrance.

The naming of a child in Mark's culture was a major affair. Relatives often competed with gifts for the right to give a child its seldom-used, sacred, African name. Such names always stood for something. One of Mark's grandparents won the right to name him and called him *Thanyani*, which means "The Wise One." George was named *Ndwakhulu*, which means "Big Wars," because he came at a time when Mark's parents were constantly fighting and arguing. Florah was named *Mkondeleli*, which means "Endurance"; she was born at a time when the family was experiencing hard times.

Whenever Mark and I went for walks at night down a lonely dirt road between open grass fields at the edge of which were fish hatcheries, breathing in the misty, fresh North Carolina country air, I loved the feeling of his warm hand gently holding mine, and of the baby stirring within me, hard, bony, and substantial. Sitting on the front porch, wedged together on a narrow wicker loveseat, we would talk hopefully about our child and the future, watching the winter rain pelt the brick steps, soaking into the moist earth, enriching it. Mark was convinced our child already loved classical music and African folklore, so he would pop a Bach cassette into the stereo and press the headphones against my rounded belly or relate one of his mother's stories. Each day he would kiss my stomach good morning and good night, usually when I was half-asleep and unaware that he was having a lengthy conversation with the baby.

About one month before the baby was due, Stedman Graham came to our house for lunch. Mark had been playing tennis with him regularly since he moved down to High Point to head a public relations firm, but I had not seen him since June 1987 in New York, when Mark's family arrived. He was much taller than I remembered, and he smiled down at me, shook my hand, and said, "Been a *long* time. When's the baby due?"

"January twentieth," I replied.

By the time we sat down to eat, Mark and Stedman were engrossed in a discussion about South Africa, life, and acting on one's instincts. As they talked, Stedman kept looking at me as if he wanted to say something.

At last he paused and, after a great deal of hesitation, said, "I have to confess something to you, Gail. When I first met you at JFK that day Mark's family arrived, and I saw that you were white, it really upset me. It upset me so much I couldn't even finish reading Mark's book. I kept asking, 'Why? Why does he want to blow his future by marrying a white woman? He could have so much more power and credibility if he focused on his role as a black leader in the struggle against apartheid.' "

He paused and waited for my reaction, but I was too surprised by his straightforward admission and frank manner to say anything.

"I don't know if you sensed this, but that's how I felt," he added.

"I didn't realize," I began. "But I did wonder why you wouldn't remove your sunglasses in a car with tinted windows, even when Oprah teased you about keeping them on."

He laughed at the memory, then said, "I remember that. And it was because of what I'm explaining to you." He turned to Mark. "I wanted to call you, Mark, and tell you not to go through with the marriage. But I felt I didn't know you well enough."

I looked at Mark. He said nothing but was listening attentively.

"But that was all before my life changed," Stedman continued. "Now I see that you two really care about each other, and love needs no justification. It doesn't have to be aware of race or prejudice or what other people may think. You two have set an example, an admirable example, of how we *should* see each other—as human beings."

I was touched by Stedman's confession, and, after a long discussion in which Mark and I revealed the internal and external pressures we had to overcome to go through with the public wedding, I thanked Stedman for being honest and having the courage to admit how he had truly felt.

"I always like to clear the air," he said. "I couldn't come to your home and eat your food without first letting you know how I once felt and how I now feel." He leaned back in his chair with a sigh, as if he had just relieved himself of a great burden. "I'm flying back to Chicago tomorrow. I can't wait to tell Oprah that I confessed to you."

I laughed, but felt grateful to him and very glad that he and Mark were becoming good friends.

By the middle of January I could not sleep. I tossed and turned restlessly, extra pillows stuffed between my knees and behind my back and along my side, unable to get comfortable. Considering how pear shaped I had become and how many pillows I had, I'm surprised I did not pitch Mark out of bed every time I turned. I tried in vain to relax. All I could think about was a newborn baby screaming in a delivery room, glistening and red. One night, when I had finally drifted off to sleep, I was awakened by a dull pain in my lower abdomen that went around to the small of my back. It went away, then came again. Contractions.

I sat up in bed and watched Mark, sleeping like a baby in the gray early morning light, swaddled in a white comforter. When Mark awoke I scratched his back and said, "Hi."

"Hi," he replied sleepily. "Did you get any sleep?"

"I've been up since three," I said. "I've been timing my contractions."

His eyes opened wide in amazement, and he started shaking. I could not tell how much was real fear and how much was a theatrical attempt to make me laugh, which I did.

"D-d-did you s-s-say c-c-con-contractions?" he gasped.

"It's all right. They're not painful yet. Just uncomfortable. This could go on for twelve hours. No need to rush to the hospital."

Mark pranced around happily all morning, talking nonstop to my stomach, saying such things as "Finally, boy, you'll be coming out to deal with the real world and earn your keep. No more perpetual fiestas and siestas."

The contractions kept going all day until, at one in the morning, I realized it was time to head for the hospital, which was half an hour away in High Point. Mark gripped the steering wheel nervously, glancing at me with concern whenever he could take his eyes from the ice-crusted road, asking every two minutes, "Are you all right? It's not going to be born in the car, is it?"

Twelve hours passed in a phantasmagoria of white walls, the faces of nurses and doctors, strange voices asking me questions, the rapid beat of the fetal heart monitor, music, the soothing sound of Mark's voice reading me a Sherlock Holmes story I was too distracted to follow.

The pain came in waves, rising to a crescendo and then fading. At the peaks I thrashed back and forth in agony, felt Mark's hand gripping mine, heard his voice coaching me through it. Strands of damp hair stuck to my sweating face and neck. I breathed so hard and rapidly I hyperventilated: Faces and hospital equipment swirled before my eyes and my limbs went numb. "It's a girl!" the doctor said.

I looked down to see a tiny blue creature, with groping hands and kicking feet, resting in Dr. Farabow's hands. Mark cut the umbilical cord, and the baby, after being turned upside down and spanked, let out a shrill cry. Tears of joy rushed to my eyes. Mark kissed me. I stared at Bianca Ellen (named after Mark's grandmother Ellen Mabaso) in amazement when they put her in my arms. She looked so tiny, so helpless, so fragile. She was the same color as I, with blue eyes and thin, straight hair: It would be months before her hair would grow thick and curly, her eyes would turn brown, and her skin would darken into a beautiful light brown.

That night after Mark left the hospital, I lay in the darkened room and longed for Bianca, who was fast asleep under the harsh fluorescent lights of the nursery down the hall. She had been a part of me for nine months, and I missed having her close to me, feeling her roll and kick within me. A powerful feeling of love for my husband and my baby rose within me and grew stronger and stronger until, by dawn, I was giddy and weeping with happiness. Because my mother had suffered from intense and long-lasting postpartum depressions after the births of my two brothers and me, I feared that I too would fall into dark despondency. To my surprise I was flooded with a joy so intense it made me sob.

"What's wrong?" cried a middle-aged nurse in a gleaming white uniform as she rushed into my room and turned on the light. She had heard my sobs and come to my rescue.

"Oh, it's . . . it's nothing," I said, red-faced and gasping for breath. "It's just that I'm so happy I can't bear it!"

The nurse smiled knowingly. "It's your hormones," she said. "They're out of whack. You'll come back to earth soon enough."

But I didn't come back to earth—I remained perpetually high for days. As soon as the nurse left my room I took out some paper and wrote a note to Bianca's father. It read,

Dearest Mark,

Thank you for holding my hand through the pain, for brushing the hair away from my forehead, for coaching me through it all, and for loving me and Baby Bianca so much. My heart is so full of love that it brings tears to my eyes just to think about our baby, about you, and about how deeply I care for and need you both. I love you more than words can say.

Forever yours,
GAIL

When the day staff went home at three and the new shift came on, a young woman in white, fresh out of nursing school and with her hair high in a sand-colored pony tail, burst exuberantly into my room and, after chatting ceaselessly about sundry topics I've long since forgotten, caught sight of Bianca fast asleep in the padded cart beside the hospital bed. Stepping closer to examine the baby, the nurse fell silent.

"She's a cute little thing," she said. "My, she's sort of got a brown tinge to her, doesn't she? Is your husband dark?"

"Yes," I replied, then smiled to myself. I knew she probably meant dark in terms of having an Italian's olive skin, brown hair, and brown eyes, as in "tall, dark, and handsome." The nurse, being the talkative type, lingered in my room long after her duties were done, telling me all about her Southern upbringing. She spoke quickly, jumping from topic to topic with ease like a monkey swinging from one tree branch to another, and with her Southern accent and Southern belle mannerisms, reminded me a bit of Scarlett O'Hara in *Gone With the Wind*. When the door swung open and Mark entered the room, she seemed petrified. She leaped backward a little.

"Are you looking for someone?" she inquired.

"Yes, my wife," Mark replied.

"Have you checked at the front desk to see which room she's in?"

"Here I am," I said, smiling at Mark, who came toward me, took my hand, and leaned over to kiss me. The nurse, trying to mask her surprise, hurriedly excused herself and left the room. About fifteen minutes later she returned with a group of nursing students, saying she was giving them a tour of the maternity ward. I felt the three of us—Mark, Bianca, and I—were on display like some curiosity exhibit at a fair. But I was too absorbed in Mark, my new baby, and my own happiness to care what strangers thought of our black-brown-white family.

For the first two weeks after Mark proudly and ceremoniously brought Bianca and me home from the hospital, none of us got a solid night's sleep. Mark and I slept in the bed directly beside her crib, jumping up at each squeak and squeal she made in her noisy slumber, making sure the blanket was tucked snugly about her little face, making sure her little knit cap stayed on her head, making sure her diaper was dry—even as she slept. We played the role of the worried, anxious new parents to the hilt. Mark enjoyed changing diapers so much that I kidded him about making it his permanent responsibility.

After two weeks of walking around like zombies, pacing the nursery by night and quieting Bianca in the sun room by day, our lives regained some normalcy. In February, which is Black History Month, Mark traveled to various colleges across the country. He was loath to leave us but he had committed himself to the lectures months ago.

I tended to Bianca and welcomed the steady flow of cards, flowers, and baby gifts that arrived at our doorstep, including a huge wicker basket from Oprah and Stedman filled with teddy bears, baby clothes, lullaby tapes, powder, and chocolates.

The other young mothers in my neighborhood, who had held a surprise baby shower for me, wished to see Bianca. They called on the phone and asked if they could "drop by." Being new to motherhood, I had no idea it was customary for friends and neighbors to deliver baby gifts in person and take a peek at the infant. I thought they wanted to see the baby merely because they were burning with curiosity, as I had been all through my pregnancy, to find out how a baby with such different-looking parents would look. They would bend over the crib or stroller and, seeing dark hair, a fairly wide nose and tan skin, would exclaim, "Oh, she looks just like Mark!"

But she's my child too, I would think to myself. Seeing my hurt expression, they would sometimes add, "Oh, but she has your long fingers" or "She has your cheeks." Mark was the only person who thought Bianca resembled me. He would lean over the baby and whisper, "Why do you look so much like your mommy and so little like me? You're just as pretty as your mommy, too."

Eager to get back in shape, I started exercising as soon as possible after delivery. I ran the same route I had before Bianca came along, but now I would run it while pushing a stroller. I still went for long bike rides along the winding country roads north of Kernersville, but now I would ride with Bianca right behind me in a cushioned bicycle seat and wearing a child's lightweight biking helmet. To save gasoline and get in an extra workout, I would sometimes ride to the grocery store and bring home bread and other items in a backpack.

One day, as I fastened Bianca into her bike seat outside the grocery store, an elderly Southern gentleman strolled by and stared at my baby. It was a hot, sunny day in the middle of summer. I was wearing shorts and a tank top and Bianca's arms and legs were bare. He gazed at five-month-old Bianca for several minutes, then said in a slow drawl, "That baby sure is turnin' brown."

"Yes, she has a nice color, doesn't she?" I said. Bianca had slowly been getting darker as the melanin came out in her skin.

"You must set her out in the sun an awful lot," he commented. When he got no reply he said, "You set her out in the sun?"

"No, she's only outside when I am."

"I don't know that it's healthy for a baby to be out in the sun so much." He shook his head in wonder, and turning to walk away muttered to himself, "That baby sure is brown."

Small children were always the first to make some remark on the difference between my color and Bianca's. One little boy tugged insistently at his mother's skirt, pointed to us and shouted, "Hey! Look! That's a white lady and that's a brown baby! Mommy, how come that white lady's got a brown baby?"

The mother bent over her child and whispered, "Don't point! How many times do I have to tell you—"

"But how come there's a white lady with a—"

"Some children are adopted," the mother explained. She looked up and, seeing that I had heard everything, asked, "She *is* adopted, isn't she?"

"No, she's mine," I said proudly.

It surprised me how many mothers boxed their children's ears or scolded them whenever the kids would ask, out of innocent curiosity, how a white mother could have a brown baby. The mothers probably thought they were training their children not to point, pry, or be impolite, but their scolding might later have a harmful effect. It might serve to teach them that it is wrong for a white woman to have a brown child. Instead of scolding and chastising, I wished the mothers would explain and reassure. Many of our prejudices, I believe, develop in this manner. Children have a natural curiosity to know, they are seldom judgmental, but we adults instill in them our prejudices and narrow views.

I envied Mark, who never had such encounters when he took

Bianca out in public. A proud black father with a cute, curly haired, light-skinned brown baby in a frilly dress draws only praise and admiration from passersby. Bianca's lighter skin did not necessarily mean that her mother was white: She could have been a light-skinned black woman, which, in the eyes of society, was perfectly acceptable. But when I appeared in public with Bianca, there was little doubt that the father of the child was black.

My white friend Connie, who has a black husband, James, and three biracial children, is frustrated by the constant stares and comments she gets when she takes her children out in public.

"I just get so sick of it sometimes," Connie said. "The reality of it hit me after having three. I'll be loading three kids, two strollers, and five bags of groceries into my car and someone will walk up to me and say, 'Oh, they're so cute. Are they yours?' What am I supposed to say to that? No, I'm just their nanny? Of course, they're mine, lady!"

"I didn't really see James as a black man, I just saw him as a man I loved," Connie said. "Now my kids have to grow up. They have to face the fact that they're mixed. Are they going to be black or are they going to be white? Since they have their father's last name, I assume they'll be black. But my son says he's not black. He says he's brown. I say, 'Dylan, you can be anything you want to be, as long as you're proud of who you are.' "

One day as Connie drove down a major boulevard in Greensboro with her children, the driver in the next lane leaned out of his window toward her and yelled repeatedly, "You goddamned nigger lover!"

"I was in shock," Connie said. "Tears gushed down my face. Long after the man stepped on the gas and took off, I was still in shock. Another time I was sitting in my car at an intersection, waiting for the light to change, and a pickup truck pulled up in the next lane. I heard someone say, 'Look at the nigger lover and her baby niggers!' Then I heard a second voice, 'I think I'm going to throw up.' "

"How does it make you feel when you hear things like that?" I asked.

"Angry. I hate it. My motherly defensiveness makes me want to beat the crap out of them. I know it's their problem, not mine, but they're saying something about my family. But if I've had a really good day, I just feel sorry for them and pray for them. God forgive them. They don't know what they're doing." She pushed her thick wavy hair away from her face and watched her curly headed one-year-old daughter, Lily, play with Bianca on the carpeted floor before us.

"To me everybody is the same, they only look different," Connie said after a thoughtful pause. "I think God created everyone different to see how much love we can have for each other. I believe He intended to find out how much people could love and care about each other even though they're different on the outside. Your blood is red whether you're green, red, polka-dot, or whatever."

Having friends in situations similar to mine helped me accept the fact that my daughter did not look like me and never would. But she was my daughter, my own flesh and blood, and I loved her deeply. A white American college student named Marya, whom I met through Mark's brother, George, was engaged to a black South African and, on seeing Bianca, expressed a strong desire to someday have a little brown baby of her own.

"Do people stare at you at the grocery store when you're carrying her around?" Marya asked.

"Yes, and they're probably thinking, 'Poor white trash.' "

Marya fell over laughing. "That's so funny. It can really make you crazy, Gail. You have to keep laughing. As serious as it is, you can't let it bother you."

"They probably think, 'She must live in an abandoned mobile home on the edge of town. A single mother on welfare with a whole brood of half-breeds.' "

"Got raped or something."

"Poor thing."

We laugh, and it is our laughter that saves us from being harmed by the venom of racists.

When Bianca began to walk and then run, she would often run excitedly around stores and airports, exploring stairs, escalators, and hallways. Wanting her to grow up to be adventurous and brave, I would let her wander, keeping an eye on her from a short distance. Whenever she headed for trouble, I'd run to catch up with her and take her by the hand. When other adults saw me heading toward her they would say, "Are you looking for this child's mother, too?"

"I *am* her mother," I'd say with a laugh and a smile. Because, after a while, I no longer cared that people could not immediately tell I was Bianca's mother, and such questions began to amuse rather than irritate me. It struck me as particularly humorous whenever someone thought Mark's little sister Diana was Bianca's mother.

The more I grew to know and love my baby, the less skin color and hair texture mattered to me. In fact, I began to envy Bianca for her beautiful year-round tan, big brown eyes, and dark little curls. I would take her for long walks in the woods when she was just a few months old, holding her close to my chest in a Snugli and talking to her about my childhood, my writing, my dreams. I vividly recall one day in late April, when I walked with her in the saturated, dripping, moist green woods around Salem Lake on the outskirts of Winston-Salem. It was raining, and as I held my child tight against me inside my windbreaker to keep her warm and dry, I told her of my long struggle to become a writer and why I loved writing.

"A writer uses everything she's ever known, seen, thought, felt, believed, experienced," I told Bianca, who closed her eyes when she heard the soothing sound of her mother's voice. "Nothing lived is wasted. In any other career, the past is only important in so far as it helped you get to your current position. But not for a writer. Everything in the past and present is vital in creating the future and all its amazing possibilities, every detail and gesture and memory."

Bianca had fallen fast asleep. Her soft cheek rested on the edge of the Snugli and her head bobbed slightly with each step. I stood on a jagged rock jutting into the lake. Lightning flashed and thunder clapped and the soft rain became hard, pelting the stony surface of the water. Bianca stirred and awoke, then looked about her with blinking eyes. I bent down to touch the warm water with my fingertips, then sprinkled a few droplets on Bianca's head, which was still soft and throbbed with each heartbeat.

"I baptize you in the name of the Father, and of the Son, and of the Holy Spirit," I said, repeating the words I had heard my father recite so many times. I hoped my baptizing her might somehow protect her from the barbs and pitfalls she would encounter in life and help her grow to be strong, loving, and hopeful. But baptizing her myself, in the atmosphere that combined solitude and nature—the two elements that never failed to fill me with inspiration and awaken my inner spirit—was more meaningful to me than any church baptism could have been.

When the rain subsided I held Bianca up so she could see the pine trees, the cloudy gray sky, and the silvery expanse of the lake. "God made all this, Bianca," I whispered in her tiny ear. "And He made you too."

Bianca looked about her in wonder during our long walk back home along the winding dirt road circling the lake. I talked to her the whole time, telling her things I probably could never have told my closest friend. I talked on and on, about how secure I now felt in my marriage and how I suddenly felt certain Mark and I would weather all storms, would find our own happiness and purposes in life. In a way, being part of an interracial couple made me less dependent on society's goals and rewards for those who blindly obey its authorities and customs. It made me less eager to please, to see my whole life as preparation for subordination to my socially approved husband. It made me look inward, to the spirit, to the heart, to the mind, to the soul. If at the end of our brief days here on earth, we are able to say honestly, with a clear conscience, that we have loved, that we have given, that we've helped others less fortunate than ourselves, that we have grown, that we have obeyed the golden rule, then our souls will look forward with eagerness to whatever lies beyond the grave.

"I never really believed that before, Bianca," I said. "Ever since my parents' divorce, I didn't believe that love could last. I used to think that people inevitably grow apart, and that it's only a matter of time before things fall apart. But now I know, deep inside me, that love can last a lifetime. Perhaps I never knew how deeply I could feel attached to someone until you came along."

My faith in my relationship was strengthened not only by the birth of Bianca but also by the publication of *Kaffir Boy in America*. Suddenly our marriage was public knowledge, and I no longer felt a need to hide the fact that I was married to a black man from anyone, ever. Mark, too, began to blossom into a truly dedicated and proud husband, father, friend. When six-month-old Bianca and I accompanied him on much of the promotional tour for his book in June 1989—joining him in New York, Long Island, San Francisco, and Minneapolis—I saw a profound change in him.

During a book signing at International House, the dormitory where we had lived as journalism students, Mark did something he had never done before. I stood in the back holding Bianca while Gordon Evans, president of I-House, introduced Mark. Mark discussed apartheid and described the effects of America's lingering racism and his struggles as a foreign student in America. His tone was gentle and thoughtful. As he ended his speech, in front of a room crowded with people, he thanked I-House for providing the environment in which he could meet someone "as intelligent, beautiful, talented, and caring" as I. Mark looked directly at me as he spoke, and I blushed. Following the speech everyone congratulated us on our "beautiful" daughter. Mark and I beamed with pride. We had come a long way from the day we met in this very building, pledged our hearts to each other, uncertain what the future held in store for us.

PART 2

THE LARGER PICTURE

9

BEING A MIXED COUPLE IN THE SOUTH

MARK'S VIEW

Not too long ago across the South, interracial relationships were not only forbidden by law but black men were often lynched by white mobs on the slightest suspicion of being involved with a white woman. Even after passage of the 1963 Civil Rights Act, the Ku Klux Klan and its sympathizers continued terrorizing interracial couples and families.

One young man Gail and I met, Trevor Nightingale, was only a toddler in 1974, but he vividly remembers the burning cross. He and his white father and black mother returned to their modest home in York, South Carolina, one night to find a blazing wooden cross in their front yard.

The cross burning was just one incident in a string of harassments meant to drive the family out of town. Trevor's parents, Charles and Alice, received obscene phone calls and were shouted at from passing cars. Klan members held rallies in a vacant lot near their home. Charles assured the FBI he would be willing to testify in court, because cross burning without a permit is a federal offense, but the case was mysteriously dropped.

Townspeople spread the rumor that Charles was an ex-convict who had to settle for a black woman when he was unable to get a white wife. When the Nightingales dared to join an all-white square dancing group, they could not find three other couples willing to form a square with them. When traveling across the state, they were sometimes stopped by suspicious state troopers who asked them questions and checked their identifications.

At that time in York, many businesses illegally maintained separate white and black entrances. York is a small town twenty miles east of Gaffney, the location of Limestone College, the school that I first attended when I arrived in America in 1978.

York was the county seat and had a history of racial bigotry. The races simply did not mix on any level. The only other mixed couple in town could not stand the persecution and fled to nearby Charlotte, North Carolina.

"Believe it or not, my parents actually liked living in York," eighteen-year-old Trevor said in his deep voice, leaning back in his chair in the Ridgewood, New Jersey, home where he lived with friends of his parents. "My father just laughed at the threats. My parents could not believe people could be so backward and intolerant. My parents were Bahá'í pioneers, and felt they were setting a good example for racial harmony simply by being a mixed couple."

The Bahá'í Faith is an international religion that strives, through nonracial and nonviolent means, to create world unity and a peaceful society free of all forms of prejudice. It encourages interracial marriage, pointing to it as one of the basic steps toward racial harmony and integration.

"As Bahá'ís, we try to love everyone," Charles explained in a letter to Gail and me. "Even, at times, the unlovable—the so-called rednecks. As a couple these challenging experiences unified and strengthened us. Many fine people approved of what we were doing. We tried to show blacks that they must forgive, and to teach whites to overcome their inherent but false sense of superiority."

The couple has since moved to the Bahamas, where they run a Bahá'í peace council in Marsh Harbour on the island of Abaco, which was settled, ironically, by white South Carolinians.

Many defenders of the New South would argue that this cross-burning incident occurred seventeen years ago in a small, isolated town in rural South Carolina. Such things do not happen anymore, they would say. But how much has the South really changed?

The first few months after moving from New York to North Carolina, my senses were keenly on the lookout for the "New South." I behaved with the same tense wariness and suspicion as your average Northerner. When cashiers made eye contact with me, smiled, asked me whether I wanted paper or plastic bags, and told me to have a good day—I walked away bewildered by their congenial demeanor. Was it authentic or mere show?

Each time Gail visited me from New York, I watched people's eyes and tried to gauge their reactions to us. In the supermarket Gail would laugh and joke with me, touching my arm affectionately from time to time, talking rapidly about her week in Manhattan, completely oblivious to the eyes of strangers fixed on us. Sometimes I would send her to find an item I knew was on the other side of the store, just to separate us so people would stop gaping. It made me feel denuded. I didn't know what they were thinking or how they might react. Though I had lived in and traveled throughout the South, Southerners were still foreigners to me. I needed time to feel them out on the subject of interracial relationships.

Gail and I provoked the most attention when we exercised together at a local fitness center, perhaps because there is something erotic about straining, heavy breathing, and stretching and bending one's body. We went to the gym every other day. By the end of each hour-long workout both of us were usually drenched with sweat. I had nothing on but running shorts, a tank top and a towel draped around my neck. Gail usually wore a Lycra bodysuit and tights. As in most gyms, the walls and pillars were plastered with plate glass mirrors.

Each time I walked over to Gail to correct her technique on a particular Nautilus machine or give her encouragement, I saw, by glancing in the mirror, that nearly every eye in the gym was fastened on us. Some white men occasionally muttered under their breath. But as time went on and people saw us together often, most stopped staring.

Though we behaved normally in public, Gail and I were not reckless. We knew that many people were opposed to our union and that some of them were capable of showing their opposition in violent acts. We were aware of the vicious murders that took place in Salt Lake City on August 20, 1980, when two black men, eighteen and twenty, were gunned down near a city park by an avowed racist while they were jogging with two white girls. The murderer, Joseph Paul Franklin, publicly admitted to the killings in a television interview from prison.

"I'll say that it was just because they were race mixing," said Franklin, a former member of the Ku Klux Klan and American Nazi party. "Had they not been race mixing, you know, it would have been a totally different story." Though he claims to spend most of his time in his cell reading the Bible and praying, he said he did not regret the Utah slayings.

In 1986 Franklin received his fifth and sixth life sentences for killing an interracial couple in Madison, Wisconsin.

One day an old pickup truck pulled up alongside our Honda Accord as we were driving from High Point to Winston-Salem. Gail was sitting beside me in the passenger's seat. It is interesting to note that whenever she drove and for some reason I had to sit in the back, we encountered almost no stares: I was, perhaps, presumed to be her servant.

The truck kept pace with us, not attempting to pass, which made me turn to examine the driver. I saw a wild-haired, sunburned white man grinning down at the two of us from his bouncing rig. Suddenly the truck lunged ahead, swerved in front of us and slowed down abruptly. In a flash I saw the Confederate flag draped across the back window and the chained tailgate heading straight for us. I slammed on the brakes to avoid crashing into it. I stretched my arm across Gail to keep her head from sailing forward into the windshield. The man's laughing face loomed in his rattling rearview mirror.

"What does he think he's doing?" Gail cried.

"Don't ask," I said, switching lanes and dropping behind to create distance between us and the pickup.

"Did you see the way he leered at us? He looked like Mr. Hyde with that maniacal smirk on his face."

"Just forget about it," I said. "These people get their kicks out of harassing mixed couples. Don't get all flustered over it—that's exactly what he would want."

We drove on in silence, but I knew neither of us could simply forget the experience. We could not when there were other white men in North Carolina who felt the same way about us.

Many of the incidents that once disturbed us now make us laugh. When we were first married, Gail and I walked from our apartment to the nearest bank branch and said we would like to open a joint checking account.

"I'm sorry, that's not possible," said a well-dressed middle-aged white woman behind a large shiny brown desk, staring at us as if we were a pimp and a prostitute trying to set up a business account.

"Not possible?" Gail said. "Why not?"

"We can only open joint accounts for people who are related by blood or by marriage."

"But we *are* married," Gail said.

This news discomposed the bank officer a bit, for she shifted in her chair and shuffled through some papers on her desk. Finally she said, "Well, you have to have at least two hundred dollars to open a checking account."

I looked down at our clothes, which were casual but neat, and wondered what she took us for.

"Yes, we have that much," I said.

"I'll need some identification. Do you both have North Carolina driver's licenses?" the officer asked.

"I do," I replied, "but my wife hasn't yet exchanged her Minnesota license for a North Carolina license."

"Then I'm sorry, we can't open an account."

"Let's go," I whispered to Gail. I knew the woman had a problem dealing with us as normal human beings and I did not want to waste our time arguing with her. We went to another branch of the same bank and had no trouble at all opening an account. In fact, the officer at the second branch, a young white woman, said there was no rule that required a North Carolina driver's license to open an account.

Several humorous incidents involved my sisters Linah and Diana. Whenever Gail, my sisters, and I went out in public together, people automatically assumed that one of my sisters, not Gail, was my wife. This occurred quite often in crowds of elderly women who flocked about us after church services.

"So you must be Mark's wife," one woman said, clasping fourteen-year-old Linah's hand with both her own and grinning through her perfume and powder. "We're so happy to have you living in High Point."

"I'm Mark's sister," Linah said, glancing at Gail and trying to contain a fit of laughter.

But the woman was apparently hard of hearing, for she continued her speech, informing Linah that "you and your husband" would make wonderful new church members.

These incidents were not confined solely to the South. Whenever we traveled in the North we encountered similar obstacles.

When I traveled to Philadelphia during a book tour, Gail accompanied me and checked into the hotel room with our suitcases in the afternoon. Because I was the scheduled guest on an evening call-in talk show, I was unable to join her at the hotel until later that night. When I arrived at the reception desk, I identified myself and requested a key.

"I'm sorry, but someone named Mathabane has already checked into that room," a clean-cut white man, not long out of college, informed me.

"Yes, that was my wife," I replied.

The young man looked puzzled, then suspicious, and I knew he was wondering how a black man could be connected with the tall blond woman who had checked in hours earlier.

"May I see some identification?" he said.

I showed him my driver's license, which he examined carefully. He conferred in whispers with two other employees behind the desk, both young white women, then picked up the phone.

"Hello, Mrs. Mathabane?" he said. "There is a man here who claims he is Mr. Mathabane."

"Great. Send him up," Gail said.

"Well, you see, uh, there might be some mistake here and I wouldn't want to . . . I mean, just as a precaution, uh, could you describe your husband for me?"

"He's wearing gold wire-rim glasses and a suit, and he's black!"

"Oh, all right, ma'am, I'll send him right up."

The young man, with reddening cheeks, apologized profusely for the inconvenience and handed me the key without delay.

Once I reached our hotel room, Gail and I fell into each other's arms and laughed over the incident, but we also knew that we never would have experienced that insulting scene if she had been black or I white.

Gail, who had never been discriminated against because of the color of her skin, was getting her first taste of racism and it bedeviled her. I wished I could protect her from it, but I knew this was only the beginning of the trials she would have to confront for being married to a black man.

These trials of the white partners in interracial relationships, though just as frustrating and dehumanizing as those experienced by the black partners, are seldom acknowledged. Black critics of mixed couples especially fail to realize how much the white partner has to endure, has to sacrifice, to remain true to his or her beliefs.

When Gail and I moved to Kernersville in June 1988, it was a small, rural town twenty miles north of High Point. Sandwiched between Winston-Salem—home of RJ Reynolds Tobacco Company—and Greensboro—site of the first civil rights sit-in at F. W. Woolworth's downtown lunch counter—Kernersville had slowly evolved from a town of small tobacco farmers into a bedroom community for people who commuted to work in the larger surrounding cities.

Despite an influx of corporate Northerners into Kernersville's new housing developments, the town retains much of its provincial Southern feel. Barefoot children still play in the yards of large dilapidated farm houses along winding country roads; white-haired men with weathered faces and faded bib overalls still gather at Farmer's Feed and Seed to shoot the breeze in their drawling North Carolina dialect; flocks of blond children and their parents still crowd the Moravian and Methodist churches on Main Street every Sunday; loyal citizens read the biweekly *Kernersville News* cover to cover and keep up with the latest weddings, church picnics, and high-school sports scores; groups of shirtless young men still harvest the tobacco fields and hang the leaves to dry in fragrant bunches; old women in floppy hats and gardening gloves still prune their meticulously groomed flower beds at dawn; horses and goats graze peacefully in the pasture around the corner from our home.

"What is it like living in the South as a mixed couple?" Scott Ross, host of CBN's "Straight Talk" asked me on camera in his Virginia Beach television studio.

I explained, just as I did to all our Northern friends, that despite having to sometimes deal with remnants of the Old South, we liked the slow pace of Southern life; the friendly politeness of strangers;

the abundance of fresh air and trees; the low cost of living; the tranquility in which one can relax, read, think, and write; and the strong sense of community among neighbors indispensable to raising healthy children.

Many people, particularly Northerners, seem disappointed when we cannot relate harrowing stories of persecution at the hands of hooded Klansmen.

There have been times, though, when I have wondered just how tolerant people truly are in the South. One Sunday morning in 1990, two days before Christmas, I took a stroll alone. Dressed in a white jogging suit and a heavy winter coat, I went farther than usual, into a new housing development, absorbed in listening to poetry on my Walkman and admiring bare tree branches against a leaden sky. As people drove past me, dressed in their Sunday best and on the way to church, I would wave and cast them a neighborly smile.

I had walked nearly half an hour in the new development when a sheriff's patrol car suddenly pulled up beside me. The deputy, a large mustachioed man in a blue uniform, rolled down the window, and said, "You live around here?"

"No," I replied. "I live just beyond those trees." I pointed in the direction of our home about a quarter mile away.

The policeman stepped out of the car and hovered before me. "Three people have called the police station to report seeing a suspicious man," the policeman said. "You fit their description."

"Really?" I said, startled.

"May I see your ID please?"

"I don't have any with me," I said. "I usually don't carry an ID when I go for a walk in the neighborhood."

The officer continued looking at me, presumably baffled by the accent, the self-assertiveness. I saw the confusion in his face. I proceeded to explain who I was. There was only one South African black writer in Kernersville.

The officer, apparently recollecting my name (I had been featured several times in the local media), said in an apologetic tone, "Listen, I was only doing my job. I was told to come out here and find out who you are."

"I'm curious—who called?"

"There goes one of them right now," the officer said, nodding to a white man driving past who stared straight ahead. It was a man I had waved to and smiled at as I walked past his home.

I returned home, upset and shaken by what had happened.

"See what I mean about white stereotypes toward blacks?" I said to Gail. "Those three whites who reported me to the police thought of only one thing when they saw me: thief. They hardly gave me the benefit of the doubt. To them every strange black man in their neighborhood is simply a robber scouting their homes. This is what I mean when I say there's little difference between white attitudes in America and in South Africa.

"And to think that some of those whites saw me on their way to church!" I continued. "They presumably called about me from the church phone, just before singing all about loving one's neighbor and being followers of Christ's teachings. What hypocrisy. And, Sweets, it's two days before Christmas!"

After my anger subsided, I attempted to come up with other explanations for the incident. I always did this to avoid seeing racism behind every white man's wrong action against blacks. Homeowners, I reflected, are always worried about theft, about the safety of their homes and families. Strangers—regardless of race—walking through their neighborhoods are bound to raise suspicions.

I recalled that on two separate occasions I had seen strangers walking through our neighborhood—in one case a white teenager and in the other a young black man. I had felt an urge to notify the police immediately as part of the community watch program, but I did not. Instead I approached the young black man and spoke to him. He turned out to be an ambitious entrepreneur selling home cleaning products. But when a neighbor and I approached the white teenager, he panicked and fled. The police caught him as he headed for the highway. He turned out to have a police record for burglary.

There was an interesting twist to my encounter with the police. Three days after the incident a white man approached me in a department store and introduced himself as one of the people who had called the sheriff on me.

"I'd like to apologize," he said. "Someone broke into one of the houses in our neighborhood recently and I guess all of us are a little on edge. I didn't mean any harm. I hope you understand."

"I do," I said, shaking his proffered hand. The man ended by inviting me to visit his home.

GAIL'S VIEW

When Mark said he wanted us to move to the South, I thought he was deranged. The race riots I had witnessed in my junior high school in Texas remained indelibly in my mind, and I was as well versed as any Northerner about the Klan and its persecution of blacks and mixed couples. Under no circumstances could I see myself settling in the South.

"The South has changed, Gail," Mark said, trying to convince me to move with him to High Point. "When I was in North Carolina I saw more progress than up here. You won't believe some of the things I saw."

"Yeah, like Ku Klux Klan rallies full of Confederate flags, rednecks, and racial slurs."

"That's the stereotype," Mark said. "I went to North Carolina full of them, but many were dispelled. I felt more at home down there than up here."

"Of course you felt at home," I said. "It's probably just like South Africa. And who wants to have Jesse Helms for a senator?"

"Gail, you don't understand," Mark said. "You just have to see things for yourself. I'm not saying the South is a paradise. Far from it. There's still awful poverty, ignorance, and racism in many places. But I've finally realized that the North, with all its liberal professions, hardly practices what it preaches. Up here there's the kind of racism that leaves black people numb with rage and schizophrenia. In the South at least you know who your true friends are. In the North people smile in your face and then stab you in the back."

"But what about us?" I asked. "When I come down to visit you, I don't want people staring at us bug-eyed wherever we go. At least in New York City we just blend in with all the various shades of white, brown, and black."

Despite my opposition and the warning of friends that he was making a serious mistake, Mark moved to North Carolina. I remained in New York, where most of my family and friends lived.

For several months I coped with the stresses of a commuter relationship.

But with each visit to High Point my attitude toward the South changed. The greatest transformation was in how I felt physically; after only a few hours, I would shed all the tensions and anxieties I had accumulated by living in a crime-ridden section of Brooklyn.

Mark and I went for walks at night, sat on the balcony gazing at stars, often left the apartment door unlocked, breathed fresh air until it made me drowsy—things almost impossible to do in New York. These simple changes had a profound effect on my personality. I became aware how three years of a fast, hard, and competitive life in a big city had dulled my sensibilities and blinded me to two of the most important things in life: health and peace of mind.

I joined Mark in North Carolina following our wedding on Long Island. Once settled I became used to the relaxed pace of Southern life, found new interests and challenges, made new friends, and no longer missed New York.

I began noticing the different ways in which racism manifests itself in the North and South. During occasional visits to New York I could feel the racial tension in the air. The city's blacks and whites were becoming increasingly polarized with each racial incident: Howard Beach, Bensonhurst, Central Park, Teaneck.

Traveling by subway from the Upper West Side to Midtown during one visit, I found myself trapped in a tunnel during a race fight. A Hispanic woman had jostled her way into the crowded train at 116th Street, irritating many of the sardined passengers who had boarded in Harlem and were already drenched with sweat and gasping for air.

"Don't you be pushing me!" a young black woman shouted at the Hispanic woman as she entered.

"I din't push nobody," the woman replied.

"You lyin' spic!" the young black woman said, angrily pushing the Hispanic woman off the train.

The Hispanic woman fought back and managed to get aboard just as the graffitied doors slammed shut. "Stupid nigger," she muttered under her breath.

"Say what!"

As the train jolted into motion the fighting continued with threats and taunts and racial epithets, then came to blows. Trapped in the crowd, I was struck repeatedly by flailing elbows and fists but could not move out of the way.

Another young black woman, apparently in solidarity with her black sister, stood up on the bench and cried, "Here, use this!" then threw a closed switchblade over several heads to her friend.

Others followed suit. I looked up and saw a dozen knives flash open, waving in the air like bayonets over an army. I had never imagined so many people carried weapons on the subway.

"No knives! No knives please!" someone shouted.

Passengers panicked. Mechanical difficulties forced the train to grind to a halt in the tunnel, halfway between two stops. The lights went out and the fan stopped. The scuffling and screaming continued in the dark, airless cage, several feet below Manhattan's sidewalks. Hispanic passengers jumped into the fray, fighting with any black who shouted encouragement to the young black woman. The crowd shoved me about as I evaded blows.

As suddenly as they had gone out, the lights came back on and the train jerked into motion. When we reached the next station, the doors slid open and people practically stampeded over each other to get out of the train, away from the knives and fighting. I staggered onto the platform, breathless and shaking, then sprinted up the stairs onto the street.

I was thankful I had moved out of New York. But I did not yet feel at home in the South. Sitting in a High Point truck rental office one afternoon shortly after we were married, I waited for the secretary to process some forms so we could rent a moving truck to carry our belongings from one High Point apartment to another. Mark had come in briefly, then gone outside to wait in the car and finish listening to a library tape of Walt Whitman's "Leaves of Grass."

"Hey, did you know they got niggers up in Canada?" a male voice shouted to the secretary from a back room. "I didn't know they got that far north! I'll be damned. Niggers in Canada! Niggers everywhere! Ain't no place you can go these days to get away from 'em."

The secretary, who had seen Mark come in with me, flushed crimson. "Aw, shut up, you damn redneck!" she shouted toward the back room.

The man, who happened to be one of the mechanics, came to the door of the office and stared in disbelief at the secretary. He glanced around the room and, seeing no one but me and the secretary, no blacks, appeared more bewildered than before.

"Since when did you get to be such a nigger lover?"

"I ain't!" the secretary retorted.

"Then what the hell'd I do to bring on such a storm of fire? I was just tellin' you a bit of news I just got from readin' the papers."

"Well, you don't have to shout so everyone can hear ya," the secretary replied.

He eyed me carefully. Satisfied that I was thoroughly white and, therefore, not offended by his remarks, he walked away shaking his head in dismay at the secretary's impudence.

I took every opportunity to speak confidentially to older whites, born and bred in the South. I questioned them about race relations and hostilities that might be left unspoken.

"What do most white Southerners think of my being married to a black man?" I asked a middle-aged white woman who had spent most of her life in Kernersville.

"Oh, that's easy," she replied. "They think you're a whore."

Her blunt reply took me aback, and I marveled at her honesty. She went on to relate stories of her Southern upbringing, how she was taught to speak to blacks in a tone of authority, how some of the boys she had dated are now members of the Klan, how the Klan still holds meetings frequently in many North Carolina towns, which she named. "I'd be careful if I were you," she said with a meaningful look, then paused. "You know, I had to think twice after you invited me to come to your home for dinner. When I mentioned it at work, one of my coworkers said, 'You're not going, are you? She's married to a black man. You don't approve of race mixing, do you?' It threw me off a bit, made me remember all the things I was raised to believe. But I've always been somewhat of a rebel, so I decided to come."

This, too, surprised me, for I had no idea she considered she was doing me a favor by coming to my home and eating food I had prepared.

On another occasion I asked a balding but vigorous white man, raised in Virginia and the Carolinas, what Southerners thought of my marrying a black man.

"They pity you," he said without hesitation. "They feel sorry for you because a black man raped your mind and brainwashed you into marrying him, against all your best interests and every remnant of reason and good sense."

Eager to understand the source of such twisted attitudes in Southerners, the contradiction between their public smiles and private scorn, between the all-embracing Christian love they felt on Sunday mornings at church and their inherent belief in segregation and white superiority that still governed their daily lives, I read various books about the South, among them *Killers of the Dream* by Lillian Smith. In this thoughtful and well-written autobiographical work, I found answers to most of my questions about the explosive issues of race and sex in the South.

Born in Jasper, Florida, in 1897, at the end of a decade in which one thousand Negroes were lynched, Lillian Smith and her eight siblings were raised to believe in God, the Bible, democracy, and freedom, but were taught to stay away from colored children and shun the warm breast of their black mammy when they reached a certain age. Glowing memories of a pleasant Southern childhood spent in Florida and Georgia, well protected from the disturbing world of sex and race, are laced with bitterness toward the South for its hypocrisy and ignorance and provincialism and for teaching her to deny the humanity of blacks.

Just as white children were taught in South Africa, Smith was taught that her white skin was her glory and the source of her strength and pride. She was also told that white is a symbol of purity and excellence, that her white skin proves that she is better than all other races on this earth.

Her skin gave her certain "privileges," which she began to see as limitations to her freedom. It dictated which entrances she used, where she should sit and stand, what part of town she lived in, where she ate, which theaters she attended, which swimming pools she used, and whom she could love.

When Smith was just a child, her mother spotted a little white girl living in a shack in Colored Town. Believing that the child had been kidnapped by blacks, Smith's mother "rescued" the girl and raised the child in her own home. Smith and the little girl, who were about the same age, became best friends. Then one day Smith's mother received a letter from the colored adoption agency stating that the child did indeed have some Negro blood. The little girl was swiftly sent back to Colored Town, and Smith was never told why she was not allowed to see her best friend again.

The South has changed a great deal since Smith's childhood. But the attitudes she described still fester. One measure of how much they still exist in a particular area is the introduction of a mixed couple onto the scene.

On May 26, 1990, the *Greensboro News & Record* did just that. The paper published a color photograph of four teenagers: two girls—one black, one white—danced on a low wall beside a black boy in high-top sneakers and a baseball cap tenderly holding the hand of a white girl with long blond hair wearing an oversize T-shirt and bobby socks.

The photograph provoked a flood of angry letters, most of them from white readers. The debate raged for more than a month in the "Letters to the Editor" column.

"The picture entitled 'Dancing in the Park' . . . was embarrassing," one letter read. "Why did you allow staff photographer Joseph Rodriquez to choose such a distasteful, demoralizing, suggestive pose for the newspaper? I have heard many derogatory remarks from friends and out-of-state visitors regarding this picture. It was an awful picture and I'm disappointed in your newspaper."

Another letter began, "I was startled by the picture on the local front page. Why did you show a picture such as this? This promotes race mixing and shows what kind of paper you print. I have talked to several people in my area and they, too, were very upset. This kind of media coverage is not appreciated by the general public. I think there should be an apology."

A third read, "I'm sure you've managed to fan the flame of racial hate with the photo of 'Dancing in the Park.' What's next, photos of burning crosses? Very poor judgment."

A few letters, in response to the above three, argued that the photograph portrayed racial harmony and urged Greensboro residents to be more tolerant toward mixed couples. These letters were all penned by women, perhaps because women are more likely than men to accept love in whatever form it takes, even black-white.

One insightful response came from a woman who wrote: "I've

been living in the South for 13 of my 28 years and during none of those 13 years have I seen any progress in the fight against racism in this area. I am constantly embarrassed by the racist attitudes of those whom I otherwise consider to be good, decent, moral, loving people. The saddest testimony of all is my willingness to tolerate this racist attitude in my friends, because after 13 years I realize I might very well be friendless if I didn't."

"Disillusioned people such as the reader who opposed 'race mixing' need to re-examine their own moral values and decide if what they believe is truly right," wrote a black female high-school student. "I find it distasteful and demoralizing that such attitudes continue to exist. Instead of seeing a group of young people having fun, they chose to view the scene in their own twisted way."

A white Southerner in Siler City, a rural community thirty miles southeast of Greensboro, rebutted this and other conciliatory letters. "Interracial marriages are unbiblical and immoral," he wrote. "God created different races of people and placed them amongst themselves. To abolish racial separatism and promote interracial marriages is to do away with God's workings. . . . If mixed marriages are necessary for racial harmony, count me out. I will not sing or dance to that tune. There is nothing for white Americans to gain by mixing their blood with blood of other peoples. There will only be an irreversible damage for us." The letter sounded as if it had been written by an Afrikaner in support of apartheid.

Mark and I have often wondered if we are partly protected from many of these hidden, hostile attitudes because we recently moved to the South from New York and, therefore, don't "know any better" or because Mark is a black South African and is thus not regarded with the same unjustified contempt as the descendants of slaves or because Mark is friends with Stan Smith and Oprah Winfrey and has written two bestsellers.

To find out whether white Southerners did indeed treat us differently from other mixed couples, I proposed to write an article on interracial couples in North Carolina for *Winston-Salem Magazine*. The idea was readily accepted by the magazine's editor, Mary Rearden, and I began my research.

What I discovered startled me: Mixed couples were hard to locate. Of the handful I found, most refused to be interviewed. Others agreed to be interviewed but wanted to remain anonymous for various reasons: fear of losing their jobs, fear of losing respect, fear of disappointing members of their family who do not yet know about the relationship, and even fear of losing their lives. One white guidance counselor at a Forsyth County high school spoke of death threats from his black girlfriend's former black boyfriend.

There were courageous exceptions. When Madelyn Ashley, a white clinical nurse specialist who works at Bowman Gray School of Medicine in Winston-Salem, married her husband Richard, a black graphic artist, she was hesitant to tell her boss.

"I didn't want to hide anything, yet I wondered how my boss would react. I didn't really fear losing my job. Richard was more important to me than my job. I don't tell my patients that my husband is black. When they make racist remarks I have to bite my tongue and change the subject. I don't understand racists. My grandmother encouraged me to be a nurse but told me, 'You don't want to take care of Negroes. They have a special disease, you'll catch it if you touch them.' But I don't care what others say or think. I'm proud of Richard. I get angry at myself for feeling the need to hide him from some people."

When Madelyn finally told her boss, he reacted not only with congratulations but he drove all the way to Chapel Hill to attend the wedding. But Madelyn was one of the lucky few. Most of the mixed couples I interviewed for the article lived in fear that their superiors at work would discover that they had fallen in love across racial lines and fire them. Thus loving human relationships are transformed into "dirty little secrets."

Jane, a slim young woman with blue eyes and waist-length blond hair, applied for a job as an exercise instructor for the elderly at an exclusive North Carolina country club. During the interview, the employer quizzed Jane on her private life, and even asked who her boyfriend was and where he worked. Her black boyfriend, Hal, is a member of the top forty band called The Society. She was not offered the job.

"To this day I wonder if I didn't get the job because Hal is black," Jane said. "All they had to do was find out that The Society is a black band."

Paula, a black teacher who is in love with a white man named

Rudy, feels uncomfortable going out in public in Winston-Salem where she may run into coworkers or people from the black community who know her, out of fear that word may get back to a former black boyfriend who has threatened Rudy's life. They began dating in 1986 and broke up for a year because of the enormous pressure Paula was feeling. During the breakup Paula nearly married a black doctor, but returned to Rudy instead.

"I'm still very aware that Rudy's white, but I thought that in time I'd get over it," Paula said. "It's getting better. I'm not as afraid to go out with him as I used to be. But I've gotten criticism from black males. They say, 'There are a lot of black guys out there who are dying to be with you. Why do you stay with that white guy?' I explain that I'm with Rudy not because he's white but because he's a really nice guy. They just can't accept that as a reason."

I met another mixed couple, whom we'll call "Nat" and "Kate," at the Dixie Classic Fair who let me interview them only if I kept their names secret. Neither of them took off their dark sunglasses throughout the interview. Kate, who is white, is afraid her parents in New Jersey will somehow find out about the relationship.

"Nat visits me a lot," Kate said over the din of screaming children and game vendors shouting for customers. "He once answered the phone when my mother called. She asked, 'Who was that?' I told her it was a neighbor who didn't have cable who came over to watch a ball game. A lot of excuses have been made. A lot. I hate lying to my parents but my mother would go nuts if she knew. When I was one year old my parents bought me a black baby doll so I wouldn't be prejudiced against black people. But as far as dating and marriage go, I'm sure that's out of the question. I don't want to hurt them, and what they don't know can't hurt them."

Nat, who had been shooting baskets in an attempt to win a huge fluorescent stuffed animal for Kate, joined our conversation.

"I just wish everyone would accept us," Nat said. "My family knows we're dating, but as long as I'm happy they're happy. They used to think one-dimensionally, you know, blacks gotta be with blacks and whites gotta be with whites. But once they got over the initial shock that I was dating a white woman, they accepted it. The people I work with feel the same way I do: It doesn't matter if the person you love is black or white or tan or purple. My friends accept it because I pick friends who aren't prejudiced. They wouldn't be my friends if they didn't accept it."

Many interracial relationships in the South don't survive the pressure exerted on them by society. Both Nat and Richard had previously had relationships with white women that failed.

"They just don't want to take it," Nat said. "The relationship usually ends mutually. I don't know which side gives in faster, black or white. They're just not willing to make the effort to make it work."

"It takes a very strong-willed, independent person to be part of a mixed couple," Richard told me. "One has to be confident in one's self and one's feelings. You have to have the firm conviction that what you are doing is right and that anything against that is 'their' problem. I don't think a lot of people have the individual strength it requires to be part of a mixed couple. To be an individual in America is very difficult."

My completed article appeared in the January/February 1990 issue of *Winston-Salem Magazine* beside a large black-and-white photograph of Mark, Bianca, and I under the heading "Color-Blind Love." The phone at the magazine started ringing off the hook, and letters came pouring in.

"We find this sort of thing disgraceful," one caller told my editor. She introduced herself as a representative of a group of thirteen female senior citizens who were upset by the article. "And that photograph—why, it looks like an advertisement for that sort of thing! Just what exactly are you trying to promote?"

My editor, Mary Rearden, was asked why she printed an article by someone as "brazen" as I, was grilled about my credentials as a writer, and was told she lacked good judgment in running the piece.

"Don't you read the Bible?" another caller asked Mary. "It states right there in the good book that God doesn't want any race mixing."

"Who's your publisher? Is he from South Africa?" another asked.

"No, he's Italian," Mary replied.

"Oh, I guess he *would* be a foreigner."

From call to call Mary held firm and, after the controversy had blown over, told me she was glad she had run the piece and shaken the dust off some old beliefs. She even had long conversations with some of the callers, listening patiently to their arguments and then refuting them point by point.

For my part, I received numerous letters from the sisters, mothers, and friends of mixed couples as well as some from mixed couples themselves thanking me for writing the article. Those letters in themselves were enough to negate all the ridiculous criticism the article provoked and convinced me that we mixed couples, if we ever want to be fully understood, accepted, and respected by society, have to be willing to tell our human stories in order to combat stereotypes about us; we have to speak out against bigotry, black and white, wherever we may live.

10

IN THE LIMELIGHT: AM I BETRAYING MY RACE?

MARK'S VIEW

I have written at some length about external events that happened to Gail and me, but much more occurs internally, inside each partner in a mixed couple as they adjust to life together. At first, once I entered the limelight, I had difficulty reconciling the private life I shared with Gail with my public persona as a writer increasingly considered by people as a spokesperson for the anti-apartheid struggle.

This conflict reached a peak following my family's August 27, 1987, appearance on the "Oprah Winfrey Show." A few weeks after the show aired nationwide, *Kaffir Boy* reached number three on *The New York Times* bestseller list and number one on the *Washington Post* list. Suddenly I was catapulted into the limelight. People felt justified in intruding on my private life. They expected me to behave in a certain way and say things that confirmed their perceptions of me as some sort of black leader. I have never claimed to be such a person. Everything I have written and said on the issues of apartheid and racial justice have been at the prompting of my conscience.

Scores of letters began arriving at my High Point apartment each week from readers across the country. Dozens of other readers wanted more immediate contact than letter writing afforded, so they started calling at any hour of the day or night, often bubbling with emotion.

I was deeply touched by this show of support. It strengthened my belief that when political issues are presented to the American people in human terms, many of them really do care and seek to do something. At first I responded to each caller, sometimes spending hours speaking to total strangers about my life, the situation in South Africa, the importance of education to young blacks, and how concerned Americans could help the struggle against apartheid by sending books and educational supplies to South African ghettos.

But soon the calls became too many and disrupted my family life and writing schedule. I was in the process of writing *Kaffir Boy in America* and was facing a deadline. Gail offered to start screening the calls. Most came from black women desperate to speak to me.

"Is this where Mark Mathabane lives?" one young woman asked Gail one afternoon.

"Yes, it is," Gail replied.

"*Oh, my God! Really?* Is he home? I've just *got* to speak to him. I just finished reading *Kaffir Boy*. I couldn't put it down. I feel like I know him."

"He's not here right now," Gail said.

The caller was deeply disappointed. "I saw him on Oprah's show and ran right down to the store to buy his book." She talked excitedly about *Kaffir Boy* for several minutes, then said, "Who's this? His secretary?"

"No, his wife."

"*Wife?*" the caller exclaimed. "I didn't know he was *married!*" After a short silence, in which she was apparently recovering from her shock, she said, "Well, you sure are one lucky woman."

Many of the calls ran along these lines, and it was hard to tell whether Gail was flattered or annoyed by them. The most bothersome calls were the ones that interrupted our sleep at about two or three in the morning. Some came from women who had met me briefly at a lecture, whose names and faces I could not recall, and who attempted to get me on the phone by telling Gail they were good friends of mine or had recently visited Alexandra and had important information regarding my family.

It soon became clear that in the minds of many readers of *Kaffir Boy* I remained an eighteen-year-old black rebel, a survivor, just as they had left me on the last page of the book. Part of my appeal, I believed, was that many female fans assumed I was still single. I knew the appeal would fade when they learned I was married and might eventually turn to disappointment and even scorn when they learned I had fallen in love with and married a white woman.

Some black male friends who knew of my relationship with Gail and were eager to see my career as a writer blossom, bluntly told me that my credibility as a black spokesperson would be seriously undermined if it were known that I was married to a white woman.

"The careers of many black leaders have been ruined by such relationships," a black friend said one afternoon.

"But I'm not a leader," I responded. "And Gail is my wife. I married her because I love her. Surely people will understand that."

"Not in America," my friend said. "Especially not in the black community. Your relationship with Gail, especially given what you and other black South Africans have suffered under apartheid at the hands of whites, will be seen as the ultimate betrayal of your blackness. I know the origin of your relationship with Gail, but many people don't. They'll simply conclude that you're another black man who, on becoming successful, marries white."

"But Gail fell in love with me when I was dirt poor, unknown, and repeatedly rejected by all the compatible black women with whom I sought to have serious relationships." My friend knew of the rejections. "Don't I have a right to wonder what is now so attractive about me—my success or my own person? I think it would be foolish to abandon, in the name of racial solidarity, friends who stood by my side during hard times."

"I understand and sympathize with your position," my friend said. "But I'm advising you as a friend, as someone who knows the black community. Gail will prove a liability."

Unsure how to take my friend's advice, I decided to play it safe until I could reconcile the demands of my private and public life. At times I subtly discouraged Gail from attending my lectures, especially before black audiences. Whenever she was present, I asked her to sit in the back of the auditorium and be as inconspicuous as possible. Aware of my confusion about how to best present our relationship to the public, and not wanting to make me or herself uncomfortable, she complied.

When she showed up at a lecture at Randolph-Macon College in

Virginia, attended by a predominantly black audience, I was angry with her, though I had invited her. She was the only white at the table of black students who treated me to dinner after the lecture. Their faces did not conceal their shock on hearing me introduce her as my wife. There were awkward silences, gaps in the conversation, and I could tell many of the students were offended and wondered how she could possibly relate to the issues of race they were discussing.

Our drive from Virginia to North Carolina was miserable. I was defensive of my base actions all the way home. I insincerely accused Gail of a gross lack of knowledge of African-American history, of an inability to truly understand what it is like to be discriminated against all your life just because of the color of your skin. I told her that I still had doubts whether it was right for me to marry a white woman, given the black community's expectations of me. Aware that such remarks wounded Gail deeply, and ashamed of my actions, I tearfully apologized to her. But the tug of war between my public and private life continued.

Sensing that she was the reason behind my strange shifts in moods, Gail started voluntarily staying away from my lectures, even if I were speaking right in High Point. When I was asked to speak in support of High Point's black library, which the city was threatening to close in order to build a new library in a predominantly white section of town, part of me wanted her to be there.

"Would you like to come?" I asked as I straightened my tie.

"I'd like to, but I'm not going to," Gail said.

There was a strained silence. I felt torn. She was, after all, my wife. I knew she enjoyed attending my lectures.

"You can come if you want," I said.

"I'd probably be the only white person there," she said. "They'd resent me. They'd resent you. Not everyone in High Point knows about me yet. I don't want to turn the black community against you."

I went to the lecture alone. My speech was well received and many people flocked around me afterward to compliment me on my book and ask what they could do to help blacks in South Africa, but as I signed autographs and answered questions I could not help wondering how different my reception would have been had Gail been there. Would it really have mattered?

My public image kept growing. In different American cities, large and small, complete strangers, black and white, would accost me, with amazement in their eyes, and say, "Hey, didn't I see you on the 'Oprah Winfrey Show'?" They stopped me in airports, grocery store aisles, on the street when I was jogging, at check-out counters, in the post office, in the library. On a visit to Manhattan, Gail and I were stopped half a dozen times as we made our way down Fifth Avenue.

"Hey, look! It's Kaffir Boy!" some would shout.

It startled me to hear those words, for I had not been called a "kaffir"—the equivalent of the American word *nigger*—since I was in South Africa.

Whenever strangers engaged me in a conversation, Gail would often walk ahead several paces and wait for me, inconspicuously. She did it voluntarily, believing that her presence would detract from my popularity. I hated this dual, secretive life and vowed to put an end to it, one way or another.

It was not until 1989, with the publication of my second book *Kaffir Boy in America,* that I finally proudly made my marriage to Gail public knowledge. I insisted that my publisher, Scribners, include in the photo section several pictures of Gail and me, including our wedding photo. I devoted one chapter of the book to the essentials of our relationship. The back flap of the book mentioned that our first child, Bianca, had just been born.

Again friends warned me that the book would never sell, that people who otherwise eagerly wanted to read about what had happened to me since coming to America would be instantly turned off by the sight of the photos.

"There's no reason you should include those controversial photos," someone said. "Let people buy the book and find out about Gail upon reading it."

"My love for Gail is more important than the success of the book," I said. "Those readers who won't buy the book just because of Gail are probably identifying with me for the wrong reasons."

In June I appeared with Stan Smith on Oprah's prime-time special "Just Between Friends," which was broadcast nationally. Again, rather than have Gail stashed away during the taping, she was there beside me and my siblings, cradling Bianca in her arms. The issue of my marriage inevitably came up.

In one scene Oprah lay on her bed, having one of her regular marathon long-distance phone conversations with her own best friend, Gayle King Bumpus. They were discussing me.

"Mark married a white woman, you know," Oprah said.

"Oh, really?" Gayle replied.

As Gail and I watched the program, I was sure Oprah's friend was not the only black woman to express surprise at hearing Oprah's words. In fact, I felt that many black women across the country reacted with far more than a mere one-line exclamation: Many reacted with shock, disappointment, and outrage.

I had a confirmation of that when I began a nationwide publicity tour for the book shortly after the special aired. During an appearance on a talk show on one of New York City's popular radio stations, the interviewer, a young radical black man very much into Afrocentricity, surprised me by how he led the program. He didn't explain *Kaffir Boy in America* nor ask me what it was all about. He simply introduced me and then opened the phone lines. Angry calls from black women poured in. I suspected a setup. I had half a mind to walk out but decided to stay and state my case, without apology.

"How dare you marry a white girl?" someone said.

I asked the caller if she knew what sort of person Gail was. She didn't. But that didn't matter, she said, the fact that Gail was white was enough to make her an "enemy." I told the caller that all whites were not my enemies and that I judged them as individuals. Failure to do so, I added, was not only wrong, it was racist. It made it easy for white racists to rally whites behind their pernicious agendas in the name of us against them.

"Your marriage to a white woman is an insult to your mother and every black woman in this country," another caller said.

I responded that the last person to blindly hate whites or anybody because of the color of their skin was my mother. She valued her soul too much to harbor hatred in her heart.

My forthright answers surprised many. But I was fed up with playing games with my emotions, with hurting a woman whose love of me was unqualified, with apologizing for a friendship that was above reproach and that people had no business prying into. Just as I had opposed tribally arranged marriages in South Africa, I opposed racially arranged marriages in America. I could never live with myself knowing that I had married someone not because I loved that person, but because society approved of the match and it was the politically correct thing to do.

The next day I was to appear on the "Today Show." I awoke early that morning in a New York hotel room to find Gail fast asleep beside me, her head resting on my shoulder. Bianca slumbered in the crib next to our bed, a five-month-old bundle nestled in a soft pink blanket. I slipped silently out of bed, showered quickly, and dressed in a dark blue suit.

Watching my two darlings asleep, I wondered if I would, once again, have to defend my love for them, this time on national television.

I kissed both gently and left the hotel room. The cab pulled up in front of NBC and I got out. The studio was brightly lit and buzzing with activity. I was taken to the powder room and received facial makeup. From there I returned to the greenroom and waited, reading the morning papers and watching other guests grab a hurried breakfast of doughnuts and coffee. I was informed that my interview had been shifted to the next segment.

This is the "Today Show," I thought, the number one morning program in America. How will this important interview go?

Finally I was led on stage. Bryant Gumbel and Jane Pauley greeted me cordially. During a commercial break I was miked and Bryant took a seat beside me and we chatted. The cue came on that all was ready. Bryant's questions came in rapid succession, for we only had a few minutes. I answered them clearly and succinctly.

"What expectations did you have of America before you arrived?"

"What parallels do you see between the lives of black South Africans and American blacks?"

"Your parents and other family members are still in South Africa. Has their situation improved at all?"

The interview ended without Bryant once alluding to my marriage to Gail. He had stuck to the issues raised in the book. I shook hands with him warmly. He had won my respect for his sensitivity and professionalism. Off camera he did ask me, with an unassuming air of friendly curiosity, how Gail was doing and what it was like to be a new father.

* * *

One afternoon in the fall of 1989 I received a small package post-marked Jamaica, Queens. Its contents jolted me. They consisted of a gruesome photograph of a lynched black man dangling, bloodied and beaten, from a tree limb. His neck was broken, his legs and arms contorted. On the back someone had scrawled, "This is what happens to *traitors* of the black race!!!"

The photo and note horrified and frightened Gail. My editor at Scribner's, Ned Chase, suggested I contact the police for protection, but I decided against it. I refused to be intimidated.

Yet it pained me to think that there were blacks in America who used the same tactics that the Ku Klux Klan used to intimidate, harass, and deprive blacks with whom they disagreed of their civil and human rights. To me both attitudes were racist and to be condemned.

More evidence of black prejudice came in letters. A woman from Plano, Texas, wrote that she enjoyed reading my second book until she noticed it contained photographs. When she saw the wedding pictures, she immediately stopped reading.

"Seeing you married to a white woman was shocking," she wrote. "The problem I have with you and others of your kind is that in talking Black and sleeping White, you betray your audience."

Someone sent me an article that appeared in *The Black American* that was supposedly a reprint of a speech made by South African President P. W. Botha to his cabinet. The following paragraph was underlined:

> Our Combat Unit is now training special White girls in the use of slow-poisoning drugs. Ours is not a war that we can use the atomic bomb to destroy the Blacks, so we must use our intelligence to effect this. The person-to-person encounter can be very effective. As the records show that the Black man is dying to go to bed with the White woman, here is our unique opportunity. Our Sex Mercenary Squad should go out and camouflage with Apartheid Fighters while doing their operations quietly, administering slow-killing poison and fertility destroyers to those Blacks they thus befriend. We have received a new supply of prostitutes from Europe and America who are desperate and too keen to take up the appointments.

No letter accompanied this unbelievable article. I assume the sender probably thought he or she was doing me a favor by warning me that Gail was a spy hired by the white South African regime to kill me or weaken my resolve in the fight against apartheid.

Not every black woman who read *Kaffir Boy in America* responded this way. Some wrote me and said that after initially being angered and embittered at learning that I had married a white woman, they later, after their visceral reactions had subsided, found it in themselves to accept us and respect our feelings for each other.

Dothula Baron-Butler, a black writer in Richmond, Virginia, who raised her two teenage sons alone, wrote to tell me about the evolution of her feelings toward my mixed marriage. "I understand the criticism and ridicule you may have received for marrying a white woman," she wrote. "I must admit that when I first heard the news, I felt like many others—that you had been tempted by the 'forbidden fruit.' But after reading your book [*Kaffir Boy in America*], I understand. You and Gail are truly soul mates. It just so happens that one of you is white; the other black. True love knows no color."

11

FOR BLACK WOMEN, THE PAIN RUNS DEEP

GAIL'S VIEW

When Mark and I first married, I knew nothing about the shortage of available black men or the pain my love for and commitment to Mark might cause some black women. I thought the most vehement opposition to our relationship would come from whites. Once I convinced my family that I was doing the right thing by marrying Mark, I believed I had overcome the greatest hurdle I'd ever have to face. Having been warmly and lovingly received by Mark's family, I assumed the African-American community, too, would see and judge me as an individual.

It was not until I accompanied Mark on a publicity trip to Philadelphia that I realized that I—an individual—was regarded as "the white woman" who stole a black man. I was made to feel that I had committed some sort of unspoken crime against the black community, particularly against black women, by marrying Mark. I felt it as soon as I followed Mark into an all-black radio station. The faces I saw did not greet me with smiles but stared at me coldly, with an air of revulsion. Mark must have sensed it too, for he quickly went into the sound booth with the radio technicians without a word or glance in my direction.

The term *militant black* took on a threatening new meaning for me. For the first time I felt like an intruder, an enemy, who had wandered into hostile territory, surrounded on all sides by people who hated the color of my skin and all it represented. No one spoke to me, not even to tell me where I might sit down and wait. I found an empty conference room in the back, cluttered with dusty equipment and stacks of paper, and collapsed in an ancient overstuffed armchair. The minutes crawled by like hours. I longed to be black, if only to save myself from such torment.

Later that day, while Mark was doing another interview at the student radio station at the University of Pennsylvania, I crossed the street and entered a campus bookstore to kill time. My interest in the 1960s led me to pick up a thick book of black-and-white photographs and thumb slowly through it, studying pictures of hippies, yippies, political activists, and riots. Paging through a section on civil rights, the image of an angry, defiant black woman caught my eye. Reading the caption, I realized what had provoked her anger: Black men were "turning against" their black sisters, "abandoning the struggle," and "betraying their race" by sleeping with white women. I imagined the furious black woman leaping from the pages of the book and shaking her fist in my face. "You honky bitch! You slut! White trash!" I could almost hear her shout. "Why don't you leave that black man alone? Mark is one of US. He should belong to a BLACK woman! You stole him! You had no right!"

I slammed the book shut, shoved it into the row of books lining the shelf, and hurried back to the radio station, shaken and bewildered. I was so upset I could barely articulate my revelation to Mark. When I finally did, he seemed surprised.

"Didn't you know?" Mark asked. "Of course black women are going to be upset at you, at us. I know it's unfair. But we just have to get used to it. Maybe someday, when they get to know you as an individual, they'll think differently about us."

Knowing that I was loathed by black women made me feel miserable. Since my days as a minority white student at Pearce Junior High in Austin, Texas, I had admired black women. At Pearce, where I felt insecure and lost, I envied the black girls for their strength, confidence, toughness. They had the courage to challenge teachers, make demands, and speak their minds. I envied them for their hair, which looked different every day: cornrows, Afros, pony tails, braids, all knotted up with colorful beads and transparent colored balls.

I watched in awe and admiration as they danced down the long tables in the cafeteria, where a jukebox belted out Motown tunes in the corner. They made up the cheerleading squad, the basketball team, the track team. They were full of life and laughter, while I, on the other hand, felt stifled by the puritan streak that deprives so many whites of their vibrancy and emotion, riddling them instead with guilt complexes that make them go through life perpetually in need of shrinks.

When I got to Columbia Journalism School I was sent, along with most of my classmates, into rough New York neighborhoods, often alone, to cover story topics ranging from teenage pregnancy to prostitution and drug addiction. While reporting in such neighborhoods I met some incredibly strong women—all of them black and determined to survive in a cruel, unpredictable world of violence, poverty, and desperation.

One night in a lower Manhattan twenty-four-hour court of arraignments, notoriously known as "night court," I sat on a hard, wooden bench under buzzing fluorescent lights watching a long line of defendants, practically all of them young black men, stand before a white judge one at a time, with anger in their eyes and their knitted caps balled up in clenched fists.

Suddenly the young black woman beside me, who appeared about eight months pregnant and with whom I had briefly spoken during a break, burst into tears. I knew she was there to see her boyfriend appear before the judge. Instinctively I slid down the bench and put my arm around her, trying to comfort her. Hot tears rolled down her cheeks.

"He got six months," she murmured, trying to catch her breath. "He won't be with me when our baby is born. He din't have to do it. I tole him I got money. But he be too proud. He say he won't take none of my money, that I'm his woman and that it ain't right to take money from your woman. Ain't that just like a man to be so stubborn?" She looked up at me inquiringly, her large, wet brown eyes gazing directly into mine.

"Just like a man," I replied.

"Jostling," she muttered. "What the hell's that? That's what they charged him with. Jostling. I swear they come up with the strangest charges, then they never explain what they's meanin'. I could do a better job than that judge. He don't know what he's doing. You got to look them in the eyes. It's the eyes that let you know. My boyfriend din't mean nobody no harm. But murderers go free and he gets six months."

Her anger seemed to dry her tears, and a look of determination came into her eyes. It was about three in the morning when she and I left the court building and headed for the uptown subway. As the train rumbled and raced through Manhattan, she talked openly and quickly about her life in Harlem, her excitement over her coming child, and her boyfriend. The farther we got from night court, the more confident she became.

"I din't need him anyway," she said. "He was a pushover. He was always in my face. I guess it's better like this. I can handle my life on my own, you know. Men just get in the way, always gettin' in trouble. And it ain't like I'll be alone. It'll be me and my baby from now on. We'll be out there together, takin' on the world." She looked at me curiously. "You Pisces?"

Her sudden question took me aback, but I replied, "Yes; I'm a Pisces."

"Yeah, I knew it," she said. "So am I. I could tell 'cause you understand. You know what I'm tellin' you."

I had to get off at Ninety-sixth Street to change for the Broadway local bound for Columbia. She remained on the train, bound for the darkest reaches of Harlem. As the train pulled out of the station, I saw her wave. I realized then that we didn't even know each other's names, yet she had left an enduring impression on my mind: an impression of fortitude, determination, and strength in the face of utter despair and hopelessness. Again I wished I had some of the strength of a black woman like that.

I thought of Mark's sister Florah, who is only one month older than I, and how readily we had become close friends and confidantes during the summer of 1987. I particularly remembered her grit when we found out she had the early stages of cervical cancer. "Don't worry, Sweets, it's nothing. I'll pull through," she had said. And pull through she did.

I realized in that bookstore in Philadelphia, with a sinking heart, that it was going to be far more difficult to make friends with

African-American women than I had anticipated. The twisted history of America's race relations, the legacies of slavery and Jim Crow, made them see me as the enemy. By marrying a black man I had stepped over the line, I was suspect. And the fact that Mark was in the public eye, a powerful writer and friend of Oprah Winfrey, only seemed to exacerbate their resentment of me, "the white woman."

Over the years I have come to understand why my marriage to Mark has so deeply wounded, disappointed, and angered many black women. I read the grim statistics about the rising death rate of young black males, but I did not make a connection between them and my marriage to Mark until I was confronted by the anger of black women. Their anger reached me through anonymous hate letters to Mark, through the questions they asked Mark during call-in radio shows, through phone calls made directly to me. I opened my eyes, I listened, I struggled to understand their feelings.

One of these women was a Greensboro professional in her thirties, whom I'll call Sylvia. After years of striving in vain to find an eligible black man, Sylvia chose to remain single rather than accept dinner invitations from white men who showed a strong interest in her. Having grown up black in a small town in eastern North Carolina, and acutely aware of enduring taboos about interracial relationships, she grew irate when a white man asked her to dinner.

"I was *so* mad at him," Sylvia said. "The nicer he was, the madder I became. I didn't go to dinner with him. I thought he really wanted sex, and my mind went back to slavery days. Few white men back then married their black mistresses. They just wanted casual sex and often took it by force, as if it were their right. I felt safe conversing with him on the phone, but if I saw him I'd get mad. He had blond hair, which made it worse.

"I was raised in the Deep South, where racism is ingrained into just about everybody, black and white," she said. "I grew up in a county that is reputed to have the highest number of KKK members in North Carolina. You had your place. You could live only in certain areas. I believed in 'separate but equal.' It didn't matter to me that in school we got used books from the white schools.

"When I was coming up, everyone made sure I knew to avoid white men. We were told the white man was no good in bed anyway, that he had no penis. 'A white man's penis is as pitiful as his thin lips,' a friend once told me. 'His hair smells like a wet dog.' I heard all kinds of things like that when I was growing up."

Sylvia came to a book signing at a High Point bookstore one afternoon and, while Mark was talking to fans and signing autographs on the title page of *Kaffir Boy in America*, she walked up to me, asked if I were Gail, and introduced herself. She talked rapidly, as if eager to express myriad ideas at once. Several weeks later Sylvia called me and we had a long phone conversation. She told me what it felt like to find out I was white.

"I knew Mark was married, but I didn't know you were white," she said. "I found out when I read an article in the *Greensboro News & Record*. For a while I was just stark raving mad. That was my first natural reaction. And I have to tell you, a lot of other black women I know felt the same way. I don't know if it's good for me to be this incredibly honest, but there it is. I have to get it out. I was torn. Especially since Mark is successful. The more successful the black man, the greater the resentment among black women. My friends and I were extremely stunned when we found out you were white, then it passed. We shrugged, shook our heads, and said, 'He's just another black man with a white woman.'

"I still go through struggles when I see a black man with a white woman," she continued in her urgent, rapid style of speech. "There are over a million more black women in the United States than black men, and a lot of those black men are in prison or living on the streets. My attitude is based on statistics. It may also be the 'forbidden fruit' syndrome: that the black man wants a 'better' woman."

"Do you still hate me?" I asked.

"Not really. You see, I assumed, at first, that you were a Southern belle. But when I found out you were a universal person, that you'd traveled, that you were worldly and probably open-minded, then I was able to understand a little better. But it still hurts."

"In what way?"

"In *every* way. Slavery-time notions are still *so* deep. In Bensonhurst a black teenager was killed just because some white guy thought he was going to see a white girl. Hey, he was just looking for a used car! In America, people, both black and white, can't stand to see a member of their race cross the color line. Those feelings don't die. They just don't. Some ideas in the South are as old as *Gone With the Wind*. People still hang up their Confederate flags, which to me is a symbol of slavery. Those attitudes are classic, just like the film."

"So, are you saying that you still feel blacks and whites shouldn't be together?" I asked.

"You know, there's an interesting twist here," Sylvia said. "In a way, black men and white women naturally belong together. They've never really had any power. They've both served the white man, either as slaves, domestic servants, or duty-bound wives with no legal rights. And, in a way, black women and white men belong together. They are both dominant and strong. Black women had to be incredibly strong during slavery. Their husbands and children were auctioned off and they had to work hard in the fields to survive. They were poor but they still had power, pride, and dignity."

"So you still wouldn't date a white man?" I asked.

"Right now I just couldn't. But maybe I will in the future. For now I'll keep looking for that special black man."

One year later, Sylvia began dating a white man—a divorced professional. It was not an easy decision for her to make, but she had grown tired of waiting.

"I'm still going through what I call a metamorphosis stage," she said. "I feel like a hypocrite—but it was just a matter of numbers. I'm doing this because there are more available white men and I wanted to expand my options. It's *so* hard to find eligible black men, and the competition for them is unreal."

When she and her white friend go out in public, Sylvia can feel the disapproving stares, especially from black men, but she sees it as just one of the many pressures of being black in America.

Sylvia was not the only black woman to express her strong, and rather mixed, feelings toward me. June Steward, a black woman living in Oakland, wrote a review of Mark's second book for the *San Francisco Post*, a black newspaper, and sent him a copy of the published piece:

> I was delighted to see Mathabane's timely sequel, *Kaffir Boy in America,* displayed among the new arrivals in the bookstore. I immediately scanned the photos and saw . . . to my amazement and, I must admit, horror, a photo of his wife, Gail, a white woman. Stunned, I turned through the pages thinking, "It just can't be." But there she was, blonde and probably blue-eyed as she could be. I put the book back on

the shelf feeling betrayed. How could he have done this to us? How could he, in the most intimate sense, take up with the very race whose brutality he described so clearly and convincingly in *Kaffir Boy*?

For days I was angry. I refused to buy the book and I felt that I had learned as much as I wanted to know about Mark Mathabane. I hate racism and its simple-minded tenets and those people who uphold them, but I am not a black racist. I do not hate white people. So why did I feel betrayed? Because after luring me into the unutterable horrors of apartheid and making me weep and angry and determined to fight racism and all its ugliness until the day I die, he seems to turn around and embrace the Nordic ideal. He seems to be saying white South Africans are right. The blonde ideal is superior, it is the one worthy of his love, not the lowly black, kinky-headed race.

All of this simplistic thinking soon gave way to a more complex view. We are not simply black or white, we are human beings with thoughts, emotions, and spirituality that make us who we are. Indeed, we are part of a group, a family, but most importantly, we are individuals and it is to this that we must be true no matter how out of step we may be with others.

Moved by her frank discussion of her feelings toward Mark's marriage to me, I wrote a letter to June asking her to explain to me why so many black women feel betrayed and angry when they discover I'm white. June replied,

The female ideal in this country has always been the nubile blonde, girl-woman. Black women always took a back seat to this image. Our beauty, no matter how spectacular, could never stand up to the blonde goddess. So for Mark, one of the most inspiring black writers of the decade, to embrace that ideal was for me, and apparently other black women, an insult. It took a bit of personal grappling for me to get over it.

I am sorry that you have had to experience all the hatred just because of your color. You don't deserve it. None of us do. What is important is that you maintain your dedication to your ideals, be true to the love that you share, and use that love to give you courage to fight this nonsense. As James Baldwin said, "From my point of view, no label, no slogan, no party, no skin color and indeed no religion, is more important than the human being."

Having spoken to Sylvia, exchanged letters with June, and communicated with other black women who had the courage to be candid with me, I learned to be sensitive to the feelings many African-American women have when they see me with Mark. But I did not feel right forcing myself to feel guilty for having fallen in love with him. After all, Mark is far more than a black man and I am not simply a white woman. Black women, I realized, would have to make an effort to try to understand *my* position, too; I can't spend my life apologizing to black women who are upset with me.

When Mark spoke at North Carolina A&T University in Greensboro in late November 1990, where controversial black Muslim minister Louis Farrakhan had spoken a couple weeks earlier, I stayed home despite my strong desire to hear my husband's lecture. I knew that someone in the crowd would ask Mark the inevitable question: "How could you have married a white woman after all you've suffered at the hands of whites?"

As soon as Mark returned I said, "Did anyone ask it?"

"Yes," he replied. "I get that question everywhere I go."

He sounded relaxed and surprisingly carefree about the matter, as if the question no longer bothered him. But it was not until the following week, when I read about the lecture in a newspaper article by *Greensboro News & Record* columnist Bill Morris, that I realized that Mark was at last completely at ease with my being white, even before a crowd that included bitter and militant black students. Part of the column ran as follows:

> It was astonishing that such a small, soft-spoken, elegantly dressed man could deliver such an overpowering message. But as I sat in an auditorium at N.C. A&T State University recently and listened to Mark Mathabane address an audience of 600 souls—blacks and whites, students and teachers, even a few blue-haired matrons—I was, quite simply, astonished. I was also filled with joy and with something that can only be described as awe.
>
> Though he grew up with the horror and brutality of apartheid, the message he brought to A&T was one of compassion, understanding and love. He told the story of how his mother struggled against an array of "Kafkaesque" laws to get him enrolled in school when he was a boy. But it was only when a white nun intervened that Mathabane's mother was able to secure the coveted birth certificate that enabled him to enter school.
>
> "You see, child," his mother told him at the time, "not all white people are bad."

The lesson of that nun's act is with him to this day. "It made me realize that the most important thing you must judge people by is their character—the color of their heart," he said.

That remark inspired a question from a black woman in the audience at A&T. She wanted to know how Mathabane, who grew up under codified white racism, could possibly have married a white woman.

"In judging," he said in a calm voice, "I look not at skin color, but at who people are. One of the things I find disturbing, having grown up in South Africa and then coming to this country, are its contradictions. We blacks say to white South Africa, 'You are monstrous and evil' for denying the humanity of black people. Yet simply in the name of black solidarity, we begin to enforce the same criteria. If you are black you cannot marry or befriend a white person. It's the same thing I experienced in South Africa—in reverse."

Then he looked the questioner in the eye and said, "I am proud to have Gail as a friend and as a wife."

When he said that, I understood the source of my awe. Here was a man who has every reason to be full of rage toward whites but who has transcended those feelings and now works toward bringing people of all races together.

"Of all the places I've been," he told his audience at A&T, "America is one of the few places where people always talk *about* each other. That's how stereotypes persist—because people don't talk *to* each other. It is incumbent on us in a democratic society to try to understand each other, including our differences."

12

RAISING CHILDREN: BLACK OR WHITE?

Wesley and Brenda Root—he's white and she's black—unintentionally made national headlines when they tried enrolling their fourteen-year-old daughter, Mahin, at Page High School in Greensboro in August 1989. The Roots ran into problems because they refused to identify Mahin's race on the registration form.

"Our daughter is mixed," Brenda said of Mahin. "To pick one race over the other would misrepresent her heritage. Whatever I would pick is likely to follow her into high school and for the rest of her life."

Brenda's beliefs challenged the Greensboro school system, the federal bureaucracy, computer technology, and society's obsession with classifying people, as in South Africa, by skin color.

It was the first time a parent had refused to identify a child's race, and the school did not know how to handle the situation. The computer would not process Mahin's registration form unless she completed the block that asked her to select from one of five options—Native American, Asian, Hispanic, black, or white. Brenda Root marked through the question.

"They did not have a space for 'other,' " Brenda said. "But even if it had been there, I would have reacted the same way. I don't believe anyone should ever have to identify their race. We are all human beings. What does race have to do with who we are?"

Brenda was told Mahin would not be registered for school until she identified her race. Mahin had spent the previous four years at Greensboro Day School, a private school where the issue of race was never brought up. Like her parents, Mahin said she never thought of herself as black or white.

"I'm both black and white," she said. "I can't pick one without denying the other."

Greensboro school officials said they needed to report the race of all their students to the Department of Education's Office for Civil Rights (OCR), which has collected racial information since 1967–1968 to determine if schools are complying with the Civil Rights Act of 1964.

The principal at Page referred the matter to the superintendent, who handed it over to the school board's attorney, who called the Office of Civil Rights in Washington, D.C., for advice. John Woods, a public affairs officer in the OCR suggested the school "do the eyeball check" to determine her race.

Time magazine picked up the story, and National Public Radio's "All Things Considered" twice broadcast interviews with Mahin. We saw the article in the *Greensboro News & Record* and wrote a letter to Brenda Root congratulating her on her courage. This began an exchange of letters between us, and before long she arrived at our home for dinner with her daughter Mahin and a white friend named Chris Tiffany.

The Brenda we finally met surprised us. We had imagined her as a militant crusader against racism. After all, this brave woman had challenged the state of North Carolina to abandon its practice of requiring race identification on driver's licenses, marriage licenses, and birth certificates. When she discovered that a local supermarket was using shorthand to indicate black or white on the back of checks, she made sure the store's management in Charlotte knew she disapproved. When Mahin was classified as a black female after a thumb operation, Brenda wrote letters to the doctor who operated on her, the Guilford County Medical Association, and the American Medical Association, demanding that black be removed from Mahin's medical records. It was done.

In place of the outspoken radical we had imagined, we met a

petite, reserved, soft-spoken woman with hints of gray in her hair. She was dressed in red knit pants and a casual sweater. Her daughter Mahin was unusually tall for fourteen. She wore a short skirt, hose, and a pullover, and her jet black hair was in a long jerry curl. She sat down and scarcely said a word all evening. Her large eyes took in everything. She glanced from one object to the next, as if painfully shy and uncomfortable. She was not with us long before she left the room to be with Linah and Diana.

"She won't stay in here because we're talking about race," Brenda told us. "She gets terribly upset when she hears the words *black*, *white*, and *race*. We didn't raise her to think in those terms. We lived in Nigeria for six years, until 1985, and it was never a problem there. It's only since we returned to America that she's been forced to think in terms of race."

Brenda was born and raised in Cleveland, Ohio, in a musical household. Though she is black and grew up during the reign of Jim Crow, her parents, she says, were never obsessed by race. They taught her not to limit her aspirations simply because of her skin color. "Racism," her father told her, "is *their* problem, not yours." As an undergraduate at Oberlin College, Brenda majored in music and went on to the University of Illinois to pursue a graduate degree in music education. In her quiet, determined manner, she makes it clear to everyone that she is a human being first, not a woman, or a black, but a whole person.

Sheena Williams, the teenage daughter of a black American and white Iranian in Teaneck, New Jersey, encountered a situation similar to Mahin's when she signed up to take the California Achievement Test. Under ethnic background, she checked both black and white.

The proctor returned the test to her saying, "You can only check one."

"What are you supposed to do if you're a biracial child?" Sheena asked.

"Put down what you look most like," the proctor said.

"Wait a minute," retorted Sheena, who has long wavy black hair and skin the color of café au lait. "A lot of people think I'm Hispanic. You're saying that if I look Hispanic, I should check Hispanic, right? But I'm not Hispanic. I'm black and white. Children of interracial

marriages should either be able to check both or have our own separate category. And I'm not going to check 'other' because I don't want
to be a nonentity. What is an 'other'?"

The proctor became so exasperated that Sheena finally relented
and checked black.

Sheena's black friends tell her, "You have black blood in you, so
you're black," to which Sheena replies, "But my mother gave birth to
me, and she's white."

One day in her African-American history class at Teaneck High
School, the discussion turned to interracial dating and marriage.
Some of the students disapproved of such relationships. Sheena
asked the class, "Then what do you think of me?"

"Oh, your mother's not white," the students said.

"Then what is she?" Sheena asked.

"I thought you said she's Iranian."

"Yes, but she's still white."

"No she's not."

Sheena made a photocopy of a page in her brother's world history book that stated that Iranians are Caucasians.

"It's not that I'm bragging that my mother's white," Sheena told
them. "I'm just trying to prove a point: that my parents' marriage is
just the same as anybody else's. There's nothing wrong with it."

Despite society's hang-ups, children of mixed couples, contrary
to popular belief, grow up with a healthy sense of who they are, a
fact which, interestingly, the combatants in America's race war find
hard to accept.

"I was taught to be proud of who I am, and who I am is mixed,"
said Trevor Nightingale. "I don't try to avoid the fact that I'm mixed
and say, 'Yo, I'm black,' or 'I'm white.' I tell people with pride, 'I'm
mixed.' I don't really care how other people see me because I have a
strong personal identity from having been raised in different parts of
the country by strong individuals.

"I think I've had the best of both worlds with my mother being
black and my father being white," Trevor continued. "I have black
grandparents and white grandparents, so I've gotten to know both
cultures. I was raised to believe that obstacles become problems only
if you let them. My parents gave me a lot of their strength and pre-

pared me to confront prejudice. They were nonconformists, pioneers. They empowered me."

Sheena's father, Alton Williams, Jr., is a coach for a baseball league in Teaneck, a New Jersey community that integrated voluntarily in the early 1960s and, because of its reputation for racial diversity and tolerance, has attracted many interracial couples. Several of the young players are the biracial children of these couples. Most opponents of interracial marriage make the same arguments over and over again: "The children will suffer. They'll be caught between two worlds. They won't fit in anywhere. They'll be lonely and isolated." But speak to any biracial child or their parent, and you'll most likely hear a different story.

"When I read articles about the problems biracial kids supposedly have, I have to laugh," Williams said. "I look at my own children and the biracial kids I coach. I mean, these kids are ready to take on the whole world. They feel so sure of themselves. They hold their heads up. They've learned to be strong from their parents."

"I have white friends, black friends, mixed friends," Trevor said. "Having white relatives, I don't feel uncomfortable or out of place around whites. I'm not acting when I'm around them, like some blacks do. But sometimes my white friends will ask me why I hang out with blacks. That really bugs me. But it also provides me with the opportunity to explain to them who blacks truly are."

"You really have to look inside yourself and find your own inner strength, and say, 'I'm proud of what I am and who I am, and I'm just going to be myself,'" said singer Mariah Carey, whose father is a black Venezuelan and whose mother is Irish. Carey, who was named Best New Artist of the Year and Best Female Pop Vocalist for her song "Vision of Love" at the Grammys in February 1991, proudly asserts that she is not just "another white girl trying to sing black."

"Some people look at me and they see my light skin and my hair," she told a reporter, running her fingers through her long, wavy, honey-brown tresses. "I can't help the way I look, because it's me. I don't try to look a certain way or sing a certain way. I'm just trying to be me. And if people enjoy my music, then they shouldn't care what I am, so it shouldn't be an issue."

Her parents divorced when Mariah was three, and she grew up in New York with her mother, a vocal coach and former singer with the New York City Opera. Because she and her mother moved often, she didn't have many close friends or get involved in high-school music programs.

"It's been difficult for me, moving around so much, having to grow up by myself, basically on my own, my parents divorced. And I always felt kind of different from everyone else in my neighborhoods. I was a different person, ethnically. And sometimes that can be a problem. If you look a certain way everybody goes, 'white girl,' and I'd go, 'No, that's not what I am.' "

Children of mixed marriages are often accused, mostly by blacks, of trying to deny their black roots and "pass" for white. Critics say they do so for economic, social, or career gain. A biracial adult who refuses to choose between the white and black within her and prefers to be called "mixed" is unfairly accused of denying her "true race," that is, the black race.

Singer Paula Abdul, whose 1989 debut album *Forever Your Girl* sold millions, bears the brunt of many such attacks. The daughter of a French-Canadian and a Brazilian-Syrian, Abdul and her style of singing and dancing immediately appealed to African-Americans, who flocked to record stores to buy her music. When Abdul said publicly that she considers herself "Third World"—neither black nor white—many black fans felt disappointed and betrayed.

If a dark-skinned person has an Italian or Japanese ancestor, there is no reason he should deny this fact and focus his entire identity on his African ancestry. Yet Prince, the multitalented musician from Minneapolis, has been vilified by some blacks for mentioning in his press bio that he is, among other things, part Italian.

Actress Jennifer Beals, who starred in the film *Flashdance*, has been criticized for not claiming to be black. Yet she has never claimed to be white, either. Her father, a black grocery-store owner on Chicago's South Side, died when Jennifer was nine. She was raised by her mother, an Irish school teacher, on Chicago's North Shore in an upper-middle-class white environment. Having grown up in both white and black neighborhoods, and having one white and one black parent, why should Jennifer be forced to choose between her father's heritage or her mother's?

With the rise of crossover music—tunes that appeal to both black and white audiences—came an increase in the number of female vocalists who cannot be, and who rightly refuse to be, categorized as black or white. Neneh Cherry, whose debut album *Raw Like Sushi* was one of the best-selling recordings of 1989, is the daughter of a Swedish woman and an African. Sade, Sheila E, Apollonia, and Vanity are other singers who are either biracial or happen to be very fair-skinned and who have been criticized for "pretending" to be white and "denying" their African roots simply because they look beyond race and consider themselves as human beings first, not as black or white.

MARK'S VIEW

One of the things I quickly learned after arriving in America in 1978 was that this nation—despite its freedom, democracy, and claims of being a melting pot where differences are not only tolerated but celebrated—was far from the racial utopia I had imagined it to be while I groaned under apartheid oppression. This shocked and disappointed me. Yet it also challenged me. Having witnessed firsthand the bitter fruits of racism, intolerance, and separateness under apartheid, I vowed that, just as I had done in South Africa, I would never allow America's racial politics to shape my destiny by determining my values, where I should live, what I should believe, what work I should do, whom I should befriend and whom I should marry.

I knew it wouldn't be easy. Race consciousness was deeply ingrained in the psyches of most Americans. The strength of the tide I had to swim against to fully realize my individuality, to acknowledge, respect, and share in the cultures of others, was daunting.

Falling in love and marrying Gail proved a formidable test of my convictions that true friendship knows no color and that humanity is one. Another challenge, as the father of two biracial children, has been to raise them to embrace, appreciate, and affirm the best in the cultures of their parents, and by extension the best in all other cultures, against a backdrop of increasing and sometimes vicious racial polarization in America.

The most important thing I wanted our firstborn, Bianca, to know was that she was first and foremost a human being. Her worth and identity should derive from that fact and no other. Whatever she does in life should be toward helping her become a better human being—feeling, caring, tolerant, giving, loving. That way, no label can diminish her humanity nor contaminate her soul.

"Your father is black," I often tell her. "And your mother is white. You unite the best in both of us. You're a testament to our belief in the oneness of humankind. Never allow society to force you to choose between one or the other. You're both, you're beautiful and be proud."

The obsession with racial labels and categories is reminiscent of the Nazi era. It can be easily perverted even in modern times, as in South Africa where, in an interesting twist, historians and researchers are discovering that many Afrikaners, including architects of apartheid, are not pure white but have black relatives in their pedigrees, the result of their ancestors' intermarriage or illicit relationships with blacks.

In America, the irony about forcing biracial children to choose between black and white is that few black Americans can honestly claim to be purely black. Many have European, native American, Asian, and Spanish blood somewhere in their ancestry. Their culture and values are almost entirely American. And few speak an African language, a skill without which it is difficult to fully understand the fundamental tenets of African culture. One of these tenets, African humanism, affirms the universality of the human experience and maintains that a rejection of the humanity of others is a rejection of oneself. This has been the principle behind my condemnation of both white and black bigotry.

I never would have survived the horrors of apartheid with my soul intact had I been forced to choose between the culture of my father, who is Venda, and my mother, who is Tsonga. My father sought to mold me after his image, as a man devoid of feelings. My mother taught me that to feel is human. Interestingly, apartheid, in pursuit of its divide and conquer strategy, wanted me to believe that the Vendas and Tsongas were sworn enemies, that I had nothing to gain and everything to lose by claiming to belong to both, just as the purveyors of racism in America want biracial children to believe that the black and white cultures are antagonistic.

True culture, I believe, encompasses what has preserved and nourished the best in a people: spiritually, intellectually, artistically.

And taken collectively, the cultures of the world are what has preserved and nourished the human race since time began. Thus as
human beings we all have a claim and a stake in each other's culture.

Aware that the identity and well-being of our children, their
capacity to weather the misunderstanding and accusations of society
about who they are, will ultimately depend on the sort of home they
were raised in, Gail and I have sought to provide a loving household
in which they can grow up secure and confident, at ease among both
blacks and whites.

Gail and I would have had a hard time creating this nurturing
environment had it not been for our decision to involve both our
families, especially both sets of grandparents. Because Gail and I live
in America, it has been easy for Bianca to be with her maternal
grandparents. Gail's mother visits us regularly at Thanksgiving and
Easter, and we see her father at least once a year. From both she regularly receives letters, phone calls, gift subscriptions to children's
magazines, stuffed animals, books, and even biracial dolls.

Though Linah, Diana, George, and I have done a great deal to
expose Bianca to the richness, beauty, and complexities of the
Tsonga and Venda cultures of our parents, she had the greatest expo-
sure when Gail and I decided to bring both my mother and father to
the United States.

What I wanted Bianca and Gail to know were not only the tradi-
tions and customs of my parents, but also their characters and the
complexities of their emotions, especially my father's. I had not seen
my father since I left South Africa twelve years before, and our relationship had been a difficult and painful one. Memories of the verbal
and physical battles between us during my teenage years, of his
hatred of white people, were still vivid in my mind. I wondered how
he would react to my new life, wife, and child.

On August 12, 1990, Gail, Bianca, Linah, Diana, and I welcomed
my parents to North Carolina. After a grueling seventeen-hour flight
from Johannesburg, my seventy-two-year-old father, Jackson, a
short, gaunt man with wisps of gray hair, stepped off a USAir flight
from New York holding hands with my fifty-two-year-old mother,
Magdelene. Seeing them together brought tears to my eyes. It
seemed an appropriate symbol of how much their relationship had

grown, of how they had stood by each other through the trials and tribulations of thirty-seven years as a black couple under apartheid.

My father first hugged and kissed Linah and Diana, his two youngest daughters whom he had not seen in more than three years. Much to my surprise, he then hugged and kissed Gail and nineteen-month-old Bianca. As I embraced my father he felt warm, gentle, accessible, and human. His eyes glistened with tears of joy as he muttered, "My son, my son, God is alive, God is alive indeed!"

His words took me aback. The father I knew back in South Africa had seldom referred to me as his son, and he used to scoff at Christianity as a ploy through which white people had stolen land from black people and enslaved them. The father I now beheld was a far cry from the tormented soul whose twisted life I chronicled in *Kaffir Boy* and its sequel. The changes that had occurred in his character were remarkable. His affectionate holding of my mother's hand, his public display of emotion, was something new. Even the smile that lit up his brown eyes and softened his hardened face was new. I was amazed and delighted to confirm the news I had been hearing from home about the miraculous transformation of my father from an alcoholic, chronic gambler, and wife batterer into a loving father and husband, a respected member of the black community in Alexandra, devout Christian, and church deacon.

The father I remembered was a distant, stoic, inscrutable, and menacing stranger. His emasculation under apartheid had poisoned his life and turned him into a tyrant. His seven children tried desperately to love him but found his heart cold and unreachable. Whenever he came home drunk and started physically abusing my mother, I would intervene. He would turn his wrath on me, beat me, and threaten to kill me. I hated him for being so unfeeling, and he detested me for challenging his authority in the house.

But the day I left for America, something happened to make me believe that despite all the shocks my father had subjected me to, he loved me. He cried. For the first time in my life I saw tears in his eyes. He wished me well and asked that I write often and remember the family.

Little did I know how hard my father would work, during my twelve years in America, to mend his life and regain his dignity and humanity. As we caught up with our lives during long conversations on hot afternoons in Kernersville, the story of his transformation unfolded.

After I escaped from apartheid through a tennis scholarship, my father began realizing he had been wrong in disparaging my love for books and tennis, and in belittling me as "a woman with a penis."

"I found myself taking pride in what you had done," he said one evening as we took a walk around the quiet neighborhood. "I even claimed credit for it, though I knew it was mostly your mother's sacrifices which made everything possible."

My mother had never been one to bask in the limelight. She let my father boast that "a son who had inherited his brain is now a famous and successful man in America." Never one to miss an opportunity, my mother seized the moment to convince my father that his behavior—drinking, gambling, and abusing the family—was incompatible with his claims to being my father.

"You should stop drinking and come to church with me," she said. "Then people will believe that you're indeed Mark's father."

My father had angrily rejected such invitations in the past, but this time he relented. He began attending the Twelve Apostles Church of God in Alexandra, where my mother had been a member for many years. At first his attendance was sporadic, but in the last three years his faith has strengthened. He is now a deacon and helps the minister counsel church members with their problems. His enthusiasm and proselytizing have brought dozens of new members into the church. And his strong will to live—a will that enabled him to bear so much misfortune and suffering under apartheid without breaking—helped him effectively fight alcoholism.

Bianca took an immediate liking to my father. She constantly followed him around our four-bedroom farmhouse, its wraparound porch, and the yard, calling him "Dada" and conversing with him in baby talk while he responded in pidgin English and various African languages. Whenever he called her name she would run to him, and he would teach her African games and songs in his native Venda. Each evening as we sat down to dinner, my father and Bianca would sing a little song in Venda, clapping their hands and patting their foreheads to the rhythm of *tutu na-nana, tutu na-nana.*

Because my father hates being cloistered indoors, he would pace the yard or shovel mulch in the garden, even in ninety-degree heat.

Bianca was right there at his heels, picking up clods of dirt to give him as gifts.

My mother adored Bianca, the first grandchild born to one of her sons. Under Tsonga tribal tradition, only grandchildren born to sons are considered true grandchildren. The children born to daughters are considered the grandchildren of their husband's parents. For this reason Bianca holds a special place in my mother's heart, though my three sisters still living in South Africa—Florah, Maria, and Merriam—all have children who are deeply loved by my parents.

My mother would take Bianca's hands and sing and dance with her in the kitchen to African songs about the joys of childhood. Bianca, sucking her thumb and playing with the smooth hem of her pink blanket, would snuggle up against my mother on the couch as she sat knitting sweaters and caps for her, studying the alphabet, or watching television with my father. And the two often took Bianca along on their marathon daily walks.

As the weeks passed I began to see that Bianca was comfortable in all four worlds that make up her identity: white, black, American, and South African. She was growing up without stereotypes against race or culture, completely open and trusting of new people and kind strangers, unafraid and self-confident, candid in her expression of feelings.

For months her favorite phrase was "I love you," and she says it not only to Mommy, Daddy, Grampa, Grandma, Uncle George, and her aunties Linah and Diana but also to her little girlfriends at play school, her teachers, and other relatives who call and ask to speak to her. She's been maturing into a beautiful, trusting, tolerant, nonjudgmental, happy child popular among the neighborhood children, both black and white. I have no fear that she will be "caught between two worlds," as so many opponents of interracial marriage argue. Instead I'm confident she will be a much better person from growing up amid so much diversity.

GAIL'S VIEW

The only image of Mark's father I had came from *Kaffir Boy*, photographs of him we occasionally received from Alexandra, and hearing his voice once or twice on the phone as he spoke in Venda to Linah or Diana. So it was with a great deal of trepidation that I rode to the Greensboro airport to meet him. I imagined an angry man who would hate me for being white, who would frequently argue and come to blows with Mark, and who would try to run our household according to his own rules.

I was surprised when I met him. He was of a much smaller stature than I had imagined, with a gentle disposition and kind eyes. When I saw how readily Bianca sat on his lap in the van, and how he listened attentively to her toddler's babble and showed her his broken watch, I knew my initial fears were unfounded.

He impressed me as being a very proud, dignified man, who seldom let on that he was surprised or excited by new experiences. Having just completed his first flight in an airplane, he yawned and said flying was nothing remarkable. When we pulled up in our driveway, he silently got out of the car and roamed around our house, both outside and inside, without revealing that he was the least bit impressed by its comfort or size, though it was about ten times the size of the home in which his children grew up, a fifteen-by-fifteen-foot shack.

He went for long walks with Mark's mother around the neighborhood each morning and evening, and wondered why Americans remain cooped up inside their homes so much. He also wondered why we drive to the grocery store instead of walking, when it is only three miles away.

I was amazed and puzzled by many of his habits: the way he would lie in the blazing sun for hours, deep in thought, with a handkerchief over his face; the way he would carefully peruse magazines and newspapers even though he couldn't read; his saying grace at each meal; and his expectation that all the women in the house serve him. Despite his idiosyncrasies, he was extremely affable and respectful. I grew to call him "Papa."

The Mathabane children had always been expected to address their father in Venda, to show respect for his native language and his authority, but Linah, Diana, George, and Mark were much more fluent in Tsonga, their mother's language. When Mark tried, after twelve years without hearing the language, to speak to Papa in Venda, his speech was so halting that Linah and Diana burst out laughing. Mark's father merely smiled, and from then on it was understood that everyone could speak Tsonga without offending him.

I heard Tsonga, Venda, Sotho, and Zulu so much that I began to understand a bit of the languages, which always made Diana exclaim, "How did you know what we were talking about?" Sometimes, just for fun or to show off his knowledge, Papa would speak in Afrikaans. This, too, I could often understand, for Afrikaans has many German words. Papa and I would point to various things on the dinner table—bread, butter, glass—comparing the names for them in German and Afrikaans. I hope to learn as many African languages as I can—they're so poetic, so melodious—as a way to fully sharing in the rich cultures of blacks in South Africa and effectively communicating with my other family.

As the months went by, Mhani's English improved, and we were able to discuss increasingly complex topics. A diligent student, she daily studied the alphabet and the beginning readers I borrowed from the literacy center at the public library. When I listened to NPR on the car radio, she would pay close attention, smiling proudly whenever she was able to catch a word or phrase she understood. She sat for hours on the floor of Diana's room, wearing headphones, listening to English-language tapes and repeating what she heard.

"Give me your address," the tape said.

"Give me your dress," Mhani echoed proudly.

Communication between us was not easy at first, and there were a few disastrous misunderstandings, like the time I said, "Those towels are dirty," and she thought I said that *she* was dirty. She sulked alone in the laundry room all day before I found out why she was upset.

"How could you think I'd have said such a thing!" I cried.

"Oh, Gail, I didn't want to believe it. But my heart," she said, pressing her hand to her chest as if in pain. "My heart—so sorry."

We embraced and laughed over the misunderstanding. After that, each time we inadvertently hurt each other by not making our meaning clear, we always made up by embracing.

Unlike many foreigners who try to speak English, Mhani was not afraid to make mistakes as long as she could get her meaning across. Soon I was able to interpret her sentences and she, listening carefully as I spoke slowly and clearly, was able to interpret mine. Mark was amazed by how much we could communicate. I'd describe to him some in-depth conversation between Mhani and me and he would refuse to believe it.

"How could she have told you all that?" he said.

At that time I was pregnant with our second child, so Mhani and I often spoke of the differences between bearing and raising children in America and in South Africa. She described the births of each of her seven children, telling me how difficult each had been, how Granny and some women from the neighborhood had acted as midwives, how much each child had weighed, and how each had got its name. One time, while we were doing laundry, she said confidently, pointing to my rounded belly, "This one is a boy."

"How can you tell?" I asked.

"From the way you look and feel," she said cryptically.

"I don't understand."

She laughed. "There are things you cannot yet understand," she said. "Look at it this way. My firstborn was a boy. Then came a girl. Then a boy, then a girl. You see? You have a girl, so the next one will be a boy. After that you'll have another girl, then another boy, and so on."

I laughed. How could I tell her I was not planning to have as many children as she had? I got the feeling, from talking to Mhani, that it was customary in an African woman's life to raise many loved, strong, and healthy children. This was an admirable goal. But the world can no longer support too many of us, as shown by the cruel life of deprivation and early death many children in underdeveloped countries face. Also I don't know many American women of my generation who could bear the strain of raising more than three. Many don't even find the time to have one child before their biological clock runs out. Most of my friends from Brown were amazed that I was already married and had a child, not to mention a second one on the way.

Every time Mhani told me I would have a boy, I cringed inside. *Would she be disappointed if I had a girl? Would Mark?* He had assured me that he wouldn't. Yet I felt the full weight of African tradition on my shoulders, a tradition that values sons more highly than daughters. Personally, I wanted a little son so much that I was afraid to hope for one, and I kept my preference a secret, even from my journal. I was afraid that if I wrote about my desire for a baby boy and then had a girl, my daughter might be deeply hurt if she read my journal years later. Whenever someone referred to my protruding stomach as "he," I would quickly correct them by saying, "she." I prepared myself psychologically for a girl.

Because of my condition, Mhani pampered me. She forbade me to pick up Bianca, who now weighed more than twenty-five pounds, and would insist I take long naps in the afternoon and not subject myself to undue stress. She was the perfect midwife. She possessed more earthy knowledge about the emotions and psychology of child-birth than anyone I have met. She often accompanied me to my monthly checkups and thought much of what was done by the doctor unnecessary.

"A strong woman should be able to bear healthy children," she would say. "So take care of yourself and the baby will be fine."

I was surprised by how indulgent Mark's mother was toward Bianca. Because Mark and his siblings are so self-disciplined and hardworking, I assumed she had raised her children with strict guidelines and punished them when they were naughty. But she let Bianca run about freely, cleaning up her messes as she made them. She never said, "Naughty girl" or "Bad girl." In fact, Mhani would get upset if Mark or I scolded Bianca. She told me she felt "a pain in her heart" whenever she heard Bianca cry. Yet she always seemed to find a way to get Bianca to behave.

"Treat children like children and not adults," she would say.

When I saw Mhani constantly praise Bianca and call her, "Beautiful girl, clever girl, well done," I realized how she had managed to raise self-confident, secure children amid the terrors and deprivations of South African ghetto life: She had given them a strong sense of self-worth in their early years.

Whenever Bianca cried, Mhani would kneel down beside her, embrace her and ask, "Who hit you?"

At first I was offended by this, for I thought Mhani really believed we hit Bianca. Then Linah explained to me that asking, "Who hit you?" was her mother's way of comforting a child. She had frequently asked the same thing of Angeline, Given, Lionel, and Sibusiso— her grandchildren back home in South Africa. It allowed the child, who most likely was simply frustrated at not getting whatever she wanted, to pin the blame for her distress on someone else and then quickly forget it.

When Mhani played games with Bianca, like the African version of hide and seek, or tossing stuffed animals for her to catch, she would roar with laughter, thoroughly enjoying herself. Bianca would clap her hands, laugh, and jump up and down, unable to contain her excitement.

Though I felt completely at ease with Mhani and Bianca, I became a bit self-conscious whenever the three of us went out in public. It seems an interracial couple has to adjust to stares three times: first, when seen with one's spouse, then with one's child, and third with one's in-laws. People would stare at us—a white woman, a black woman, and a brown child—trying to figure out the connection between us.

Every week I took Mhani and Bianca to the Forsyth County Health Department. We were desperately trying to get Mhani's diabetes under control. The patients and clinic employees were predominantly black, and many took me for Mhani's welfare case worker or some volunteer do-gooder.

"Are you from Crisis Control or social services?" they would ask.

The black women behind the desks and in the lab had little patience with me.

"Why don't you let her talk for herself?" one nurse snapped at me when I kept answering questions about Mhani's medical history. "Can't she talk?"

"Yes, but I can tell by the expression on her face when she doesn't understand a question. She's still learning English. She speaks Tsonga."

"She speaks what?"

"She's from South Africa."

"And who are you? Her interpreter or something?"

"Her daughter-in-law," I said.

As we continued to go to the clinic each week, however, the employees got to know us and began to treat us kindly. When we told Mhani's doctor that she would soon return to South Africa, he was distraught.

"Oh, but you can't leave!" he said. "You're my best patient!"

When Mhani came to the United States, her blood sugar count was between 400 and 500—between 60 and 120 is normal. By following a strict program of diet, exercise, and regular doses of insulin, her blood sugar count steadily dropped.

I did not realize how attached I had become to Mhani until the night she collapsed on the floor, faint, dizzy, sweating, and shaking. She had been on insulin only three days, and we feared she was having a reaction. I phoned the clinic and the doctor on call told us to make her drink some sweet juice and rush her to the hospital.

"Otherwise she might die," the doctor said.

"Die!" I exclaimed. My heart started pounding and I trembled all over. No one had told me an insulin reaction could be life-threatening.

Shivering and too weak to sit up, Mhani crouched under a comforter complaining of the cold. She refused to drink any juice, insisting she would vomit if she did. Mark, Diana, and Papa carried her limp body downstairs, into the garage, and placed her in the backseat of Mark's car. Mark sped down the highway toward the hospital while I sat in the backseat with Mhani, trying to keep her from lapsing into a coma. Her eyes were half-closed and her lips were dry. I watched her chest rise and fall, afraid it might suddenly stop.

"Please don't let her die," I chanted to myself. "Please, God." I tried to calm myself, knowing that panicking would be of no help.

We became lost in a maze of side streets and nearly ran out of gas by the time we reached the emergency room. A nurse and an orderly hauled Mhani from the car into a wheelchair and whisked her through a pair of heavy swinging doors labeled "Patients only." Mark was permitted only because they needed a translator.

I was left to sit alone in the waiting room, stunned and quaking. "If anything happens to her it will be all my fault," I thought. "I'm the one who's been taking her to the doctor. I should have known about insulin reactions." The baby kicked restlessly within me, and I realized I was right in the middle of two generations—the one that is about to be born and the one that gave us birth. "If we should lose her . . ." I thought with tears in my eyes.

After what seemed like hours an emotionally exhausted Mark came out and told me her condition was stabilized, but that she would have to remain in the hospital a bit longer. I hugged Mark as tightly as I could with a baby between us. Knowing how deeply the prospect of losing Mhani had shaken me, I realized she had truly become a second mother to me. A few weeks later her diabetes was finally stabilized through a combination of diet, exercise, and insulin.

Mhani sorely wanted to stay for the birth of our second child, but Mark's father was eager to get back to Alexandra, back to his friends and family, back to the familiar sights and sounds of his homeland, back to his native language, back to being the head of his own household.

Mhani and Papa departed for South Africa in late December, laden with Christmas gifts from us to the rest of the Mathabane clan. Mark accompanied them to New York to help them with their numerous bags and boxes and to make sure they safely boarded the proper Air Zambia flight at JFK Airport.

Mark's father was almost left behind. While Mark was in line waiting to check their luggage and confirm their seats, Papa, who was squeezed into a corner with Mhani at the back of the teeming crowd, insisted on going to an upstairs bathroom unaccompanied. Upon leaving the bathroom, he became confused as to which door he had come through as there were several doors that looked the same. He took the wrong one and wandered all over the airport, lost, for nearly an hour.

I cannot imagine how confusing and strange such a modern international airport must have seemed to someone who cannot read, write, or speak anything fluently except a minor African language.

All of us, especially Bianca, missed them as soon as they had left.

"Where's Grandma go?" she would ask, looking pleadingly into my eyes. "Where's Grampa go?"

"They flew away in a big airplane to a land far, far away, but don't cry. We'll go visit them someday soon."

13

FRIENDS WHO ARE MIXED COUPLES

There is a tacit understanding among interracial couples that make friendships between them both natural and spontaneous. They have weathered similar trials, confronted the same prejudices, sought to ignore similar stares and derisive comments. Together they can laugh over the experiences they once found alienating and painful.

Since our marriage we have befriended several mixed couples, many of whom are proud of the racial harmony they represent. They have confirmed our belief that there is something profoundly moving and beautiful in love shared by people from two worlds often at odds—one black, one white.

The black women we know who married white men are usually very upbeat and optimistic about their relationships and what the future holds for their children. They encountered little resistance from their parents and siblings when they announced their marriage plans, and most were eventually accepted by their husbands' families, even the most conservative and wealthy of white families.

Evelyn and Rainer Zawadzki say they have always gone wherever they pleased and never encountered any prejudice or hostility against them in their twenty-two-year marriage, despite the fact that Evelyn's skin is the color of dark mahogany and Rainer is a full-blooded German. They met in Mexico, where Evelyn was teaching English and Rainer was a graduate student in chemical engineering at the University of Mexico.

Evelyn was born and raised on the South Side of Chicago in an all-black neighborhood. One year out of high school, at nineteen, she married her childhood sweetheart. The marriage lasted less than two years, but it produced a little girl.

Evelyn supported herself and her daughter, working full-time, and taking college courses at night. Eventually they moved to Mexico, for Evelyn had always dreamed of living in a foreign country.

"I met Rainer at a time in my life when I wasn't interested at all in marrying again," said Evelyn, a tall, beautiful woman and former model. "I didn't trust a man with something as serious as marriage. I didn't think there was anything a man could do for me that I couldn't do for myself. Besides, I hadn't met anyone I really wanted to devote the rest of my life to. But Rainer was totally different from anyone I had ever met before. He made me believe he was interested in me as a human being. He appreciated my thoughts and ideas. We had very nice intellectual conversations."

"I was fascinated by Evelyn," Rainer said. "She has a very sharp mind. I love it. Besides, I've always believed the way to a woman's heart is through her intellect," he added, smiling mischievously.

"We were at a party, and I was wearing a hot orange minidress," she said, laughing.

Born in East Germany, Rainer moved with his parents to a German colony in Mexico in 1948 when he was three years old. He attended an elite German private school, reputed to be the most exclusive in Mexico. The Germans formed a tight-knit community and never socialized with outsiders.

"Germans who married Mexicans were ostracized," Rainer said. "From society and friends I heard, 'Don't you ever try to come here with one of those darkies,' meaning a Mexican. We had to keep ourselves white-white."

Rainer was relieved when he graduated from the private school and could enroll in the University of Mexico. "I loved it," he said. "For the first time I was free of that German domination. Yet I was cast into Mexican society, which never fully accepted me. I found my German friends too snobbish and discriminatory, so I chose to make friends with Americans. I spoke German and Spanish fluently, but I was still learning English when I met Evelyn.

"I was fascinated by black people," Rainer continued. "If you're different from me, I want to find out what makes you tick. I want to know how you feel, and maybe I can share some of my feelings with you. I do the same thing when I see a Japanese or Indian. I wonder, 'What do they think? How do they perceive things?' Finding out what the difference is between us shows me something about myself I hadn't known before. The only way you can find out about yourself is by contrasting your experiences with some one else's. It's incredibly fascinating."

Evelyn's daughter liked Rainer immediately. When Evelyn and Rainer decided to marry and move back to the United States, she knew her parents would accept him, though it might take some time for them to get used to the idea.

"I was very close to my father, and I knew that if he didn't approve of my marrying Rainer initially, he would at least be very kind and polite to him," Evelyn said. "That's exactly what happened. But about one year after our wedding, when we were visiting my parents, my father came into the room and invited Rainer to go out and have a beer with him. I started to get my shoes, but my father gave me a look that said, 'I didn't mean you could come too.' I knew then and there he had accepted Rainer. I knew it was okay. From then on they were almost inseparable."

Rainer had more difficulty convincing his family to accept Evelyn. "Evelyn's parents may have had as many doubts as mine, but unlike mine, they did not voice them. My family pitched a bitch. But my decision to ask Evelyn to marry me took race into account. I had no illusions. I knew what I was getting into. I knew she was black, I knew I was white, I knew we'd live in the United States, I knew I was going against everything I had been taught."

"His sister had just become Catholic," Evelyn said, "and she went to the priest to confess OUR sins. The priest told her we had committed a moral sin, a social sin, and a racial sin. If the priest had told *me* that, I would have told him what he could do with his 'sins.' "

Despite opposition in Rainer's family, Rainer and Evelyn have had few, if any, problems as an interracial couple. They don't even mind the stares.

"When we go out, we know people are going to look at us because we're a good-looking pair," Evelyn said. "We dress and look the best we possibly can. It's only sometimes that I wonder, 'Why is that person staring? Is something wrong? Is my blouse unbuttoned?' But for the most part I want them to look. We've had a lot of people—both white and black—come up to us and say we make a striking couple. We were in Penn Station one day and a black man asked Rainer, 'Excuse me, but is that your woman? She's so pretty and chocolate. You're all right, man, you're all right.' "

Vickie Nizin, another friend of ours, is married to a white surgeon named Joel whom she met when they were both students at Howard University in Washington, D.C. They are members of the Bahá'í Faith. A petite black woman and the mother of two young girls, Vickie says she and Joel have encountered no problems as a mixed couple and actually enjoy the stares.

"I love having attention, because I feel it's an opportunity for me to provide a fresh, more wholesome, healthy perspective. We're setting a good example. It's a chance to say, 'Yes, we're a mixed couple and we're healthy and happy, we're not suffering and crazy and weird. We're not hiding. We're not freaks.' "

Vickie was born in Richmond, Virginia. The state's governor, Douglas Wilder, is her father's relative and, as a child, played with her father, Ellsworth Johnson. Though historically the maternal line of Vickie's family had been very light-skinned and well-off by black standards, the wealth was dissipated in one generation and her mother and nine siblings grew up in poverty in Richmond, under the unpredictable tyranny of an alcoholic and abusive stepfather. Vickie's mother was sent to live with relatives, who were well educated for blacks at that time.

Vickie's father, a brilliant man with a master's degree in zoology who yearned to be a physician, tried for fourteen years to get into a Virginia medical school, but it was closed to blacks. Frustrated, he gave up and studied dentistry instead. Her mother was trained as a secretary, but no one would hire her. Desperate for work, she eventually pleaded with a Jewish doctor, who trained her to prepare slides in a pathology lab. From there she went on to the National Institutes of Health and became a specialist.

Before moving to Washington, the Johnsons had three children: Vickie and her two brothers. A refined female relative made sure Vickie took ballet, wore beautiful clothes, sang in public, acquired poise and sophistication, and understood how to behave "properly."

Vickie was aware her family tree included Irish ancestors and native Americans as well as Africans, but she quickly learned that nothing mattered to strangers but the fact that she had brown skin and kinky hair. To the world she was simply black. She shopped at segregated stores, lived in an all-black, inner-city neighborhood, and attended segregated schools. As a student at Roosevelt High in Washington, D.C., in the late 1960s, she saw many of her classmates come to school high on marijuana or heroin. Only a handful went on to college, but Vickie, who expanded her world by reading voraciously, went on to Oberlin College in Ohio, then transferred to Howard.

"I am by nature friendly and outgoing, but at that school I belonged to no group," Vickie said. "I belonged to myself. I found that was the only way to survive."

Growing up in a segregated world and hearing her parents discuss civil rights and social justice, Vickie was aware of racial tensions from an early age. "My parents did not want us to hate anybody, but we could see and feel how wounded they had been by racism."

There is one story Vickie heard quite often. When he was fourteen her father happened to be in an all-white neighborhood right after a robbery. A police officer saw him and, because "all blacks look alike," gunned him down. Her father lay in a coma for a week, then his heart stopped. On the way to the morgue he groaned, startling everyone around him. He had a long difficult recovery, but he made it.

"You can imagine my father has no reason to love anybody who's white," Vickie said. "And yet my father is a man of great vision." He accepted Joel, and if he has any reservations, they spring not from the fact that Joel is white, but from the fact that Joel attended medical school and is now a practicing physician: He is doing all the things Vickie's father dearly wanted to do but wasn't allowed to do.

Joel's parents, Conservative Jews from the Bronx, urged Joel to break up with Vickie and, for a month, succeeded in making their son have second thoughts. They wanted their son to prosper more than they had, to marry a woman who would advance his career and raise their grandchildren in the Jewish faith. They arranged dates for Joel with Jewish women. They did not even want to hear Vickie's name.

"The first time they met Vickie they liked her, because she's a very likable person," Joel said. "But as soon as they realized we were talking about marriage, their attitude switched one hundred and eighty degrees."

"They thought it was okay as long as he didn't marry me," Vickie said. "He could have lived with me, and disgraced me, and it wouldn't have mattered. It would have been okay as long as he didn't marry me."

During a long separation, when Joel was in New York doing his internship and Vickie was still in Washington, D.C., finishing her college degree, Joel realized his feelings for Vickie were more important to him than his parents' disapproval. But Vickie insisted they not marry until his parents gave their consent, which was required under Bahá'í Law.

"I wanted very much for us to be married," Vickie said. "I couldn't imagine going through life without Joel. Yet I didn't resent his parents. I wanted them to accept me, and there was no way I'd let hostility come between us. I went out of my way to be pleasant and loving toward them. His parents are truly good, kind, generous people, and I could tell it bothered them that they couldn't find it in themselves to accept me."

Realizing how committed Joel and Vickie were to each other, his parents finally gave their consent. "We were very strong," Vickie said. "People could sense it. Our relationship grew very solid from all the tests we were put through. We could sustain."

When Joel's father fell ill from cancer, he gave up the last of his reservations and treated Vickie as a daughter. They're now grateful they waited for his parents to come around, for it gave them time to get to know each other better, in hard times as well as good.

"I think you have to be very sure that what you are doing is right," Vickie said. "You really have to believe that we are all one people, and that interracial marriage is a very positive thing. It's more than just two people who find one another and fall in love. By your marriage you are saying, 'We are all one humanity, and we can grow closer together, even to the point of marrying. And our children will be the fruit of that common humanity that brought us together.' "

"People don't bother us because we don't present ourselves as meek little wimpettes," Joel said. "We don't ask for anybody's permission. We are accepted because we accept ourselves. We're here to accept you, we're not asking you to accept us."

Though white parents usually resist when their son announces his intention to marry a black woman, one couple we know has had no problem at all. When Eric Asimov, nephew of science fiction writer Isaac Asimov, told his father he had a girlfriend named Jackie Lee whom he'd met at Wesleyan University, his father asked, "What is she, Chinese?"

"Nope, she's black," Eric replied.

After a momentary silence his father said, "Oh, really? Well, that's nice." Eric describes his parents as "two of the best-intentioned liberals in the world."

Jackie's mother accepted the news readily, and her grandfather, though not quite as accepting, only commented, "Oh, he's white?" Jackie grew up in an integrated neighborhood in Philadelphia, attended an integrated Catholic school, and was used to being around whites. When Jackie and Eric moved to Austin, Texas, in 1983, Jackie expected trouble, but they had none. In fact people were so friendly to them they couldn't believe it. They now live in Manhattan with their son, Jack.

A photograph of the couple appeared on the wedding announcements page of *The New York Times* while they were honeymooning in Bermuda. Tourists who had seen the photo shouted their congratulations and waved.

While black women with white men seem to have a fairly easy time as interracial couples, the white women we know who have married black men have often had to struggle against enormous difficulties. Despite the fact that about 75 percent of interracial marriages in the United States involve black men and white women, it is the black man–white woman combination that sparks the most widespread condemnation among both blacks and whites.

Few things can be more difficult for the average white American than to see his daughter marry a black man. It places even the most loving and liberal white father in an emotional quandary, as it did Spencer Tracy in his role of the white father in *Guess Who's Coming to Dinner?* The desperate despair of a daughter over losing her father's love and her father's agonizing disappointment are the painful themes that often surface whenever a white woman marries outside her race.

When our friends Madelyn and Richard Ashley decided to marry, Madelyn had to sacrifice her good relationship with her father. For years after the wedding, Madelyn's father refused to meet Richard. One Christmas Eve at her sister's house, when Madelyn and Richard dropped by without knowing her parents were there, Madelyn's father ran down to the basement and refused to come upstairs until Richard was out of the house. Madelyn went downstairs to persuade him to come up, but it was no use.

"Everyone tells me Richard's a fine young man," Madelyn's father said. "But I just can't bring myself to meet him. I can't. He's stepped over the line by marrying you."

Her father, an engineer and a Methodist, was born and raised in Columbia, South Carolina, and her mother, a Baptist, was born just outside Winston-Salem. Though they raised Madelyn to believe in racial equality, they oppose interracial marriage.

"When I graduated from Chapel Hill, my parents did not come to my graduation because they knew Richard would be there. They didn't even call. My parents raised me to be a broad-minded individual, but that only went so far. I knew they would never accept my marrying a black."

When they first began dating, Madelyn let her parents believe Richard was white. Because he sounds white on the phone, he was able to develop a good relationship with Madelyn's parents by having phone conversations with them. Madelyn's mother even told her, "Richard must be good-looking, judging from his voice." Her parents invited Madelyn and Richard to visit them. Richard refused to go unless Madelyn told her parents he was black; he did not want to shock them.

When Madelyn told her parents they reacted with, "How could you do this?" and retracted their invitation. In the wedding photos, Madelyn's parents are conspicuously absent. Richard was forbidden to set foot in his father-in-law's home.

It was not until Madelyn's mother had a heart attack that her parents had a change of heart. Lying in a hospital bed, confronting the dark abyss of death, and troubled by an uneasy conscience, Madelyn's mother turned to her husband and asked, "Why have we done this to Madelyn? Why can't we accept Richard?"

Her father wept. Fortunately Madelyn's mother recovered, and as soon as she was home from the hospital, Madelyn's father invited Madelyn and Richard to visit. When the young couple arrived, Madelyn's father eagerly shook Richard's hand, as if hungry for the companionship of the son-in-law he had so long denied. He and Richard talked nonstop and spent the entire weekend fishing together. Both Richard and Madelyn are amazed by her father's complete transformation, and happy that their baby boy, Colin, has a kind and loving grandfather.

Not all white fathers learn to accept their black sons-in-law, but many of them do eventually come around. It is often a slow, gradual, and painful process, and requires parents to come to terms with their own prejudices and fears.

It took nine years for Connie, a lithe and beautiful white woman with high cheekbones and luminous eyes, to win back the affection of her father after she started dating James, now a black service manager in Greensboro. Connie, who is the middle child of seven children, drew a lot of criticism from her five sisters, who always told her she was ugly and stupid and would never amount to anything. They made fun of her and called her a nigger lover when she started dating James, whom she met at a Greensboro high school.

"My parents hated me when they found out," Connie said. "Daddy used to say he was going to shoot him. He said, 'I'll shoot the nigger.' I just sat there and gaped. I couldn't believe those words had come out of his mouth. When I first started dating James I didn't really think about how my parents would react. I thought it was no big deal."

Her father, an alcoholic who used to beat his wife and children, terrified Connie so much that she used to leave the house quietly and meet James at the end of the road to avoid a scene.

"He used to beat all of us," Connie said. "He just went down the line. He beat us over anything, nothing in particular. With belts and sticks. I always thought the reason he drank was because of us kids. We were pretty obnoxious. I mean, we weren't the "Leave It to Beaver" family. He used to beat my brother so bad I had to clean the hair and blood off the bathroom wall. We would run from him. If we saw him coming we'd run upstairs and hide in our rooms. If he got irritated over something he'd just come upstairs and smack one of us upside the head. He's been sober for more than ten years now, and he doesn't remember any of this stuff."

Of all the girls in the family, Connie was the only daughter who fought back against her father's violence and rebelled against his authority. Her friends believe that, because of her defiance, Connie is now much stronger than her sisters.

James's parents did not approve of his dating a white woman, but he was twenty at the time and financially independent, working his way through college, so they had little control over him. Raised in government projects in Greensboro in the late 1950s, James says he lived in a real rough, all-black neighborhood.

"You grew up fast there," said James, the middle of six children. "I always ran with boys a lot older than I was. I had to do what they did. Toughened me up. Breaking in, stealing, causing trouble, you know, going into people's windows and taking stuff, then taking it to the playground and breaking it, just to be foolish. I used to wake up early in the morning and come back when it was dark. I loved to fight. I fought all the time, every day just about. I'd start fights over nothing, just to fight. It's just something you did. You didn't think about it."

James attended an all-black elementary school, for Jim Crow laws still ruled the South. His father sorted letters by zip code at the post office all day, then worked at an all-black university at night as an assistant programs director. But these two incomes were still not enough to keep the family out of government housing.

Busing began when James entered fifth grade. "That first year was wild," James said. "We more or less just stared at each other, trying to figure out what was really going on. It was the first time I'd had contact with white kids. It took me only about three weeks to make some white friends, 'cause I was aggressive and outgoing from hanging out with those older boys. But after that first year of integration, we came back for sixth grade and it was completely segregated again. All the white kids had left. They'd gone to private schools or schools across town. By seventh grade there wasn't even a white teacher left."

By the time James entered high school, attempts at integrating the Greensboro public school system were starting to work. He was bused to a predominantly white high school, and, though he had had very little contact with whites, he began dating white girls.

"People told me not to, but I wasn't one to listen," James said.

"My parents never talked to me about stuff like that. I've always done what I want."

James knew Connie's father was against him, but he continued to date her. When Connie's father found out his daughter was still seeing James, he kicked her out of the house. One day her mother came home from work and told Connie, "You've got to leave."

"Why? What have I done?" asked Connie, then nineteen.

"Your daddy just wants you to get out. You've got to be out of here by five o'clock."

Connie, shaken and crying, hurriedly packed her things and, with her mother's encouragement, moved in with James, who had a job delivering pesticides to tobacco farmers. Her mother, knowing Connie had nowhere to go and no money, pleaded with James to let Connie move in with him.

"Can Connie stay here?" her mother asked James in a hysterical tone, still huffing from carrying suitcases up two flights of stairs. "She doesn't have any place to go. Do you mind if she lives here for a while?"

Connie began living with James, though neither of them felt ready for such a commitment. They felt the decision had been foisted on them by circumstances. Connie found a job waiting tables at a steak house and, to make their money go further, she and James decided to look for a more affordable apartment. Connie found a one-bedroom apartment on Spring Garden and signed the lease in her name. When James showed up with his belongings, he was accosted by the landlord.

"We stayed in that apartment only one night," Connie said. "The landlord told us to get out. James came to the steak house and told me what had happened. I was hysterical, crying, mad. We were real naive. We didn't know a landlord could react like that."

They finally found an apartment that would accept them, and after settling in, Connie discovered she was pregnant. She kept this fact from her parents until she could no longer hide it. The pregnancy made James feel restless, uneasy, and trapped. When he began attending college, he stayed away from home most of the time.

James started dating another woman, a blond-haired, brown-eyed woman he met in his art class. He would spend hours talking to his new girlfriend on the phone in front of Connie and his infant son.

He would take weekend trips with her. Then he left for Chicago. Connie remained in Greensboro, the unwed mother of a biracial infant she named Dylan.

"I couldn't go home after James left me," she said. "I found a roach-infested apartment on McGee Street and moved in with my baby. To pay rent I had to work two jobs, as an aerobics instructor by day and a waitress by night. I never saw Dylan. He stayed in the nursery from eight in the morning until ten at night."

Connie, feeling deeply wounded and angry at James, tried to go on with her life. "I was so depressed. I wanted to kill myself. I knew I couldn't work two jobs and raise a child. I never made more than enough money to survive, and I saw Dylan only on Sundays. I was still hurt. I thought, 'This isn't right, this isn't fair. I had his child! What's he doing leaving me for her?' I never hated like I hated him. If I had had a gun, he'd be dead. I'd go through spells of crying and loneliness. It was hard to raise a child when I was so depressed."

James returned from Chicago after two years of working for an advertising firm there, and tried to make amends. He had had a change of heart, turned to religion, and accepted his responsibility as a father. He was eager to establish a good relationship with his son, but Connie was still too hurt to let him back into her life.

"He'd come over anytime, never call," Connie said. "I'd try to keep the door shut on him. He would come by to take Dylan to church. He said he was praying for me. I thought he was joking. I didn't know he'd been saved. Finally he told me he'd been born again. That didn't mean anything to me. I wasn't going to church then. I was mad at God. I was mad at the world."

Connie confided her problems to her friend Nancy, the manager at the gym where she taught aerobics. Nancy, also an ardent Christian, started ministering to Connie, telling her that religion was the only answer to her problems.

"Every time she said the name Jesus I'd weep," Connie said, "because I knew in my heart that she was right. I knew I had to learn to forgive James and his girlfriend. It says in the Bible that you have to forgive one another, faults and all. It took me a long time to forgive them. It drove me crazy just to think of them together."

Gradually Connie and James started living together again. They did not sleep together for months. "We had to learn to be friends all over again," Connie said. "It took forever to trust him again. When we finally decided we were ready to get married, Dylan was five. Everyone who knew our story—all the struggles we'd been through—were wild with joy. The wedding was great, a real celebration."

In the wedding photographs, Connie's father beams proudly, apparently delighted by the way everything turned out.

"After Dylan was born my relationship with my father started to improve," Connie said. "I mean, you can't refuse a child, not a baby, mixed or not mixed."

Nine years into their relationship and four years into the marriage, James and Connie now have three children and a home of their own. James works for Connie's father, and the two of them have become good friends.

The trust between James and Connie grew slowly but steadily. When Connie was pregnant with her second child, a little boy named Joshua, she awoke from a nightmare, gripped by panic and drenched in sweat. She grabbed James by the arm and whispered, "You're going to leave me again, aren't you? Just like the first time. I know you will!"

"No, it's different now," James reassured her. "We both know the Lord and I love you. I'm not going anywhere. We're married."

By the time Connie bore her youngest child, Lily, she knew everything would be fine. "James is such a good father. I mean, he's wonderful. He's the only one who puts up with me," she says with a laugh.

It is not only white fathers in the South who have trouble accepting their daughters' decision to marry across racial lines but it happens in the North too. And even the birth of a grandchild is sometimes not enough to move the stony hearts of disappointed fathers.

Our friends Sarah and Amil are a case in point. Sarah, the daughter of hardworking second- and third-generation Irish Catholics who had settled in New England, was disowned by her parents when, at age seventeen, she fell in love with Amil, a nineteen-year-old black student at Wesleyan University who had grown up in the South. Twenty-two years and three children later, she and her parents are still estranged.

"It *did* hurt to be rejected by my parents," Sarah said. "For me it was like going through a divorce. I went through the same phases: hurt, anger, resentment, fighting, grief, sadness. I wrote letters to them at certain points in my life; I showed an openness to reconcile. They never responded. It's been such a long time, I don't even cry about it now."

Sarah met Amil in 1968 at a college dance when she was a student at Hartford College for Women and Amil was at nearby Wesleyan. Both of them were very active in protests against the Vietnam War. "In 1968 young people were very open," Sarah said. "They spoke their minds. Amil and I were totally open with each other. We're each other's first loves."

Even before she met Amil, Sarah, who was living at home and commuting to college, had clashes with her parents over her political activism. She was involved in a Puerto Rican rights group, had traveled to Puerto Rico, and had tutored impoverished black children in north Hartford for no pay. When she was only twelve and thirteen Sarah would argue with her father as they watched civil rights marches on the evening news.

"He would make some negative comment about blacks and I would disagree," Sarah said. "It was just something inside me. As I got older I acted on it: I became active in the black consciousness movement."

The year 1968 was, in Sarah's words, "a pretty heavy year." Like many of her generation, she went through that phase of rebellion that created what came to be known as the generation gap. Her parents supported America's involvement in Vietnam and she opposed it. Parents and daughter were on opposing sides of nearly every political issue.

"But our arguments over Vietnam had no deeply personal meaning," Sarah said. "My relationship with Amil, on the other hand, became a major issue."

Sarah began visiting Amil at Wesleyan on weekends. Afraid of their reaction but feeling compelled to speak the truth, Sarah told her parents all about Amil only one month after meeting him.

"They freaked out," Sarah said. "They forbade me to see him. They ordered me to come straight home after school. They threatened to take away my car, but they knew I needed it to get to my classes. I was living at home to save money so I could afford to transfer to Mount Holyoke, but I decided to put that goal on hold and move out."

Her parents told her, "You'll end up in the gutter. You'll be on welfare. You'll have lots of children. No one will accept your children. All blacks are in the gutter. Are you going to pull this whole family down into the gutter with you, after we've worked so hard?"

Desperate to put an end to their daughter's relationship with Amil, Sarah's parents took her to a Catholic priest and explained the whole situation. The priest counseled Sarah to Honor thy mother and father, and told her that this commandment was more important than caring about people of different races.

"I wanted to stick with Catholicism, but it became impossible," Sarah said. "Priests who counseled me after I moved out always said the same thing: Honor thy mother and father. They didn't have a world view or a political consciousness."

Her parents cut off all financial support and all ties of communication. Sarah moved in with a family and worked for her keep, but caring for five children and a household, working a part-time job, and keeping up with her studies was too much for her. Finally she found a family that took her in and treated her more like a family member than a domestic servant.

Sarah and Amil traveled to Washington, D.C., for nearly every major march or political protest; they helped organize student strikes in 1970, educational programs on Vietnam, and black history seminars. At the time many whites actively supported the black consciousness movement, so Sarah was seldom the only white at a meeting.

Sarah started getting feedback from black women who knew she was with Amil. While some of them were supportive, others accused her of tearing the black community apart. They asked, "What do you want with him?"

"When you care deeply about someone and you believe in a world of interracial harmony, it's not pleasant to be told you've stolen a man," Sarah said. "Sometimes the pressure would make me pull back from the relationship, and we'd let things cool off. We wanted to make sure we weren't wrong for each other. But we were never wrong for each other."

Amil was part of that subculture of black intellectuals who did not have the traditional goals of making a lot of money and establishing himself in a career. He let his hair grow into a huge Afro. He had no car, little money, and no concern for material things. He wanted to explore ideas, search for his true identity, spend more years in college if need be. While these characteristics did not attract black women who sought men who could provide them with stability and financial support, they appealed to Sarah and deeply impressed her. In many ways Amil was more comfortable with radicals—both white and black—than with the black middle class.

Yet Amil felt strong ties to his heritage and to the black community. He believed in the philosophy of black self-help. He felt the African-American community had to unite and work together. At times he felt tremendous pressure coming from within himself to break up with Sarah. He was torn between his love for her and his commitment to the movement, to his people.

In 1971, during one of their periodical breakups, Amil moved to Halifax, Nova Scotia, to attend graduate school in oceanography. He dated a black woman for a while, but did not have the same feelings he did for Sarah. He and Sarah began writing again and were soon engaged.

After graduating from the University of Connecticut in December 1972, Sarah moved to Nova Scotia to be with Amil. Five months later they were married by a Unitarian minister in a gathering of a dozen friends. Sarah, with her long flowing brown hair parted in the middle, wore purple and Amil wore white.

One year after the wedding their first child was born, a son. Sarah wrapped the baby in blankets and put him in an open dresser drawer, for they could not afford a crib and there was not much room in their basement apartment. They were given a used baby carriage that had no tires; only the metal rims of the wheels were left.

Sarah sent her parents a note announcing the birth of her first child. For weeks she was hopeful that her parents might be gladdened by the news and have a change of heart. When she received no response she went through another period of grief over the rift between her and her parents. When their second child was born, a daughter, Sarah hoped that perhaps the thought of a little girl might make them want to visit. Still, no response, followed by another period of sadness for Sarah.

"It doesn't matter to my parents that time has proved them wrong," Sarah said. "They know we don't live in the gutter. They know I'm a college graduate and a schoolteacher. They know my husband is a successful businessman. They know we own our own home. Yet they've shunned their grandchildren. They're racists. They just don't like children of different races.

"It's not sad to me anymore," she continued. "Time heals the wounds. It's as if my parents died a long time ago. I regret having fought with them so much. I don't like fighting and anger. But you can't divide yourself to please your parents. My parents have a negative world view and no respect for my husband or children. It would be more damaging to have a relationship with them now than not to. They would have to change.

"You have to make what you can of your life," she said. "If you please racist, intolerant parents, does that mean you would then have a happy and successful life? No! You should make a better world with your husband and the family you create. It's far more important to really love the person you marry than to please others. You need that rock to make it through the storms of life."

14

MIXED COUPLES IN SOUTH AFRICA

In "City Lovers," a famous Nadine Gordimer short story, the South African Nobel laureate powerfully depicts the complexities and often tragic consequences of interracial love affairs under apartheid. In a scene repeated many times in real life, the clandestine affair between a German geologist and a young Coloured (mixed-race) woman is reported to the police by suspicious neighbors and the landlady.

One night, just as the woman is stepping into the bathtub, there is a loud knock on the door. She pleads with her German lover not to open the door, even threatening to jump out the window if he does. But, insisting they have nothing to fear, he locks her in his wardrobe and answers the door. A group of police officers, introducing themselves as the vice squad, barge in with a search warrant and begin scouring the premises for evidence, tearing the sheets from the beds and gathering feminine toiletries and underwear.

"We have reason to suspect you are cohabiting with a Coloured female," the head officer says. "In defiance of the Immorality Act."

After a tension-filled search, the policemen discover the locked wardrobe and demand the key. The German, acting forgetful, claims to have left it at his office. Their suspicions aroused, the police break the lock and open the wardrobe. The Coloured woman is squatting, naked but for a towel, beneath a row of men's shirts. One of the officers zooms in with his camera and shoots a series of photos of her in her misery and degradation.

After being taken down to the station, they are led to separate rooms, fingerprinted, ordered to strip, and examined by a physician for signs of sexual intercourse. The moving story, which was made into a film, ends with a shot of the Coloured woman's grimacing face as she lies, naked and humiliated, in a sterile room, her heels in stirrups, as a white doctor prepares to search for further "evidence," with cold metal instruments, inside her vagina.

This story might be seen in a different light now that apartheid is crumbling and the Prohibition of Mixed Marriages Act and the Immorality Act were abolished in 1985, but it loses none of its power. Mixed couples may have become a more common sight on the streets of Johannesburg and Cape Town, but their relationships still provoke the same indignation, the same scrutiny, the same sense of tragedy, and the same intense emotions as in "City Lovers."

One mixed couple in South Africa, a black man named Jerry Tsie and his white Afrikaner fiancée, Annette Heunis, has drawn so much attention that the story was featured in *People* magazine in June 1988. Jerry, a security guard at a gold mine who dreamed of coming to America to study martial arts, grew up in a black township outside the small mining town of Odendaalsrus. He met Annette, who worked at a photo shop in the white section of town, when he went there to drop off a roll of film. Soon he was visiting the photo shop frequently, and the two fell in love. Annette felt confused, for she knew her father and stepmother, Afrikaners who were so strict they forbade Annette to date a white seminary student because she was "too young," would vehemently object.

On Valentine's Day 1987 Jerry, then twenty-one and two years older than Annette, declared his love for her. Testing the waters, Annette asked her stepmother, "What would you do if a black man came to the apartment?"

"First I'd shoot him dead," her stepmother replied. "Then I'd give you the biggest hiding of your life."

The couple conducted their relationship in secrecy for months, then Annette moved into Jerry's family home in the black township. Thrilled to have his *palesa*—"beloved flower," in the Sotho language—with him at last, Jerry excitedly told neighbors and friends.

Overnight the pair were local celebrities, and black people stopped by just to see them kiss.

Because it was illegal for whites to live in black townships under apartheid law, their life together was precarious and often terrifying. Each time a car pulled up outside the house they thought it was the police. They were harassed by anonymous callers. Taxi and bus drivers in the township were not licensed to transport whites, so Annette had to quit her job and tend to domestic chores with Jerry's mother in the cramped shack, shared by fifteen people, without electricity or an indoor bathroom.

Annette's parents were furious and refused to accept Jerry. Despite Annette's attempts to reconcile with them, they rarely spoke to her.

"I could choose Jerry or I could choose my parents—I could not have both," she said. "It was terrible, because I love my parents very much."

At last report the couple was living in Bophuthatswana, a black homeland where mixed-race couples were allowed to live together even before F. W. de Klerk repealed the Group Areas Act in 1991.

Susan Bazilli, a white Canadian lawyer, went to South Africa in 1986. For two years she worked in defense of black activists from Alexandra accused of seeking to overthrow the apartheid regime. She has helped hundreds of black South Africans; has become familiar with Alexandra, Soweto, and other black townships; and has won the respect and affection of many families, including Mark's.

Since her arrival in South Africa, Susan has seen a sharp increase in the number of mixed couples on the streets of Johannesburg. She related the story of an acquaintance, a white South African lawyer we will call Nan, and her black South African boyfriend, Tsepo.

Nan fell deeply in love with Tsepo, one of her defendants. She was delighted when she learned she was expecting a child, but a month before her due date, Tsepo was sentenced during a major treason trial and sent to prison on Robben Island. The baby was born while Tsepo was in prison. Nan brought the baby to the prison, but Tsepo was not allowed a contact visit. He could see his child only through a glass window. He yearned to hold her.

Nan's family disowned her when they learned of the interracial relationship. After Tsepo's release from prison, he and Nan were married in 1990 in Johannesburg. They now live with their child in Mayfair, a Johannesburg community that was once white Afrikaner and is now predominantly Indian. Quite a few mixed couples live there as well.

Johannesburg, South Africa's New York City, has slowly changed from a predominantly white city to a largely black one, in the same manner in which American inner cities evolved. In Hillbrow, a downtown section of Johannesburg, there are now sixty to eighty thousand blacks.

Mixed couples are a common sight in Countryview, South Africa's first truly integrated community of about 150 families, located halfway between Johannesburg and Pretoria.

Andrew and Mary Moorosi—he's a black South African and she's a white Canadian—moved to Countryview after a landlord evicted them from their apartment in Hillbrow. One time when Mary was sick and had to lean on Andrew as they walked down the street, an irate white man ran up to them and shouted at Andrew, "What the hell's going on here?" They've had no such problems in Countryview, which they believe is leading the way in showing that South Africans can live together as people with no racial strings attached.

"White hostility against mixed couples is based on protecting 'our women,' " Susan said. "A white woman and black man walking down the street are subjected to verbal, and sometimes physical, attacks by white men. It's happened to me lots of times, even when I'm just walking with one of my defendants and discussing preparations for a trial. I've been called a *Kaffir boetie* ["nigger lover"] many times. But now that so many blacks live in Johannesburg, it doesn't happen that much. It still happens in the 'dorps' [small Afrikaner towns]."

Susan says that some liberal whites in South Africa are so eager to appear free of prejudice that they prefer to date black people. "It's suddenly trendy in anti-apartheid circles to be with a black person. I think it's even becoming a problem. A lot of whites seem to think having a black lover proves they're not racist. Realizing this, some of the more sexist African men use it to their advantage. They may say, 'Prove your nonracism to me, baby.' You see more and more white women with biracial children, and they're usually not married."

At the memorial service for David Webster—a white anti-apartheid activist and lecturer at the liberal University of Witwatersrand who was assassinated—Susan saw more than half a dozen biracial babies with their white mothers.

While some mixed couples choose to live in Coloured neighborhoods or in integrated areas like downtown Johannesburg, the black townships were legally off-limits for mixed couples until the Group Areas Act was repealed in 1991.

"If you two were to live in Alexandra," Susan told us, "it would be the white system that would create problems for you, not blacks."

Unlike the United States, where the black power movement has caused many blacks to oppose interracial relationships, South African blacks are usually very accepting of them.

"There is no doubt the black community in Alex would accept you," Susan said. "But there would be legal issues and questions of safety. With the increasing violence in the townships, nothing's predictable. I've driven through Alex at night hundreds of times. People know me, they recognize my car. But I drove through Alex in a rental car one night and they saw me as just a white woman in a car. They smashed my back and side windows with bricks. A girlfriend from Los Angeles was with me and she was scared to death. She wanted to get out of there as fast as possible. If she hadn't been with me I probably would have stopped to find out who threw the bricks and let them realize they'd attacked a friend. But the violence is starting to scare even me."

The more polarized blacks and whites become, the more dangerous it is for interracial couples to be seen together.

"It's the instability and uncertainty of life here that makes life stressful, maybe even life-threatening, for mixed couples these days," Susan said.

Though the instability and violence of the ghettos has made life hard and dangerous for the few white women living with black men in South Africa's townships, circumstances are much better for white men who marry or live with black or Coloured women. The reasons are obvious. White men hold the best jobs and receive the highest incomes in South Africa. In South Africa a white man earns roughly ten times more than a black man. And white men who marry across racial lines are usually not rejected by white society or forced to relocate.

It is interesting that two of South Africa's leaders who for years had regarded each other as enemies have interracial relationships within their families. Tembi, the daughter of President Oliver Tambo of the African National Congress, is married to a white London banker. Willem, the younger son of President F. W. de Klerk, is married to Erica Adams, the daughter of a mixed-race Cape politician. Only five years ago such a marriage would have been more than illegal; it could have destroyed de Klerk's political career.

Interracial love, while not new in South Africa, is just coming to the surface now that the last apartheid laws have been scrapped. As a result, it still enjoys a sort of vogue with the media and the public. Yet mixed couples across the country, once their relationships are made public, face the same problems with families, friends, and employers as in America. There is also the constant threat of violence from white right-wing groups, and most decline to be named in the press because of fear for their safety. In the liberal northern suburbs of Johannesburg, where racism is still widespread, mixed couples are frequently invited to parties, where they are exhibited by hosts eager to show how "progressive" they are.

Another much-publicized Johannesburg interracial marriage has been that between black South African singer Mara Louw and her Scottish husband, William Thomson. The couple shares a three-bedroom home in Johannesburg's all-white northern suburbs, where Mara is often mistaken for a hired gardener by whites and black domestic workers when she tends her flower garden.

"That's because they don't expect a black housewife in a white suburb," Mara said, laughing.

"*O senya makgowa,*" one Tswana-speaking elderly domestic told her repeatedly. "You're spoiling those white people."

Despite the occasional awkwardness of having a white husband and living in the white suburbs of a country rigidly divided along racial lines for decades under apartheid, Mara believes that the fact that she and her husband come from different cultural backgrounds and have different skin colors is "no big deal."

"Life gets simple when we don't look at the color and culture of a person," Mara says. "The more we regard ourselves as people, live together and aim for harmony, the quicker we'll build a peaceful South Africa."

William, who emigrated to South Africa ten years ago, praises South Africa's blacks. "They are warm and friendly with an interesting view about life. There is a strong indication from their part that there is a possibility South Africans can live together in peace if apartheid is scrapped."

William has been to Mara's home in Soweto many times, and the neighborhood seems proud of him. "They find me interesting," he said, "especially when I start juggling Zulu words in an attempt to impress them." He laughs about the time he tried to excuse himself by saying "I'm tired" in Zulu, but accidentally said "I've soiled myself."

Mara and William met at Club 58 in 1985 in the Hillbrow section of Johannesburg, an area that has shifted from all-white to racially mixed. By then Mara had released her first single, "Good Love," and an album titled *Ipi Ndela* and was also working as an actress. Mara, who was then appearing in *My Name Is Alice,* went to the club for a drink. It happened that both she and William had just ended their respective relationships.

Their friendship blossomed into a relationship, though it would have been illegal for them to marry. Shortly after the Prohibition of Mixed Marriages Act was repealed, the couple married at the Johannesburg Magistrate's Court in March 1987.

As often happens when a mixed couple lives in a hostile environment, the couple leads a rather isolated existence. They seldom socialize. Mara hardly knows her neighbors in the wealthy northern suburb and remains locked in her house much of the day for security reasons. The only welcome gift she received from her neighbors was an anonymous letter in which a neighbor complained about their dog.

When the couple goes out in public, William says, most whites assume that Mara is his maid, not his wife.

Mixed marriages are even occurring in conservative parts of South Africa, strongholds of right-wing and Fascist parties where residents are known for their vehement opposition to even the slightest changes in apartheid and the status quo. Robert Beyl, a white businessman, and his black bride, a Soweto taxi owner named Stella Nkhethoa, were the first interracial couple to marry in Orange Free State, a vast territory settled in the mid-1880s by trek-Boers, the forerunners of today's Afrikaners. Orange Free State is one of the areas white opponents of integration and democracy in a unified South Africa want to turn into a whites-only homeland.

Stella met Robert in 1983 when she first brought her taxi to his service garage for repairs. After a two-year friendship, they fell in love but kept their relationship secret. Once they decided to marry, the couple ran into a number of difficulties—for instance, the Group Areas Act made it difficult for them to find a suitable place to live. They eventually bought a house in 1989 in the Coloured township of Bronville, halfway between Welkom and Virginia in the northern Free State, but this was possible only after the couple was legally married.

Despite the obstacles, Stella is confident the union will last. "If you love each other you never have to worry about problems or what people will say," she said. "Your love will be strong enough to get you through."

In another rigidly conservative area, in the East Rand town of Boksburg, a thirty-two-year-old, Afrikaans-speaking white man named Percy Button married a Zulu woman, Mabel Tshoko Zwane, in magistrate's court. The mayor of Boksburg, Beyers de Klerk, and one of his councillors were present to "observe President de Klerk's five-year plan in action." It was the third mixed marriage to take place in Boksburg in the two years since the Mixed Marriages Act was abolished.

Though the numbers are small, these marriages are significant. They represent a change in the way whites and blacks in South Africa view each other, pushing them to see each other as human beings with needs and emotions, rather than as enemies in an impending race war.

Some of the pressures on these couples are different from those felt by mixed couples in America. For instance, among South African blacks there is very little opposition to interracial marriages. On the contrary, such marriages are joyously celebrated, with great fanfare and tradition. The white partner in the marriage is made to feel welcomed and a member of the family and community. Despite the color differences of the partners, their marriage is seen as a celebration of love between two human beings, seldom complicated by questions of racial politics and power.

One interracially married couple, Tahirih Senne and Bill Linton, talked about the differences between the way they are treated in South Africa, Tahirih's homeland, and in America, where they live. Bill, an architect and Yale graduate from Boston, and Tahirih, a programmer analyst for the U.S. Congress, have helped start an interracial marriage support group in Washington, D.C., to create a forum where couples can share common concerns and experiences.

When the couple arrived at Jan Smuts International Airport in Johannesburg in December 1989, on their way to get married in Mmabatho, Bill was overwhelmed by the warmth and affection showered on him by Tahirih's family and friends.

"I was kissed, I was embraced, I immediately felt I was part of the family," Bill said. "Every place we visited I found myself treated with kindness and respect. I was frequently introduced to neighbors. My love for Tahirih was being reciprocated by everyone who knew her. I was made to feel at home and accepted without doubt or suspicion. It's different in America. When you live in the United States you breathe in racism every day. It's so deeply ingrained that most whites can't even recognize the extent to which it affects their lives. The racially charged atmosphere in America still generates irrational fears that tell me I'd be in danger in a place like Soweto, especially during an upheaval, but I'd probably have nothing to fear. As a white you really stand out in a black township, you're watched closely at first. But once people find out who you are and why you're there, once you treat them as equals, you're accepted without hesitation. Blacks would even want to protect you."

"We walked hand in hand around Johannesburg," Tahirih said. "We got a lot of stares, but people were polite enough not to say anything. The white community is slowly changing. While we were there I heard of another mixed couple, a white lecturer and his black wife, who applied to the city council to move to a white suburb. The council granted them permission. I think that, eventually, whites in South Africa will deal with mixed marriages better than many whites in America. Afrikaners don't deny their prejudices. In the United States overt bigotry isn't socially acceptable anymore, so there's a big gap of denial."

One of Tahirih's black girlfriends from South Africa said, "It's nice that you and Bill are getting married, but that's not for me." An

American acquaintance said more directly, "How could you have grown up black under apartheid and marry a white?"

Tahirih grew up in the Transvaal, the daughter of two schoolteachers. The family moved every two or three years from one black township to another, from Rustenburg to Hammanskraal to Kgabalatsane to Ga-Rankuwa. At fourteen she enrolled at a boarding school in Rustenburg, and at sixteen she moved to Johannesburg, where her father had been appointed Consul General by the Bophuthatswana government. She attended an integrated university in Mmabatho, pursuing coursework toward her bachelor's degree in economics.

Her parents were members of a local group of Bahá'ís. The Bahá'í movement began spreading in South Africa's black townships in the 1950s, despite the barriers posed by apartheid laws.

By attending meetings with her parents, which were racially integrated and therefore under surveillance by the police, Tahirih came in contact with whites on a human level, which rarely happened in the lives of most black children growing up in racially polarized South Africa. Most whites, having grown up isolated from the townships and homelands, do not believe blacks are fully human, and in turn many blacks, seeing only the brutality of the white police, believe whites are inhuman, devoid of compassion or sensitivity. At these meetings Tahirih saw whites and blacks relating to each other as human beings with shared hopes and fears for the future of South Africa.

"We used to wonder if the white kids were real, and they wondered the same about us," Tahirih recalled. "We would touch each other's hair, just to see what it felt like. When they skinned their knees, their blood was red, like mine. The barriers between us started to break down."

As a child in South Africa, Tahirih heard rumors about the tragic fate of mixed couples that circulated through the townships. She heard the story of a German man living in Johannesburg who fell in love with a beautiful black woman. The man was arrested under the Immorality Act and died in police custody. Other mixed couples were forced to flee South Africa.

Tahirih left South Africa in 1982 on a Fulbright scholarship. When she arrived in America she attended Hood College in Frederick, Maryland, completing her bachelor's degree before going on to American University for her master's in economics. Initially she felt let down.

"Because of the way America was portrayed in South Africa, I had high expectations of harmonious race relations in this country," she said. "When I got here I realized that attitudes have hardly changed—only laws have."

After graduating from American University in 1987, Tahirih went to the Green Acre Bahá'í School in Maine for a weekend seminar on women's rights, history, and racial issues. While playing volleyball she met Bill, a tall, white American. They became engrossed in a conversation that seemed to have no end.

Born and raised in the Boston area—first in Westfield and later in Acton, Massachusetts—Bill had almost no contact with blacks. There were only one or two blacks in his high-school class of four hundred.

"Growing up in the sixties I was aware at an early age that racism was wrong. In school we learned about the civil rights movement, and my parents taught me to treat all people fairly, but in Acton there was no way to practice my beliefs in equality because there were virtually no minorities."

After graduating from high school Bill went to Yale University in New Haven, where he had a black roommate who became a close friend. After graduating from Yale Bill moved to St. Louis to pursue a graduate degree in architecture at Washington University, became active in St. Louis's Bahá'í community, then returned to Boston.

During the summer of 1987, Bill often went to the Green Acre Bahá'í School in Maine about an hour from his home. When he met Tahirih on the volleyball court, he was struck by her British-African accent and wondered if she were from the Caribbean. After the volleyball game they had lunch together. The atmosphere was open and warm, the friendship spontaneous. They returned to their respective homes and jobs but began corresponding. They arranged another weekend visit to Maine, then attended a three-day conference together at Princeton. They started visiting each other on weekends, shuttling back and forth between Washington, D.C., and Boston. This commuting went on for more than two years.

When they had been dating three or four months, it suddenly dawned on Bill that the relationship might fall apart. He started feeling self-conscious with her in public. He wondered how strong their commitment would have to be to weather the obstacles they would inevitably face. He knew his parents would not be happy about it.

"Without realizing it, I started wondering what people were thinking about us," he said. "And the fact that some might disapprove bothered me."

But one weekend things changed. While visiting Tahirih in D.C. for a couple of days, it started snowing harder and harder until a full-blown blizzard developed. His return flight to Boston was canceled three times. Instead of leaving him alone to wait for the next plane, Tahirih took time off from work. During those days together, they recognized the depth of their feelings for each other.

"I became aware that I had been worrying too much about other people's opinions and had overruled my own feelings, so I told myself, 'I don't care what they think.' Getting past that threshold changed the relationship for me. It became my conviction that, 'This is the right thing for me.'"

Before they decided to marry, Bill and Tahirih talked to other mixed couples about their experiences. They learned it would be a challenge, but that with patience, persistence, and love even difficult situations could be resolved.

"In an interracial marriage, all normal marital problems are attributed to race," Bill said. "Being forewarned of this makes it easier to work out your problems as individuals, not as a black person versus a white person. One of the main benefits of being a mixed couple is that you're constantly learning from each other. You're reassessing your cultural assumptions all the time."

Bill's parents were reluctant at first to grant him permission to marry Tahirih. They had many concerns: "Where will you live? What about the children? You won't fit in. You won't be accepted. What do you have against white girls?"

Because Bill and Tahirih were Bahá'ís, they had to seek their parents' permission to marry.

Instead of arguing with his parents, Bill planned dinners and events during which each of them could become better acquainted with Tahirih. This forced his father to interact with Tahirih and the barriers between them gradually came down. Tahirih ceased being a stereotype and became an individual. When Bill's parents finally gave their consent to the marriage, it was given unreservedly.

Bill's father told his son, "I'm so happy for you. As a father I have to say that I feel closer to you through taking the time to get to know Tahirih. I feel I'm part of the wedding now."

Tahirih and Bill, in expressing their dream of someday seeing truly nonracial societies both in South Africa and America, offered these observations:

"Today black-white marriages are shunned," Tahirih said. "Tomorrow they'll be appreciated. Reasonable people of all races feel comfortable with a mixed couple, because they know they're in the presence of people whose relationship is a testimony that color doesn't substitute for character, that prejudice can be overcome, and that people of different races can find common ground in mutually respectful friendship."

"Racism is completely emotional and irrational," Bill said. "Most people agree, at least intellectually, that it's wrong. But they seldom do anything more than just talk about it. Many of the most prejudiced people adamantly deny being prejudiced. My grandmother insists she's not prejudiced because she chats and has tea with her black cleaning woman."

"A lot of people believe in racial harmony as an ideal, but that only goes so far," Tahirih said. "Intermarriage is not part of their idea of racial harmony. They can form shallow friendships at work with coworkers of other races, but those tenuous ties end when it's time to go home. We are one human family, but the divisions between us seem so real to us now, and so deep."

EPILOGUE

It is fitting that *Love in Black and White* be published in 1992, the twenty-fifth anniversary of the landmark Supreme Court decision legalizing interracial marriages. Yet two-and-a-half decades after the 1967 court ruling, as has been shown by the stories in this book and by movies such as Spike Lee's *Jungle Fever,* the issue of interracial love is still highly charged and riddled with taboos, misconceptions, sexual myths, and stereotypes.

There still is intense pressure not to date or marry across racial lines. Even platonic interracial friendships are increasingly frowned upon, particularly on high-school and college campuses. Political correctness, racial exclusivity, and cries for racial purity, from both blacks and whites, have smothered the idealism of the sixties, a decade when many advances were made in fighting bigotry and improving tolerance and race relations in America.

Many Americans seem to have given up on the ideal of an integrated society. Two segregated, opposed, and hostile camps have emerged. More and more, blacks and whites are hurling accusations of racism at each other and arguing rancorously over civil rights, affirmative action, and racially motivated violence.

With such tension and acrimony, it is not surprising that individuals who dare to fall in love across the color line find themselves caught in the cross-fire. They're doubly detested because they are proof that racial harmony can become a reality, that the misunderstanding, suspicions, fears, and hatreds between black and white can be replaced by trust, cooperation, mutual respect, and even love.

It's ironic that as the battle lines between blacks and whites in America become sharply drawn and entrenched, in South Africa, once the prototype racist state, the walls of legalized segregation have crumbled. As a result, interracial relationships are finding greater acceptance. African National Congress leader Oliver Tambo has a white son-in-law, and President de Klerk's son is marrying a Coloured woman.

While a new era of hope in race relations has dawned in South Africa, many in America believe that the best days in racial coopera- tion and harmony are past. Some have even given up on the dream that visionaries like Dr. Martin Luther King, Jr., died for. Appropri- ately, in these trying times for race relations, interracial couples have begun speaking out against racism and feeling proud of the racial harmony their union reflects.

Children of mixed marriages, fed up with being labeled and forced to identify with the race of one parent and reject the other, are forming support groups at universities across the country. At the Uni- versity of California at Berkeley, the Multi-Ethnic Interracial Student Coalition, known as Misc., has sixty members. Multiracial student groups have also sprung up at the University of Michigan, Harvard, New York University, Stanford, Kansas State, and UCLA. There are twenty chapters nationwide of the Association of Multi-Ethnic Amer- icans, based in San Francisco, which is fighting for the creation of a "multiracial" classification on standardized forms.

Births to black-white couples increased fivefold between 1968 and 1988. When our second child was born, the unease and self-con- sciousness we had felt at Bianca's birth was gone. Color, finally, no longer mattered to us. With tears of joy filling our eyes, we hugged and kissed each other in front of the entire hospital's childbirth staff the minute our son Nathan Phillip arrived January 20, 1991.

We called Diana at home to tell her she had a new nephew. She screamed with delight and got Bianca equally excited. Diana dropped the phone on the floor and jumped around the room with Bianca shouting, "Nathan! Nathan! It's a boy named Nathan!"

"Nafen! Nafen!" Bianca echoed.

When the family in South Africa was informed of Nathan's birth, Mhani and Granny ululated and danced with joy. They shared the

good news with practically the entire ghetto, and held a celebration
to which friends, relatives, neighbors, and strangers were invited.

"I *told* you you'd have a boy," Mhani said jubilantly over the
phone. "I prayed so hard for you, my American daughter and my son
Mark. Now God has blessed you. Now, when are you bringing my
beloved grandchildren over to visit me, to see Africa? They're half
African, you know."

"Soon, Mhani, soon," we assured her.

Grampa, now in his late eighties, eagerly welcomed his new
great grandson into the world. When he received the birth
announcement he sent Nathan a letter which read:

Dear Nathan Phillip,

I am sure that you know in your very bones and blood and brains
that even beyond the love that just greeted you at your birth, you are a
part of a larger whole—our family. We love you. We believe in you. We
will give you the best of what we are and of our love. Thanks for joining us, and for just being you.

None of us are really "on our own." We must share, or we cannot
live. We *never* can do it alone. For now, we want you to be as cozy and
close to us as you can. As you grow up and away from us, we will miss
your being that close, but you and we will find ways of sharing what
we both need—to have, to be, and to give. You have taken the gift of
life, which love has given you, and, with your heartbeat and breath and
sigh, you tell us how glad you are to be alive, and to join us. You
already know, down to your tiny toes, that we need each other.

Love,
GREAT GRAMPA

Time and understanding have healed the rifts we once felt
between ourselves and our extended families.

Gail's father flew down from Minneapolis to see his new grandson. Bianca led him around the house, from her tape player to her
toys to her kiddie videos, saying over her shoulder in an insistent
voice, "Grampa, c'MON!" He followed her obediently, marveling at
how much her confident, adventurous, and fearless personality
reminded him of Gail as a child. After all the pain and misunderstanding Gail and her father had been through over our relationship

it is heartwarming to see him affectionately and unreservedly embracing his biracial grandchildren.

We appreciate the kind words from initially skeptical family members and friends, though we long ago agreed that whether society accepted us or not, as long as we had each other and faith in our love, we would find ways of being happy and fulfilled.

Writing this book has meant far more to us than merely telling a story about interracial love. Reading each other's versions of our early relationship led to a greater understanding of one another and our past, strengthened our love, fueled our dedication to fighting bigotry, and made us hopeful that blacks and whites can relate as human beings, can reduce and even eliminate the tensions and barriers that now divide them. Meeting and interviewing other mixed couples inspired us, made us proud of our relationship, and confirmed our belief that we are not fugitives from the "real" world or social outcasts, but living proof that blacks and whites do not have to hate each other.

Racism is essentially a problem of the heart. Pervert the human heart, which was made to feel and to love and to care, and you get cancers like racism and injustice. If in our hearts we truly accept one another as fellow human beings, many of our intractable problems would have solutions, and there would be no limit to the good we could do in making our world a better place for all.

INDEX

Sudi (biracial child), 50
Supreme Court, U.S., xii, 259
Swimming, racism and, 133–34
Sylvia (Greensboro professional), 204–6

Tambo, Oliver, 251, 252
Tambo, Tembi, 251
Tammy (Gail's roommate), 96, 106, 108–9
Teaneck (NJ), 214
Teaneck High School, 213
Telephone threats, 7–8, 68
Tennis, 8–10, 14–15, 24–25, 157
  Mark's scholarship for, 24
Texas, 26–34
  black-white relations in, 27–34
Third World Week, 37
Thomson, William, 251–52
Tiffany, Chris, 211
Tiki, 31–34
Time (magazine), 211
"Today Show" (TV show), 197
Tracy, Spencer, 235
"Tsepo" and "Nan" (mixed couple), 248
Tsie, Jerry, 247–48
Tsonga culture, 6, 217, 218
  childbearing and, 151–53
  names in, 156–57
Tsonga language, 132, 134, 135, 148,
    222–23, 226
Twelve Apostles Church of God, 220

Vanity, 216
Venda culture, 217, 218, 220
Venda language, 222–23
Violence, 237–38, 250, 251. *See also* mur-
    ders
  Afro rakes and, 27–28
  battered women and, 6–7
  of blacks against blacks, 24, 198

police brutality, 21–22, 67, 87, 246–48
  race riots, 29, 180
  of white gangs, 108
Virginia, ban on interracial marriage in,
    xi–xii
Vogel, Naomi, 68–69

Washington, D.C., black-white marriage
    in, 115
Webster, David, 250
Wife-beating, 6–7
Wilder, Douglas, 232
Williams, Alton, Jr., 214
Williams, Sheena, 212–13
Winfrey, Oprah, 127, 128–30, 158, 162,
    195–96
Winston-Salem (NC), 188
Winston-Salem Magazine, 186–90
Witherspoon, Kim, 100, 101
Women
  battered, 6–7
  black. *See* Black women, American;
      South African women
  feminism and, 5–6, 18, 49, 74
  as housewives, 49
  purchase of wives, 6, 87
Woods, John, 211

York (SC), 171–72

Zawadzki, Evelyn, 229–32
Zawadzki, Rainer, 229–32
Zwane, Mabel Tshoko, 253